POURING DOWN WORDS

SUZETTE HADEN ELGIN

San Diego State University

POURING DOWN WORDS

Prentice-Hall, Inc., Englewood Cliffs, New Jersey

Library of Congress Cataloging in Publication Data

ELGIN, SUZETTE HADEN.
   Pouring down words.

   Bibliography: p.
   1. English language—Style. 2. English language—
Rhetoric. 3. Communication. I. Title.
PE1421.E4   808′.042   74-22139
ISBN 0-13-686352-3

10 9 8 7 6 5 4 3 2 1

Printed in the United States of America

Prentice-Hall International, Inc., *London*
Prentice-Hall of Australia, Pty. Ltd., *Sydney*
Prentice-Hall of Canada, Ltd., *Toronto*
Prentice-Hall of India Private Limited, *New Delhi*
Prentice-Hall of Japan, Inc., *Tokyo*

ACKNOWLEDGMENTS

p. 2. **Robert A. Barakat, "Arabic Gestures."**
Copyright, *Journal of Popular Culture*, Spring 1973. Reprinted by permission of the publisher.

p. 12. **N. Scott Momaday, *House Made of Dawn*.**
From page 95 (hardbound edition) *House Made of Dawn* by N. Scott
Momaday (Harper & Row, 1968). Reprinted by permission of the pub-
lisher.

p. 29. Tom Wolfe, "The Last American Hero is Junior Johnson. Yes!"
First published in *Esquire* Magazine From *The Kandy Kolored Tangerine Flake Streamline Baby* by Tom Wolfe, copyright 1965 by Farrar, Straus & Giroux, Inc., publisher. Reprinted by permission of the publisher.

p. 36. Peg Bracken, *Appendix to the I Hate to Cook Book.*
Reprinted by permission of the publishers, Harcourt Brace Jovanovich, Inc.

p. 44. Marshall McLuhan, *The Gutenberg Galaxy.*
Copyright © University of Toronto Press. Reprinted by permission of the publisher. Translation by Marshall McLuhan of an extract from *L'Enseignement de l'écriture aux universités médiévales* by Istvan Hajnal (Budapest, Academia Scientiarum Hungarica Budapestini 1959).

p. 46. Malvina Reynolds, "A Song of San Francisco Bay."
From *The Highway*, words and music by Malvina Reynolds, copyright © 1965 by Schroder Music Co. (ASCAP). Used by permission. "A Song of San Francisco Bay," copyright © 1968 by Malvina Reynolds.

p. 47. L. F., "The Veil: a darkness at noon."
Reprinted by permission from *Aramco World Magazine*.

p. 50. Don H. Berkebile, "GM, You Can Relax Now."
Copyright 1973 Smithsonian Institution from *Smithsonian* Magazine, May, 1973, by Don H. Berkebile.

p. 55. Patrick C. Easto and Marcello Truzzi, "Towards an Ethnography of the Carnival Social System."
From the *Journal of Popular Culture*. Reprinted with permission of Ray B. Browne, editor.

p. 58. Axel Olrik, "Epic Laws of Folk Narrative."
Jeanne P. Steager, translator, in Alan Dundes, *The Study of Folklore*, © 1965, Prentice-Hall, Inc. The article originally appeared as "Epische Gesetze der Volksdichtung," *Zeitschrift für Deutsches Altertum*, Vol. 51 (1909) 1–12.

p. 60. Frank Hamilton Cushing.
From *Zuni Folk Tales*, edited and translated by Frank Hamilton Cushing. Copyright 1931 and renewed 1959 by Alfred A. Knopf, Inc. Reprinted by permission of the publisher.

p. 65. Tom Glazer, "Going Down the Road."
Copyright © 1970 by Tom Glazer. From the book *Songs of Peace,*

Freedom and Protest by T. Glazer. Published by David McKay Co., Inc.; reprinted with permission of the publisher.

p. 68. Meredith Tax.
"Women's Songs," from *Sing Out!* (Jan./Feb. 1971). Reprinted by permission.

p. 79. Clifford Simak, "A Death in the House."
From *Galaxy* Magazine. Reprinted by permission of Robert Genest, editor.

p. 109. Morris K. Udall, "The Right to Write."
"Congressman's Report" to constituents by U.S. Rep. Morris K. Udall, Sept. 15, 1971. Reprinted with permission.

p. 114. Bill Garvin, "Mad's Guaranteed Effective All-Occasion Non-Slanderous Political Smear Speech."
Copyright © 1970 by E. C. Publications, Inc. Reprinted by permission of *Mad* Magazine.

p. 116. John D. Rockefeller, III, "For Revolution."
From *Intellectual Digest*. Reprinted by permission of the author.

p. 121. William Temple, *Religious Experience.*
James Clarke & Co.—Attic Press, Inc., Greenwood, S.C. Reprinted by permission.

p. 122.
From *Language in America,* edited by Neil Postman, Charles Weingartner and Terence P. Moran, copyright © 1969 by Western Publishing Co., Inc., reprinted by permission of The Bobbs-Merrill Company, Inc.

pp. 122, 130. Alan Watts, *Beyond Theology.*
Copyright © by Pantheon Books, a Division of Random House, Inc. Reprinted by permission.

p. 122. William James, *Varieties of Religious Experience.*
Reprinted by permission of Alexander R. James, Literary Executor.

pp. 123, 129, 131. Stephen, *The Caravan.*
Copyright © by Random House, Inc., and The Bookworks. Reprinted by permission.

p. 124. A. J. Ayer, *Language, Truth and Logic.*
Published by Victor Gollancz, Ltd., London. Reprinted by permission.

p. 130. Idries Shah.
From the book *The Pleasantries of the Incredible Mulla Nasrudin* by
Idries Shah. Text and illus. © 1968 by Mulla Nasrudin Enterprises, Ltd.
Published in 1971 by E. P. Dutton & Co., Inc., in a paperback edition.
Reprinted by permission.

p. 134. George B. Leonard, "Notes on The Transformation."
Copyright © 1972 by George Leonard. Reprinted by permission of the
Sterling Lord Agency.

p. 141. R. D. Laing.
From *Knots*, by R. D. Laing. Copyright © 1970 by The R. D. Laing
Trust. Reprinted by permission of Pantheon Books, a Division of Random
House, Inc., and Tavistock Publications.

p. 145. Robert Bly, "Where We Must Look for Help."
Reprinted from *Silence in the Snowy Fields*. Wesleyan University Press,
1962. Copyright © 1962 by Robert Bly, reprinted with his permission.

p. 145. James McMichael, "Corn."
From *Poetry*, November 1970. Copyright © 1970 by The Modern Poetry
Association. Reprinted by permission of the Editor of *Poetry* and the
author.

p. 146. John Haines, "If the Owl Calls Again."
Copyright © 1962 by John Haines. Reprinted from *Winter News*, by
John Haines, by permission of Wesleyan University Press.

**p. 149. E. E. Cummings, "my father moved through dooms of
love."**
From *Complete Poems 1913–1962*, published by Harcourt Brace Jovanovich, Inc. Reprinted by permission.

p. 151. Marie Borroff, computer poem.
Reprinted with permission from the January 1971 issue of the Yale
Alumni Magazine; copyright by Yale Alumni Publications, Inc. Reprinted
by permission of the publishers and the author.

p. 153. Edwin Morgan, "The Computer's First Christmas Card."
Reprinted from Edwin Morgan, *The Second Life* (Edinburgh: Edinburgh University Press, 1968); copyright © 1968 by Edwin Morgan
and Edinburgh University Press.

p. 155. Judson Jerome, "Poetry."
Reprinted by permission of *Writer's Digest* and Ann Elmo Agency, Inc.

p. 171. Arrow Shirt Commercial.
Used with permission of The Arrow Company (Arrow Shirts).

p. 174. Advertisement for the Mount Airy Lodge.
Reprinted by permission of Ronald T. Logan, Manager.

p. 184. Arthur Berger, "Marvel Language: The Comic Book and Reality."
Reprinted from *ETC.* Vol. XXIX, No. 2, by permission of the International Society for General Semantics.

p. 188. Stephanie Harrington, "Enticers, 1970, on TV, Who Do They Think You ARE?"
Copyright © 1970 by The Condé Nast Publications, Inc. Reprinted by permission of the publisher and the author.

p. 200. Harper Lee.
From *To Kill a Mockingbird* by Harper Lee. Copyright © 1960 by Harper Lee. Reprinted by permission of J. B. Lippincott Company.

p. 201. Mike Cook and Paul Gillespie, "Aunt Arie."
From *The Foxfire Book* by Eliot Wigginton. Copyright Doubleday & Company, Inc. Reprinted by permission of the publishers, Doubleday & Co., Inc.

p. 209. Robert Waddell.
"The Grammar of Jargon," from *Style and Rhetoric,* pp. 76–81.

p. 217. J. L. Dillard, "The Validity of Black English and What to Do About It."
From Black English: Its History and Usage in the U.S., by J. L. Dillard. Copyright © 1972 by J. L. Dillard. Reprinted by permission of Random House, Inc.

CONTENTS

PREFACE

In contemporary society more people spend more time in communication than in any other waking activity.—*Lee Loevinger*

More time than in any other waking activity. That's a lot of your time. Time you spend reading, listening to the radio, watching TV, reading signs and directions and instructions, looking at movies, listening to classroom lectures, talking to friends, filling out credit applications and job applications, preparing reports and taking examinations, taking part in classroom discussions, interacting with customers, talking with members of your family, following signs on the freeway. Alvin Toffler tells us, in *Future Shock*, that the average American takes in between 10,000 and 20,000 printed words every single day, and manages to see or read or hear 560 advertisements during that same day (not to mention more than an hour spent listening to the radio and several hours spent watching television).

The common denominator in all this activity is *language*. It's pouring down words, all day, every day. You are surrounded by, inundated with language from morning till night, every day of your life. And what does this mean to you? It means that language is your business, as it is everybody's business, unless you are one of those rare individuals who is going to be able to isolate himself or herself totally from society. It means that the day when the analysis and understanding of all language other than simple conversation could be left for the scholar and the expert is long past. It means that you must, in self-defense, become an expert on language yourself.

This expertise has to be a two-way matter. First, you must be able to deal with all that language coming down, in at least the following ways:

1. You decide whether to notice the language sequence or not.
2. You identify the sequence as a particular *kind* of language —political speech or novel or advertisement or the most utter nonsense.
3. You decide what motive lies behind the sequence, what effect it was intended to have on you, as listener or reader.
4. You process the sequence—read it, or listen to it, try to understand and perhaps to remember it.
5. You evaluate the sequence—to determine whether it is (a) logical, (b) relevant, (c) honest, (d) useful, (e) a source of pleasure, and, if appropriate, whether it is beautiful or not.

Secondly, not only must all of us function in response to language, we must also be responsible for our own portion of other people's language environment. We have to decide if we are going to respond, we must choose the kind of language most suitable for that response, we must be aware of our reasons for responding, and we must do the best we can to communicate the result in an efficient and understandable manner.

The need to take language seriously, to consider it a part of our environment that can be polluted just as surely as our air and water and our food, has been summed up by George Gerbner as follows:

Never before have so many people in so many places shared so much of a common system of messages and images—and the assumptions about life, society and the world that the system embodies—while having so little to do with creating the system. In sum, the fabric of popular culture that relates the elements of existence to one another and shapes the common consciousness of what is, what is important, what is right and what is related to what else is now largely a manufactured product.

Given, then, that it is clear that language is an important part of our lives and that language processing is something we cannot afford to be ignorant about, what can this book—which is itself another part of the language downpour—do to help?

The purpose of the book is to help you learn how to fulfill the language function, both as processor and as producer. We will go about this by looking at a number of different kinds of sequences of language, and by trying to answer three basic questions about each sequence we are examining:

1. What is it?
2. How is it put together?
3. What is it for?

Enjoy the book.

POURING DOWN
WORDS

INTRODUCTION: THE NATURE OF LANGUAGE

The subject of this book is human language. If its subject were algebra, astrology, carpentry, or music theory, you could be reasonably certain that it would present a set of basic terms, concepts, and facts. You could probably also expect the experts in those fields to agree as to what those basic terms and concepts had to be.

Where language is concerned, however, there often seems to be more conflict than agreement. Even defining the term is no simple matter. Discussions of what a text on language ought to cover result in violent and sometimes passionate disagreements. Under the circumstances, the best we can do is to choose among the many alternatives and to remember that there are undoubtedly hundreds of other ways of looking at these matters.

DEFINING HUMAN LANGUAGE

We will begin, then, by taking up the question of the *definition* of a human language. A human language is, first of all, a system of meaningful sounds, or in the case of the deaf, a system of meaningful gestures. We hear all around us sounds that are made by human beings. We hear them coughing, hiccuping, humming, rattling garbage can lids, tapping their teeth with pencils, snoring, and whistling. But there are no words made up of such sounds. Of all the enormous variety of possible human sounds, only a few are meaningful, and these constitute human language. In the same way, the deaf speaker of sign language sees thousands of gestures made by other human beings, but only a small set of these gestures is meaningful. We might therefore propose the following statement as a definition of a human language:

A human language is a system of meaningful sounds or gestures.

But this definition is inadequate. By this definition, the famous "language of the bees" would be a human language. The bee returns to the hive and communicates information to the other bees about the location of nectar by performing a systematic set of dance movements. Bees thus have a system of meaningful gestures.

Arabic Gestures

ROBERT A. BARAKAT

1. Hit the side of the face with the palm of one hand, head tilted slightly to one side, eyes open wide. MEANING = SURPRISE.

2. Gently blow smoke into a woman's face. MEANING = DESIRE.

3. Move right arm up from about waist level to over right shoulder, keeping palm up; head is tilted back and eyes are raised upward. MEANING = SWEARING AN OATH.

4. Grasp chin with tips of right fingers. MEANING = NEED AS-SISTANCE.

5. Clench both fists at waist level with thumbs extended in opposite directions. MEANING = ANGER.

6. Hold right hand with palm down at left side of body, then move it quickly from left side to the right and turn the body slightly as the hand is moved. MEANING = DON'T BOTHER ME. GO AWAY.

7. Touch tips of right index finger, second finger, and thumb to mouth and bow slightly at the same time. MEANING = RESPECT.

8. Press right palm on stomach and move hand in a circular motion. MEANING = HUNGER.

The difficulty here lies in a common misuse of the term *language* itself. We are accustomed to hearing about the "language" of the bees and the "language" of flowers, and the distinction between such "languages" and real language is not something we ordinarily think about. In fact, neither the communications system of the bees nor the code we use to send messages by the careful choice of flowers in a bouquet is actually language at all. It's necessary that we get this distinction clear in our minds in order to improve our definition.

Both the so-called language of the bees and the language of flowers share a single characteristic that is not a characteristic of real language: they are *finite*.

Bees can communicate on only two possible topics—the distance from the bees to the nectar and the direction they must fly to reach it. Nothing else can be discussed in this system. Bees cannot communicate about the weather or the beekeeper or discuss what they plan to do the following day. No real language is restricted in this fashion.

You know, because you speak a human language, that no such language is restricted to a particular set of topics. Anything that exists in this universe and a multitude of things that don't exist can be talked about in any human language. If something is discovered on Tuesday that was not known to exist on Monday, and there are no words in the vocabulary that apply specifically to it, we can still talk about the discovery, and we all know how to add new words to our vocabulary as we need them.

The language of the flowers contains a set of utterances, each one corresponding to a particular flower as shown on page 4. To send someone a bouquet of fern, heather, hyacinth, and yellow roses thus means "I feel lonely, sad, jealous, and forsaken." This bouquet communicates, but it is not language. Everything that can be said in the "language" of the flowers can be rather quickly listed. No real language is like this. And, as with the "language" of the bees, the subject matter is rigidly restricted; you can only discuss emotions. You cannot talk about physics or auto body work or the best way to get to the nearest town, and there is no possibility of ever doing so.*

You might wonder if a computer could set down all the possible utterances in any human language. The answer is "no"—a computer could make a longer list and make it faster, but it could never reach the end of the possible meaningful sequences of even one language.

If you think about this for a moment you will have no difficulty understanding why it is true. Look at these examples:

a. I went to the store.

---

* Unless, of course, we change the code and make "fern" mean "sparkplug."

b. I went to the store and I saw a friend.

c. I went to the store and I saw a friend and I said hello to him.

d. I went to the store and I saw a friend and I said hello to him and we went in together.

e. I went to the store and I saw a friend and I said hello to him and we went in together and the first thing we did was. . . .

Clearly, no matter how long such a sentence grows, it would always be possible to add one more "and" and put some more words after it.

Now look at the following set of sentences:

a. Mary said that the steaks were raw.

b. Mary said that Bill knew that the steaks were raw.

c. Mary said that Bill knew that Elizabeth claimed that the steaks were raw.

d. Mary said that Bill knew that Elizabeth claimed that Harry had forgotten that the steaks were raw.

e. Mary said that Bill knew that Elizabeth claimed that Harry had forgotten that Noah told him that the steaks were raw.

Again, no matter how long such a sentence grows, it is always possible to add one more "that" followed by another sentence.

It's not that such sentences are *probable*. Certainly they are not. Only small children connect a series of sentences with "and" as in the first example. No one is likely to keep embedding one sentence in another indefinitely as in the second example, because people don't talk like that. But the point is that *only* in human language is it *always* possible to make a sentence, no matter how long, still longer. Thus, there is no way that all the sentences of a human language could be listed, ever, and this characteristic of infiniteness is one of the defining characteristics of a real language.

We can now revise our previous definition:

A human language is a system of meaningful sounds or gestures which can be used to produce a potentially infinite number of meaningful utterances.

The other things popularly called "languages" do not meet this definition and in fact are only sets of signals. Therefore, from now on we can drop the phrase *human* language and say simply *language*.

You can see that to know a language includes the *ability* to produce an infinite number of meaningful utterances from this system of sounds or gestures. A mynah bird that can recite all of Shakespeare's sonnets cannot be said to "know" English. Such a bird can be taught to say "the donkey is going down the road" and he can be taught to say "the calf is sick." But although he can say all those words and say them in the proper order, he can never say "the calf is going down the road" or "the donkey is sick" unless someone has taught him those two specific utterances.

TEACHER.   Ferrabeau, give me the rule for the use of the comma.

FERRABEAU.   Easy. Commas go in the *pauses.* Like at the end of every sentence. Like when you cough. Like when you decide to talk about something else.

So far as we know, the creative use of language—the ability to produce utterances without having been taught them—is restricted to human beings. The mynah bird can never utter one sentence that he has not been specifically taught, while you, as a speaker of a human language, could easily produce fifty sentences you had never before heard or read. It is precisely in this creative aspect of human language that the infiniteness of language lies.

Now we can set down a final definition:

A language is a system of meaningful sounds or gestures which can be used creatively to produce a potentially infinite number of meaningful utterances.

WHY STUDY LANGUAGE?

Nobody knows what the first language was, or how language began. Nobody knows exactly how the language ability works. But we do know that everyone is born with the ability to learn and use a language, and that this ability is one of the defining characteristics of a human being.

A child begins to speak at about eighteen months of age, no matter what language he or she is exposed to, and by the time he enters school he knows his language—in a way that the mynah bird can never know it. This is not to say that a child enters kindergarten with an adult vocabulary, but rather that he has command of the grammatical principles that allow him to use his language, that he can produce the sounds that are part of it, and that he knows how to relate these sounds to their meanings. In other words, he speaks and understands his language.

At which point, in the early years of his schooling, the child finds that he is expected to study "language." This study comes under various names, depending on the school and the level of education. It may be called "English" or "Language Arts" or "Composition" or "Rhetoric" or a number of other things, but it amounts to studying language.

And here you are, after all those years of elementary and secondary school, studying language once again. It is very reasonable that you should be wondering why.

The answer lies in the fact that communication depends upon language, and that difficulties in communication are a terrible handicap to you in carrying on your daily life. Language pervades everything you do, in a way that is totally unlike many other subjects you might choose to study. You may, for example, go through life without knowing anything about ballet because ballet is divorced from the daily life of most people and is in a separate area of optional knowledge. Language isn't like that. We have to deal with it, no matter how we feel about it. We have to talk to people, we have to listen to them, and we have to try to understand what they say to us. We have to read newspapers and textbooks and magazines. We have to read and follow printed instructions. We have to fill out endless sets of forms. We have to write letters, reports, and directions. The only way to escape from language is to escape from human society, and that alternative is not open to most of us. It is therefore important to learn everything about language that we possibly can.

There are lots of ways of going about this. It seems, however, that since it is as a part of daily life that language is most crucial to us, it is in that context that it should be studied. In this text, therefore, we will look at the language of a number of areas that all of us can reasonably be expected to have to learn to deal with in our everyday existence as human beings.

There is the language of the media, of television, and movies and radio; we are all inundated by the media. There is the language of literature, the language of the books we read. There is the language of politics, the language of religion, the language of our folklore. We will examine all these topics, because they represent areas in which language affects us directly.

A warning is in order at this point. This is *not* a textbook on the media, literature, politics, religion, and so on. The author of this text is not an expert in any of these fields, but rather a linguist, an expert on language. Full-length books have been written on every area that will be discussed here, and a single unit cannot provide more than a cursory examination. We will be concerned instead with the *language* of each field, and that concern will arbitrarily be restricted to an examination in detail of one type of such language that can be taken to represent the whole. Just as the principles of chemistry can be learned without a detailed examination of every chemical known to exist, so can the principles of language be learned from representative examples. To do this, we will need to learn something about the structure of language sequences.

STRUCTURE OF LANGUAGE SEQUENCES

Structure matters. If you wanted to build yourself a house, and you tried to learn how by looking at the outside of houses, the chances are pretty slim that the house you built would stand up through the first day you lived in it. The structural principles that keep a house from collapsing cannot be learned from an examination of its surface shape. In the same way, we need to learn about the structural principles that keep a sequence of language from collapsing. The collapse of a paragraph may be quieter than the collapse of a house, but it is potentially just as dangerous.

Language structure ranges from the most informal conversation to the rigid restrictions of a poetic form like the sonnet. Neither of these extremes concerns us here. The following basic traditional model, however, offers a good beginning for the study of language structure. Because so much of your time in college is spent preparing assignments according to this model, we will look at it in some detail.

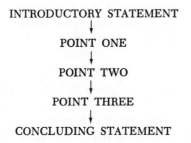

This model is the structure of logical argument and of much prose that is intended to teach or to persuade. Let's look at two examples of paragraphs constructed according to this model. The structure will be summarized first in outline form, and then the full text will be added.

Example One—Outline

INTRODUCTORY STATEMENT
Reporters have problems covering radical groups.

POINT ONE
Radicals resent spying, especially spying by those who do not share their views.

POINT TWO
Reporters tend to report only the outrageous side of radical groups' activities.

POINT THREE
Most of a radical group's time is spent organizing, but the press ignores this fact.

CONCLUDING STATEMENT
   It's not surprising that radical groups spend time only with reporters they feel are on their side.

Example One—Full Text

Covering a radical group presents problems for even the best of re-   *INTR*
porters. As self-avowed true believers, radicals do not appreciate
being spied upon by the unconverted. Furthermore, reporters often   *POINT*
make story leads out of their most outrageous statements or report   *POINT*
only their unusual or shocking activities, ignoring the humdrum routine of their workaday lives. Both the radical right and the radical left
spend most of their time in organizing, but it is only when their mem-   *POINT*
bers are caught with guns or overheard hatching wild plots that we
read about them in the papers. It is not, therefore, surprising that, as
a rule, only the reporter who has proved himself a kind of fellow   *CON*
traveler is suffered by radical groups for any length of time.
—Mary Breasted

   There is nothing sacred about the number three for the points supporting the introductory statement. If you cannot think of at *least* three points to back up the claim you are making or the idea that you want to present, then you probably either do not know enough about the subject or have not thought it through. The more supporting points you present, the stronger your argument will be. In the next example the writers offer five points, each clearly related to the idea presented in the introductory statement.

Example Two—Outline

INTRODUCTORY STATEMENT
   All known solutions to the energy problem create other problems.

POINT ONE
   Fossil fuels create environmental problems.

POINT TWO
   Hydroelectric power is limited and causes other problems.

POINT THREE
   Nuclear power is dangerous.

POINT FOUR
   Controlled fusion may not be possible and will add to environmental problems.

POINT FIVE

Solar energy is expensive and difficult to utilize.

CONCLUDING STATEMENT

There are other possibilities, but none of them changes the fact that technology alone can't solve the energy crisis.

Example Two—Full Text

Because no means of supplying energy is without serious liabilities, there are no easy technological solutions to our energy problems. The use of fossil fuels pollutes air and water, defaces the landscape through mining, and depletes a resource having other, recyclable uses—for example, lubrication and synthetics. Unexploited hydroelectric sites are in limited supply, and their development compromises other values. Nuclear fission poses hazards at every step of the enterprise, from mining through fuel reprocessing, and it creates a burden of radioactive wastes that must be infallibly contained, unerringly transported, and indefinitely interred. Controlled fusion has not yet been conclusively demonstrated to be scientifically feasible, and it will not be completely free of environmental costs when we do get it. Solar energy is unevenly distributed, dilute, and presently expensive to harness. There are other energy sources (and other defects in the ones just listed), but a more comprehensive compilation simply confirms the verdict: The "energy crisis" will not be solved by technology alone.—Paul R. Ehrlich and John P. Holdren

INTRO.

SUPP. POINTS

CONC.

The satisfying thing about mastering the structural technique demonstrated in these example paragraphs is that the same model, expanded, is what you need for full-length papers, all the way from the first composition in English One to the Ph.D. dissertation, technical manual, sales report, or any other major writing project.

Here is the expanded model; other structural units, such as sections or chapters, can be substituted for paragraphs.

INTRODUCTORY PARAGRAPH
↓
FIRST PARAGRAPH
↓
SECOND PARAGRAPH
↓
THIRD PARAGRAPH
↓
CONCLUDING PARAGRAPH

Even if experimental structures are excluded, this is certainly not the only possible language structure model; we will later examine some other models. But this model is one of the best ways to get *started* writing, and it will allow you to consistently produce material that is sufficiently well-organized to be readable. Many professional writers have learned to do this sort of thing in their head, and if you are able to do that, go right ahead. The important thing is that all your sentences fit in their paragraph, in the same way that all the doors need to fit in a house; how you personally can best achieve that fit is something you must determine for yourself.

The point of all this is not to make you into a kind of Super Mynah Bird who can produce a stream of newly memorized utterances on demand. It is not to fill you up with information, like filling a bag with rocks, to give your image a shape that we call "educated." It is instead to make it easier for you to communicate with other people, which is a skill of community, and to make your communications more interesting and more clear.

EXERCISES

1.   The following quotation is from N. Scott Momaday's novel, *House Made of Dawn*. Is the speaker's opinion one that you can agree with? Why or why not? Using the structural model presented in this unit, write a brief defense of your answer.

> In the white man's world, language, too—and the way in which the white man thinks of it—has undergone a process of change. The white man takes such things as words and literatures for granted, as indeed he must, for nothing in his world is so commonplace. On every side of him there are words by the millions, an unending succession of pamphlets and papers, letters and books, bills and bulletins, commentaries and conversations. He has diluted and multiplied the Word, and words have begun to close in upon him. He is sated and insensitive; his regard for language—for the Word itself—as an instrument of creation has diminished nearly to the point of no return. It may be that he will perish by the Word.

2.   A common student reaction to presentation of a model for composition, like the one presented in this unit, is that the model stifles all creativity you might have and puts your writing into an artificial straitjacket. The preparation of an outline is often seen as busywork. On the other hand, the major flaw in the written

language of students is total lack of organization, to such a degree that the instructor is unable to *locate* the student's ideas, let alone try to understand them. Can you argue either for or against the presentation of the model? If you are against this method of composition, can you suggest an alternative?

3. Look at the list of Arabic gestures on page 2. These gestures are a set of signals, rather than a true language like American Sign Language. Does a set of similar gestures exist for English-speaking Americans? for Americans who speak languages other than English? Make a list of as many such gestures as you can, together with their meanings.

4. A number of books have been written recently on the subject of what is called *body language*. (For example, Julius Fast, *Body Language* and *How to Read a Person Like a Book*.) These books attempt to explain what a person is communicating by the way he holds his head, the way he crosses his legs, and gestures such as tugging at the hair or rubbing the nose. Remembering the final definition of language in this unit, do you think that "body language" is really a language? If you do, explain why that is your opinion. If not, do you think this sort of language is in the same class as the Arabic gestures discussed in the previous exercise? Why or why not? (If you would like to read more about body language before answering this question, try looking in the library under the headings of body language, gestures, or kinesics. There is a long bibliography of materials on this subject in the *Southern Folklore Quarterly* for 1957, pages 218–317.)

5. There has been a great deal of discussion lately about the possibility that some of the apes, and perhaps the dolphin, may have language ability. For example, scientists R. Allen Gardner and Beatrice T. Gardner have taught hundreds of signs from American Sign Language to a chimp named Washoe, who uses these signs creatively. Linguists have known for a long time that the apes were *physiologically* unable to produce vocal speech, but that they have a great deal of manual dexterity; the Gardner experiment is an attempt to find out whether the apes' apparent lack of language is due only to their physiological difference from man.

Assume that the Gardner experiment definitely shows that Washoe has the ability to learn and to use a language. Take one of the following positions and write a statement defending it.

a. Chimpanzees should not be encouraged to use language because it will only make them unhappy.

b. Chimpanzees should not be encouraged to use language because human beings will then exploit their ability.

c. The development of language in chimpanzees would be an enormous boon to mankind.

d. Teaching chimpanzees to use language would be an inexcusable interference in their natural evolution.

e. Washoe is clearly a genius among chimps, and it is highly unlikely that another such chimp could be found.

f. Training chimpanzees to use language is a waste of time since they have no possible use for such a skill.

6. Do computer languages fit our final definition of a language? Write a paragraph explaining and defending your answer.

7. Is Morse Code a language? Write a paragraph explaining and defending your answer.

8. You feel that the statement of goals in the last paragraph of this unit is totally ridiculous. Write a letter to the editor of your school paper, not more than 300 words in length, protesting this particular abuse of the educational process.

9. Assume that you have read the letter of protest in the newspaper and you disagree with it. Write a similar letter defending the unit goals.

10. Here are some definitions of human language that have been proposed by others:

S. S. BARLINGSAY
"Language is an instrument of communication of thought."

CHARLES HOCKETT
"A language is a complex system of habits."

MARSHALL MC LUHAN
"Languages are stuttering extensions of our five senses, in varying ratios and wavelengths."

ALAN WATTS
"Language is the symbolic echo of direct experience."

ROBERT C. LUGTON
"Language is the activity in which we use some parts of our experience to systematically stand for or signify other parts of our experience."

TIMOTHY LEARY
"Language is the pattern of energy sent or received by a temporary energy package."

LUDWIG WITTGENSTEIN
"A natural language is a nexus of (presumably) meaningful games."

Is any of the definitions quoted here superior to the definition given in this unit? Write an essay of no more than 300 words defending your choice.

11. The following quotation is from Timothy Leary's article "Languages: Energy Systems Sent and Received":

The absurdity of man's language exchanges is now clear. Each of us has a static picture of the world—accidentally imprinted, and elaborated by means of chains of conditioned associations—themselves arbitrary and parochially accidental. Each of us labors under the illusion that our imprint board is reality. . . . When two human beings attempt to communicate, the absurdity is compounded—my chessboard interacting with your Monopoly game.

Is Leary right? Is his attitude optimistic or pessimistic? Is he downgrading man's linguistic ability or is he amazed that it works as well as it does? Write a brief essay defending your position on these questions.

12. The word *presupposition,* a technical term in linguistics, refers to those things which do not appear in the surface shape of a sentence, but which are nonetheless understood by all native speakers of the language. For example, in the sentence "Even John could get an A in this class" there are two presuppositions (among others): (1) John is not very bright; (2) the class mentioned is not difficult. Neither of these pieces of information appears anywhere in that sentence. Now look at the following sentence, keeping the concept of presupposition in mind, and explain why they are so strange:

a. John is an Eagle Scout, and he can't build a fire, either.
b. That flagpole lying there flat on the ground is thirty feet tall.

13. Notice that if you change the sentence "Even John could get an A in this class" to "John could get an A in this class" you no longer have the two presuppositions listed for the sentence in exercise 12. What does this tell you?

14. One characteristic common to every human language is that of ambiguity—that is, the possibility for one sequence of language to have two or more meanings. Write a sentence corresponding to each of the possible meanings of the following ambiguous sentences:

    a. Crissy fed her dog biscuits.

    b. Bill reminded the doctor of his other patient.

    c. Visiting sailors can be boring.

    d. Officer Trusty arrested the burglar in the bedroom.

HOW NOT TO DROWN
IN THE STUFF

2

This unit is going to be somewhat different from the rest of the units in this text. It differs from a scheme of organization called the "format" of the book and is intended to serve as a practical tool for using the book as a whole.

It is customary for a writer to hold to his or her main points and method of organization in a given piece of writing, for the very good reason that clarity is impossible otherwise. As a result it has become standard practice for writers, particularly in scientific and scholarly writing, to put their digressions, and any information which does not fit perfectly into their scheme of organization, in the footnotes. (The curious result of this practice is that it is a truism that the most interesting parts of scholarly articles are frequently the footnotes. But that's another story.) At any rate, this unit is much too long to be a footnote, and it seemed simplest just to put it up here at the front of the book where it logically belonged.

What we're going to do in this unit is try to find some basic strategies for interpreting and evaluating sequences of language. It's fine to say that you need to be able to answer such questions about sequences of language as "is it relevant?" and "is it honest?" and "is it useful?" and "does it make sense?" We can all agree on that. But how do you go about it? How do you look at a sequence of language and judge it as reader or listener? What do you look for? First, and most obviously, you look for plain instances of typographical errors, lies, and factual mistakes. To spot these you have to be careful. You have to refuse to accept a statement as fact until you have checked it out, when such acceptance is going to matter. Look at the following examples:

1. Nine out of ten doctors claim that the wearing of silver earrings will prevent hives.

This sentence is an obvious lie. If you are dubious, ask any ten doctors. *But be careful.* The lie here is *not* "the wearing of silver earrings will prevent hives." That may or may not be true, and no evidence is offered in the above statement either for or against it. The claim made—and the lie—is that nine out of ten doctors *say* that wearing silver earrings will prevent hives.

2. The Emancipation Proclamation was written in 1867.

Error. This is a typographical error; in this case the printer has re-versed the last two numbers in the date 1876. Publishers of books and magazines and other printed materials make a real effort to avoid this kind of thing, but the book that is totally free of "typos" has probably never been printed yet.

Most of the time such errors probably won't matter to you. If you see the sentence "the food was too salpy for my taste," you will automatically correct the error. If a date or figure is incorrect, it probably is not important; either you will notice it at once, in which case it's done you no harm, or it's not an item that is crucial to your understanding or appreciation of the sequence in which it appears. In two situations, however, you must go to a reliable source and check every so-called fact: first, when you must base a decision of your own upon that fact; second, when you are going to quote the fact or use it in such a way that other people are going to rely on it.

3. The most effective cure for warts is the boiled hind foot of a toad.

Mistake. The person who wrote this sentence is simply wrong. (If he knows he is wrong, of course, then this is not a mistake but a lie.) The second half of example 1 was also a mistake, so far as anyone knows.

You may handle this mistake just as you handle typographical errors. If you should read that the most common bird in Texas is the flamingo, and you have no interest in either birds or Texas but are reading the article because you are interested in the writer's experi-ences as a hitchhiker, it doesn't matter whether the flamingo is found in Texas or not. Nobody has time to check every statement he reads or hears, and we have the right to assume that ordinarily we can rely on the truth of what we read or hear so far as factual detail is concerned. However, if you do need to be able to rely on the factual detail, you must proceed as you did with the typos—go to a reliable source and check.

There are several things to remember here. First, when we say we can generally assume that the factual detail is correct, we are assuming that we have paid some attention to the source of the language. If the writer is known to be an extremist, or to have special personal reasons for distorting the truth, or has been proven wrong frequently in the past, then it is not safe to rely on that source. We can read or listen to what is said and enjoy it, but we should remember that the facts are not reliable. Secondly, if for some reason you check a fact and find that the writer has made a significant error, it's a good idea to check several more items. If they are also in error, it is no longer safe to assume that the writer knows what he or she is talking about.

Most of the trouble in dealing with language does not lie with such problems as we have just described. Few writers are so careless as to pepper their work with obvious lies and mistakes. The real difficulty lies in those sequences of language where the lies, mistakes, and errors are carefully hidden and cannot be resolved merely by turning to an authoritative source. Let's look at some of the most common ways in which such concealment occurs in the language you are likely to encounter.

4. The Appeal to Pity

A man is accused of having embezzled a large sum of money from the firm for which he works. The lawyer defending him, when releasing a story to the newspapers, does not discuss the embezzlement at all. Instead he devotes the story to a long recital about his client's miserable childhood, the fact that he never had a proper chance to get ahead in life, and the fact that he now has a bleeding ulcer.

This is an attempt to distract attention from the real issue—whether or not the man is guilty of the charges—by appealing to the sympathy of others. It may well be true that the man is deserving of pity, but that is an independent issue. It has nothing to do with the issue of guilt or innocence.

5. The Appeal to Force

A professor whose students have objected to the enormous amount of outside reading he requires them to do spends some time in class discussing his requirement. He concludes his discussion by saying, "and please remember that not only do I assign the reading in this class, I also assign the grades."

This is just a club in word's clothing. The fact that the man assigns the grades has nothing whatever to do with the validity of his teaching methods. The appeal to force is a crude way of winning an argument and is usually only a last resort. Its dangerousness lies not in the possibility that you as reader or listener will be misled, but rather in the degree of power the person using it has to carry out his threat.

6. The Appeal to Authority

You are arguing with another student about the behavior of baboons. He defends his own claims by showing you a quotation from a famous mathematician, whose opinions about baboon behavior agree with his.

This type or argument is valid *if and only if* the authority appealed to is an expert in the field being discussed. Thus, to appeal to a quotation by Einstein in order to back up a mathematical opinion is probably valid; to appeal to Einstein to back up an anthropological opinion is not likely to be. The proper way to deal with such an argument is to demand that either (a) other evidence be presented or (b) the authority's qualifications as expert be presented.

The most common use of this kind of argument today is in advertising testimonials, where a football player or a popular singer advises which toothpaste to buy or which cereal is more nutritious. There is no reason to expect that a football player knows any more about nutrition or toothpaste than you do.

7. The Appeal to the People

An apartment manager is trying to rent one of his apartments. Instead of telling you about the materials that went into construction or the distance to schools and transportation, he tells you that "all the best people" are moving into this area of town and that one of his apartments has been rented by Gary Cooper's cousin.

This is another distraction technique. It may be true that many fine people have moved into the area, and for good reasons of their own, but that has nothing to do with whether or not the apartment is suitable for your needs. *Be careful.* This is one of the most common advertising techniques in America today. For example, the cigarette advertisements always show a tall, strong, handsome man and a beautiful young girl, and "snob appeal" advertisements imply that those who "want only the very best for their families" buy Product X.

8. The Abusive Argument

A candidate for public office is running against a woman with strong qualifications and much popular appeal. He cannot find anything objectionable about her platform or public statements. The candidate therefore ignores the opponent's qualifications for office and devotes his campaign time to telling the public that the woman was once on the staff of a radical underground newspaper.

This campaign technique has been overdone to such an extent that it is surprising that it still works. Unfortunately it is very effective when the abusive statement happens to hit a voter right smack in the middle of one of his or her pet projects. We find the abusive argument in other forms too; we may be advised against reading the novels of a particular author because he has a reputation for some activity frowned upon by society. Although the charge against the writer may be true, the claim that the author was a jewel thief is emphatically *not* evidence that his books are worthless. This argument is particularly uninteresting when the author has been dead for a hundred years.

9. The Argument from Ignorance

A scientist writes an article in a popular magazine in which she states that there is positively no such thing as telepathy. To support this claim she points out that no one has ever presented one piece of solid evidence that telepathy exists.

Watch out for this one. It occurs in the two following forms:

$$X \text{ is } \begin{Bmatrix} \text{false} \\ \text{true} \end{Bmatrix} \text{ because it has never been proved } \begin{Bmatrix} \text{true} \\ \text{false} \end{Bmatrix}.$$

Because something has never been proved either true or false, it is not possible to state which of these terms applies to it. The absence of positive proof does not constitute negative proof, or vice versa.

10. The Circumstantial Argument

A man has been arguing with a friend who hunts for sport. He has pointed out to her that the animals she kills are helpless against the technology of modern weaponry (point one). He has pointed out that she keeps only the heads of the animals and leaves the rest, so that she cannot be said to need them for food or clothing (point two). He points out that some of the species she kills are in danger of becoming extinct (point three). The sportswoman does not dispute any of his statements, but says "I don't notice you becoming a vegetarian."

This is another distraction technique. It is a way to avoid replying to an argument by saying that the person presenting it is, because of some special personal circumstance, as guilty of the offense as the person argued against. The claim may be true, but its truth is independent of the truth of that argument. That is, the fact that a man might have killed his wife would not make his arguments against murder invalid.

11. The Circular Argument

An advertisement says that a particular tennis racket is better than any other tennis racket, offering as support the fact that many expert tennis players use it. It also tells you that the way you can tell that a tennis player is an expert is by noting that he or she uses that tennis racket.

You run into this one a lot. Another variant is:

X.   All good students get straight A's.
Y.   Really? How can you tell they're good students?
X.   Why, because they get straight A's, of course.

12. The Accident Argument

A student runs across a man's property because he is being chased by a large and vicious dog. The man signs a complaint against him at the police station in spite of the circumstances, saying "Trespassing is trespassing."

This is a matter of applying a rule that is valid in most cases to a particular case where it is not. Prosecuting someone for stealing a loaded gun from a drunken man would be another example of the same error in reasoning.

Be careful. This faulty argument is often backed up by a claim that to ignore the rule, even once, even where it is clearly wrong, would set a precedent. People say, "Oh, if we let you do that we'd have to let everybody." Point out that if "everybody" has the same good reason for needing the exception that you do, they are entitled to have the exception made; and that if they don't have your good reason then your case does not set a precedent.

13. The Hasty Generalization

A man notes that in the past six months four murders have been committed by people who were heavy cigarette smokers. He tells his children, "If you smoke cigarettes you'll grow up to be a murderer," and writes his congressman demanding legislation against cigarettes on these grounds.

This is a misapplication of a valid reasoning process. If 100 Cocker Spaniels who are fed Product Q break out in a rash, it is valid to conclude that there is something about the product that makes it unsuitable as dog food. There are instances where even one case is sufficient—for example, if one child dies from eating a certain weed, you make certain that no other child eats it, without waiting for further testing. But where the testing of a hypothesis is not a matter of life and death, there is no excuse for hasty generalizations.

14. The False Cause-and-Effect Argument

A student hands in an exam on ordinary ruled paper instead of using a bluebook. He gets a D on the exam and complains that the bad grade is the result of not using a bluebook.

The student may be right. However, if (a) the professor has made no stipulation that bluebooks must be used and (b) the student's work is only worth a D, this is an example of a false cause-and-effect argument. Remember the claim in the first example that wearing silver earrings prevent hives? Someone who wears silver earrings and does not get hives (cancer, diabetes, or arthritis) and who then concludes that the earrings are responsible is using this kind of false reasoning. It is the basis of the following joke:

A man is standing on a street corner twirling a keychain, and a friend comes along and asks him what on earth he's doing.

MAN.   I'm keeping the tigers away.

FRIEND.   You can't keep tigers away by twirling a keychain!

MAN.   It's working, isn't it?

15. The Irrelevant Conclusion

An administrator at a college wants a rule forbidding students to drink beer on campus. He convinces the authorities to establish the rule by arguing that alcoholism is a terrible disease and that public drunkenness is disgusting.

This one is dangerous because it isn't possible to argue with anything that the proponent of the irrelevant conclusion is saying. The administrator in the example is correct that alcoholism is a terrible disease, as well as in his assessment of public intoxication. There is no way that you can argue against either of these statements.

The only way to handle this argument is to insist that the conclusion has nothing to do with the argument. You must make it clear that the administrator's real claim is that if beer is available on campus all students will get drunk constantly and become alcoholics in the end. When the actual claim is out in the open it will be possible to argue the case on its merits.

One of the most insidious ways that this tactic is used today is in situations where someone tells you that they are certain that you want to do something which you cannot possibly say you *don't* want to do—but that stated objective or request is not really what they are after. For example:

> Because we are certain that you will want to add to the beauty of the campus and set an example for the incoming freshman class, we are offering you this opportunity to. . . .

. . . an opportunity to do something you genuinely don't want to do. But the implication, if you refuse, is that you have no interest in the beauty of the campus. Again, dig until you find the real claim being made and bring it out into the open where it can be dealt with.

16. The Trick Question

A policeman says to a suspect, "All right—where did you throw that bag of marijuana you were carrying?"

This is a way of hiding an unsupported claim. The most famous example of this kind is the question: "Have you stopped beating your wife?" Notice that if you answer no you are admitting that you used to beat your wife and that you still do. If you answer yes you are denying that you beat your wife now but admitting that you used to. The only way to deal with this is to demand that the question be rephrased until all the tricks are out of it.

These are by no means all the ways that language can be used to fool the listener or the reader. Weighty words, high-flown phrases, and top-heavy structure can be skillfully spun together to impress you. This writer once listened to a talk of this kind, the content of which was nonexistent, only to have a woman in the row ahead turn around and warble that she didn't understand a single word that was being said, but "I just know it has to be terribly important!"

Undefined terms are another source of problems. Phrases like "radicals say" or "conservatives claim" are meaningless unless we know what the writer means by the words *radical* and *conservative*. You have a right to insist that terms be defined.

And there is the odd problem of what is known as "charisma." Charisma is the ability someone has to spellbind an audience by the force of his or her personality, without reference to the real content of the language. Adlai Stevenson once said that people listened to his speeches and said "My, what a wonderful speech," but when they listened to John Kennedy's, they said "Let's march!" That's charisma. Nobody knows quite how to deal with it, but you can be aware that it exists and try not to let it sway you unduly.

Every day of your life you are expected to accept or reject language sequences in the form of rules and regulations, contracts, business agreements, advertisements, speeches, lectures, and a multitude of other forms. Unless you take the time to examine these sequences for flaws and distortions you have no one to blame but yourself if language gets the upper hand over you. Faced with a sequence of language you must say, "All right, here's what it appears to mean—but what is that person *really* saying? And why is he saying it?" This is something we must all learn to do.

The way to end this unit, if it were like the other units in this text, would be to add a set of exercises. But that is not really necessary. There are two ways in which you can exercise what is presented in this unit. First, whenever your assignment in another unit demands that you write something to support a position of your own, examine what you have written to find out if you are guilty of the offenses we've been discussing.

Second, look for examples. Collect any magazine you enjoy reading, some Christmas gift catalogues from mail-order houses, real estate advertisements, and two newspapers—one with an "establishment" point of view, one with some other point of view that interests (or repels) you. Sit down and review these materials as if your linguistic life depended on it. Spot every example of a flaw in reasoning, and notice exactly how the flaw is handled. You'll learn quickly. You may become so expert that you will automatically evaluate language sequences in the future for all the difficulties described above. That's the point.

THE LANGUAGE AND STRUCTURE OF PROSE NONFICTION

3

You are a student at an urban college that has severe parking problems. One of the parking lots at your school is restricted to faculty, and students may not park there under any circumstances. This means that you often get to school and find no parking space available to you, even when there are a number of empty spaces in the faculty lot.

You may be either for or against the existence of this faculty reserved lot. Write an article for the college newspaper defending your position. Be sure you state the problem clearly. Offer at least two well-motivated arguments for your claim, and stay within the newspaper's limit of 1500 words.

DEFINING PROSE NONFICTION

Prose nonfiction is probably the broadest category of language dealt with in this book. Newspapers, magazine articles, textbooks, scholarly journals, how-to books, and religious books belong to this category. Prose nonfiction can probably be best defined by elimination. If a sequence of written language is *not* poetry, fiction, or drama, and if it is not simply a list—like the contents of the telephone book—it is probably prose nonfiction.

The chances are good that you will never write a sequence of fiction outside a classroom, and even then you will write it only in an English or Creative Writing class. Because of this fact, because so few of us make the writing of fiction a significant part of our daily lives, our relationship to the language of fiction is primarily that of processor; we are on the receiving end. The same is true of poetry, the subject of another unit in this text. Nonfiction prose, on the other hand, is vital to your life as a student, since almost everything you write during your academic career falls into that category. Every essay assignment in a composition course, every term paper in a history or science course, every research paper, even the M.A. thesis or Ph.D. dissertation, is prose nonfiction.

Because of the wide scope of this type of language, we will not restrict this unit as narrowly as some of the following units. Instead, we will consider examples of a type of nonfiction that appears in as infinite variety as does the short story, and which (unlike the short story) constitutes the largest proportion of many people's reading today: the magazine article.

Approximately 10,000 magazines are being published in the United States today, and with few exceptions the bulk of their content is composed of nonfiction articles. Fifty years ago, fiction monopolized magazine space. Today the nonfiction article, rather than the story, is used on the magazine cover to entice people to buy the magazine.

Four primary types of language structure are used in the writing of nonfiction. If you have taken previous courses in composition or rhetoric you will already be familiar with them. They are:

1. Description
2. Narration
3. Exposition
4. Argument

DESCRIPTION

There is nothing at all mysterious about the technique of description or the reasons for writing it. The writer uses description to present enough facts about the physical appearance of something to enable the reader to visualize it. The amount of detail required depends on such things as whether the reader need have only a rough idea of the object's appearance, whether he must be able to identify it quickly, or, perhaps, make another object just like it. Here are three examples of description:

> The two common varieties of barberry—*Berberis canadensis* and *Berberis vulgaris*—are similar leaf-losing shrubs which grow to a

height of three to six feet. They have thorns on their dark brown branches. The leaves of the plants are alternate or in lateral clusters . . . broadest at the center, wedge-shaped at the base and smoothly pointed at the tip. When we look for the barberry in November, though, the leaves will be gone and the shrub will probably be thickly covered with football-shaped berries which hang in clusters from a common stem. Closer examination will reveal that the fruits hang almost straight down and the thorns form the sign of a cross.—James E. Churchill.

The actin molecules are small, roughly spherical particles that are arrayed in the thin filament as if to form a twisted double strand of beads. An important characteristic of the individual actin molecules is that they are not spherically symmetrical; each acts as if it had a distinguishable "front" and "back." Since the actin molecules are assembled into filaments in a "front to back" manner, the entire thin filament acquires a recognizable polarity; that is, the front sides of all the actins face in one direction and the back sides face in the opposite direction.—John M. Murray and Annemarie Weber.

Ten o'clock Sunday morning in the hills of North Carolina. Cars, miles of cars, in every direction, millions of cars, pastel cars, aqua green, aqua blue, aqua beige, aqua buff, aqua dawn, aqua dusk, aqua aqua, aqua Malacca, Malacca lacquer, Cloud lavender, Assassin pink, Rake-a-cheek raspberry, Nude Strand coral, Honest Thrill orange, and Baby Fawn Lust cream-colored cars are all going to the stock-car races, and that old mothering North Carolina sun keeps exploding off the windshields.—Tom Wolfe.

Now all three of these examples have in common the fact that they present details, aimed primarily at the reader's eye, with the intention of making that reader "see" the thing described. But the similarity stops there. In the first example, the writer wants to describe the barberry in such specific and exact detail that the reader can go out and unhesitatingly select the barberry plant from among other plants. This is important, since the article is about eating wild foods, and if the description is not clear the reader may eat a poisonous plant that has a superficial resemblance to the barberry. The paragraph will be of great interest to anyone looking for a barberry plant and of almost no interest to the rest of the reading population, because although the writer has done a good job, the article is deliberately aimed at the select group of seekers-after-barberry and at nobody else.

The second example is also directed at a specific audience.

Julia Margaret Cameron. Rosebud Garden of Girls, *1868. Royal Photographic Society Collection.*

DESCRIPTION: Describe this picture in careful detail. Try to limit your description to 500 words.

Unless you happen to be a scientist, and a biologist, you will not want to read this paragraph. The writers know that, and they would not be surprised to hear that you are not interested in the paragraph. They would be upset, however, if a biologist informed them that no one could distinguish an actin molecule from another, different molecule after reading the description.

The third example is very different. It is aimed not at a special audience but at that vast group called the General Public. This paragraph introduces the reader to the scene and gives him the feeling that he is actually seeing that stream of cars headed for the stock-car races.

If you are going to write description, then, you must first be sure who you are writing it for. If your audience is interested in what *happened*, it will resent having to wade through paragraphs of descriptive detail. If, on the other hand, the main need of the reader is to be able to identify the thing described, the detail will be welcome, and missing details will be resented.

An article composed entirely of description is relatively rare. Articles with a high proportion of description do occur, particularly in travel magazines, in magazines on mechanics and electronics which describe new products and processes in detail, in scholarly journals for fields like astronomy and botany, in household magazines, and in magazines for collectors, where items on exhibition or for sale are described. In most cases, however, description provides the setting for the rest of the article, and the skillful writer must provide just enough and not too much.

NARRATION

We usually think of narration as an element of story-telling, as in the short story and the folktale, but narration is a major component of nonfiction as well. People want to know what has happened, what is happening, and what is going to happen. Since the sixties, much prose narrative has been in the form called "New Journalism," * exemplified by such writers as Truman Capote, Terry Southern, Norman Mailer, and Ken Kesey. This type of prose is almost undistinguishable from fiction.

Michael J. Arlen, in an *Atlantic Monthly* article, discusses the difference between traditional and "new" journalism, saying of the traditional that "the American press rested its weight upon the simple declarative sentence. The no-nonsense approach. Who-What-Where-When. Clean English, it was later called when people started teaching it at college."

We see this type of writing most frequently today in the straight newspaper story; it relates the facts and sets them down in

---

* It should be pointed out that the "New Journalism" is not really new, since it was practiced long ago by people like Mark Twain. But it has only become a dominant nonfiction form since the 1960s.

some sort of order, usually putting all the major points into one leading paragraph and adding the details later. Edmund Carpenter has called this traditional form a "pyramid" and has pointed out that people ordinarily read newspapers by reading all of the first page, then reading all of the second page, and so on, despite the fact that the first page may have the beginnings of a dozen stories all continued elsewhere. Obviously, if all the important facts were not present in the story's opening section, this reading technique would be impossibly frustrating.

Michael Arlen notes that the traditional way of reporting a hotel fire was to put down things like: where the fire was and when it started; how many people were hurt in the blaze; how much property was damaged or destroyed. Much of this material would come from an official version of the event obtained by questioning the fire chief or someone else in charge. But, he goes on to say:

> Today, when a New Journalist tells it, there is likely to be *no* deference to an official version. . . . There is virtually no interest in the traditional touchstone facts, the *numbers*—the number of people dead, or saved, or staying at the hotel, the worth of the jewelry, or the cost of damage to the building. Instead, there are attempts to catch the heat of the flames, the *feel* of the fire.

Let's look at the following example of New Journalism, from an article by Terry Southern.

> Whether it's New York or Tuscaloosa, Norfolk or L.A., one factor is constant: The dressing room of the Rolling Stones is always Groove City—the juice flows, smoke rises, crystals crumble, poppers pop, teenies hang in, and Mick knifes through like a ballet-dancing matador . . . all of the funky wail of Keith's guitar turing up, and sometimes the honking sax of a solid, down-home pickup sideman, like Texas Bobby Keys. And in Buddha repose, Charlie sits twirling his sticks Sid Catlett-style. Scent of good karma.
>
> SLOW ZOOM IN ON MIRRORED FACE OF FALLEN ANGEL as Mick sits down at the lighted glass, and the makeup man leans in intensely to begin his magic ritual—transfiguration toward sympathy for the devil. I watch cautiously. It's a heavy number, a lot of head-stuff coming down.
>
> Outside in the Washington, D.C., stadium, fifty thousand fans are stomping it up to the screams of Stevie Wonder . . . while they wait it out. Like the teenies, they've been hanging in—since two

o'clock this afternoon, many since the night before. Now it's 10:30; they'll soon be impatient.

In the rest of his article, Southern does provide many facts of the who-what-where-when-why variety. But this opening is not intended to inform; it is a device for hooking the reader so that he

Dorothea Lange. Migrant Mother, Nipomo, California, *1936. Courtesy of the Library of Congress.*

NARRATIVE: What do you think is the story behind this woman? Write a brief narrative statement describing her background as if you had talked to her and were writing from what she told you.

or she will be *unable* to move to the beginning of another story. As with fiction, the reader wants to find out what happens next.

Notice that the verbs in the excerpt are almost all in the present tense, giving the vivid sense that you are *there*, experiencing the scene *with* Terry Southern, the Stones, and the fans. Notice, too, the borrowing of techniques from film-making, particularly in the first paragraph, where we see or hear one detail after another in rapid sequence, as if a camera were presenting the scene to us. The opening sentence of the second paragraph, SLOW ZOOM IN ON MIRRORED FACE OF FALLEN ANGEL, is pure undisguised film technique, and it is very effective.

If we tried to rewrite this opening in traditional style, supplying invented facts and numbers, we would get something like the following:

> On July 4, 1972, in Washington, D.C., the Rolling Stones held a concert at the city stadium. The concert, which did not begin until 11:13 P.M., attracted 50,000 fans, many of whom waited outside the stadium from the previous evening, July 3rd.
>
> Before the concern began, the Stones' lead singer, Mick Jagger, gave a brief interview in his dressingroom, which was a scene of chaos.

Which version do you prefer? The question is meaningless and must be rephrased as "Which version do you prefer *for what purpose?*"

If you are interested only in the facts, as when you read the front pages of a newspaper, you would be irritated by plowing through paragraphs like those quoted from Southern's article while you hunted for the who, what, where, when, and why. On the other hand, if you are reading for pleasure as well as for information, you will prefer the Southern technique.

There are, then, two basic styles of nonfiction narration. In both cases we find out that X happened, and later Y happened, but we find out in very different ways. One presents the facts in an orderly sequence, based on chronology, with no attempt to make them "live" for the reader. Newspaper stories, textbooks (perhaps unfortunately), and scholarly articles in professional journals use this format. Such narration in the hands of a skilled writer can of course be just as interesting and gripping for the reader as the New Journalism technique. Ordinarily, though, the intention behind such writing is to inform rather than to please.

The second technique also presents the facts, although it may omit items that would appear in traditional journalism—particularly what Arlen calls the "numbers." However, these facts will not appear together in a clump, but will be salted into a narrative that attempts to make the reader feel that he or she is actually present and taking part in the action.

EXPOSITION

In expository writing the primary intention is to inform. Pure exposition is much more common than pure description. For example, cookbooks are almost entirely exposition, as are how-to-do-it articles or books. A typical article of this type will include the following:

1. Item to be produced
2. Tools and materials required
3. Step-by-step instructions

Frequently the article will also include drawings or photographs to aid the reader in the construction or preparation of the item.

As you can see, much vivid detail would be out of place in a how-to-do-it article. If a reader is trying to build a loom, a fence, or a dulcimer, he will have no interest whatsoever in plowing through extraneous matter. He just wants to know how to achieve his goal.

In *Mother Earth News* there is an article by Jerry Friedberg on converting an ordinary car to run on propane gas. Mr. Friedberg uses the following subheadings:

1. Equipment
2. Costs
3. Tools and supplies
4. Instructions
    a. Installing the tank
    b. Installing the convertor
    c. Installing the jet
    d. Finishing the installation
    e. Adjusting the air-fuel mixture
    f. Buying liquid propane

Here is a sample paragraph from the article:

Take off the two cloth-covered tubes on the left side of the carb and unscrew the two 13 mm bolts that hold the carburetor to the manifold. (A 1/2" wrench will work if you don't have a 13 mm one). As you lift the carb off, you'll find that it's still held by a connection to the accelerator cable, the end of which passes through a little cylinder clamp which has a small setscrew in its side. Loosen the setscrew and slip the cable out . . . but be careful you don't lose the cylinder clamp, which is now free to drop out. Note where it goes and store it in a safe place.

Only someone personally interested in converting a car to propane would be likely to read this article. Although the article is well written, its sole purpose is to explain a particular task. It contains no plot, no intriguing characters, no inspiring message, and no punchline.

There are a few writers, however, who create a kind of hybrid exposition that *is* intended to be more than a simple set of instructions. Peg Bracken, for example, writes material that does tell you how to cook but can be read with interest by people who never have cooked and never intend to. Here is a typical Bracken paragraph, disguised as straightforward exposition:

As indicated earlier, the reluctant solo cook is rather a creature of habit, who tends to major in one—and only one—of several eating patterns.

1. The English Muffin with Something on It
2. The Egg with Something under It
3. The Milk Shake with Something in It
4. The Soup with Something beside It
5. The Baked Potato with Something over It

That is, when the chips are down and the freezer contains mainly what you don't feel like thawing or eating, it will be one of these you revert to. So let us take a brief look at each one.

This is a difficult style to maintain, and unless the writer is careful, it gets unbearably *cute.* Ms. Bracken does it with sufficient skill that many people read her magazine articles and books who have no interest in how to prepare an "English Muffin with Something on It," skipping the recipes the way people who hate description skip long descriptive passages.

Photo by John G. Pitkin

EXPOSITION: Study this picture and state exactly what you think the woman in the picture is doing. Try to stick to the facts and leave out emotional responses.

ARGUMENT

Argument is very similar to exposition, except that it is intended primarily to persuade, rather than to inform. The writer of argument presents facts, reasoned statements, or emotional statements in an attempt to bring the reader into agreement with his stated point of view, the *thesis* of his argument.

Unlike the political speech which also seeks to convince and persuade, the written argument is subject to leisurely review by the reader, so that the writer can afford to bring in point after point, each flanked with supporting statements. Up to the point of ridiculous excess, the more points supporting the thesis, the stronger the argument. In the examples that follow, notice that the argument uses the basic structure described in unit 1.

Look at the following example by Denis Hayes, from an article called "Can We Bust the Highway Trust?" Mr. Hayes begins by describing vividly the paved-over condition of Los Angeles, the smog, the accident toll, the health problems of emphysema, and concludes that as a result of the automobile the city "grows relentlessly noisier, dirtier, and uglier." He ends his description with a rhetorical question: "Why is this affront to public decency tolerated?" He then begins the argument.

> According to advertisements written and distributed at considerable expense by automobile makers, gasoline salesmen, and road builders, it is because the private automobile is an unsurpassed convenience for all of us—because it takes us wherever we need or want to go more quickly than we could get there by any other means of transportation, and in the most pleasing fashion imaginable.
>
> But people who drive or ride private automobiles through Los Angeles rarely if ever enjoy the experience. Any trip into, within, or out of the city is hard work at best and at worst a grating ordeal. All involved suffer a similar fate. They inch their exasperated way up waiting lines at freeway entrances, stand almost motionless bumper to bumper for as long as two hours at a time, find all available parking spaces filled upon reaching the central city, and ultimately arrive back home disgusted and exhausted by the compulsive aggressiveness that has come to characterize automobiling. Instead of enjoying an exhilarating exercise in person freedom, the motorist endures a sweaty war of nerves.

We can break down this sequence into its components as follows:

THESIS

The claim that the misery we suffer as a result of the automobile is justified by its comfort and convenience is false.

POINT

Automobile travel is characterized by endless waiting and delays.

POINT

Assuming you do arrive where you are going, you have no place to put your car and have wasted your time.

POINT

Automobile travel is exhausting and disgusting because it demands constant aggressive behavior on the part of the driver.

POINT

Automobile travel is a strain on the nervous system.

Mr. Hayes then argues each point in more detail, provides supporting evidence in the form of expert opinion and statistics, brings in additional information, and argues a compelling and convincing case against the whole idea of travel by automobile.

The skill of argument is possibly the most valuable single language skill that you can acquire. The subject used to be taught extensively in our schools. This writer learned argument as part of a high-school debating team whose coach required written briefs, made every member of the team argue first on one side of the argument and then on the other, and who was mercilessly unsympathetic toward any attempt to weasle out of the construction of a strong and sound case. Nothing I have ever been taught anywhere else has been as useful.

The following example of argument is the introductory paragraph to an article whose thesis is that the traditional assumptions about the connection between amount of time in school and amount of learning are not necessarily valid.

One of the most widely accepted assumptions in education has been that exposure to teaching is highly related to student learning—and in a linear fashion. That is, we have assumed that a 50 per cent increase in full-time schooling would result in a 50 per cent increase in the knowledge retained by students. We have also taken for granted that formal schooling accounts for the major share, if not all, of the knowledge and skills that young people acquire. Therefore, in order to improve standards, it is necessary to increase the number of years of schooling, or the number of hours a subject is taught per week, or both.—Torsten Husén.

Maurice Schell

ARGUMENT: What do you think of these young people and their activity? Are they wasting their time or doing something valuable and creative? Prepare a carefully argued defense of your position.

This paragraph carefully introduces the article that follows, setting out the situation for the reader in terms of the traditional argument for more time in school. Professor Husén then presents evidence from all of the following:

1. Studies in which children have entered school at an earlier age than is usual, therefore receiving more years of schooling, without any resulting increase in learning
2. Studies in which length of time in school was drastically reduced because of teacher shortages or other factors, with no resulting decrease in learning
3. Studies in which it can be demonstrated that the amount of learning depends heavily upon socioeconomic factors outside school rather than on in-school instruction itself

He concludes by stating that the amount of evidence against the traditional concept of schooling is beginning to have an impact on today's education, and that it is possible that we have been mistaken all along.

TEACHER. Ferrabeau, have you ever answered a question by saying that you didn't know?
FERRABEAU. Hmm. I don't know.

Most nonfiction writing is a combination of two or more of these structural types; we rarely have pure description, pure narration, pure exposition, or pure argument. The three brief articles included at the end of this unit illustrate how this combining takes place.

Remember the parking lot problem that you wrote about at the beginning of this unit? You may have taken a number of approaches to the exercise, for example:

1. You chose pure description and described the situation in detail, telling the reader about the empty faculty lots and the full student lots.
2. You chose pure narration, taking the reader through a student's hour-long maddening search for an empty parking space, driving past the empty faculty lot and around and around the full student lot, finally ending by taking a faculty space in desperation, chancing a parking ticket.

3. You chose pure exposition or argument, first stating the problem, then presenting several points for or against your position, perhaps presenting your suggestion for a solution of the problem, and concluding with a summarizing paragraph.

What is more likely, however, is that your paper contained examples of all four types of writing. You may have begun with a description or narration and switched to exposition or argument, for instance.

Whatever your original choice, rewrite your paper in one of the following two ways:

1. Write it in a new journalism format, putting the reader in the middle of the situation.

2. Devise a solution for the problem and redo your paper as a how-to-do-it article on your solution.

EXERCISES

1. A number of so-called composite stories have recently been published by New Journalists. In these stories the writer gathered data about a number of people to create a story about one hypothetical person, but the reader was not told that the supposed subject of the story was a composite. The writers of these stories defend them, claiming that they are in effect reports of real things that happened to real people; some readers, however, have demanded that such materials be labelled clearly as fiction. What is your opinion on this subject? Write a statement of 500 words explaining your position.

2. Much necessary but unglamorous labor has been neglected by our technology. Although we are able to put men on the moon, we do not seem to be able to release people from the multitude of piddling chores that make a house liveable. Choose one of these chores and consider it carefully; then write a description of a proposed solution. Give at least three solid reasons for the superiority of your solution to the current situation. (An example of past work in this area is the development of fitted bedsheets, to cut down the time spent in making beds, or the near-elimination of ironing through the use of permanent-press fabrics.)

3. Cancer kills 900 people every day in the United States, yet the research budget for cancer in 1970 was only $173 million dol-

lars. If we divide the 1970 budget by the U.S. population, we find that we spent $964 for every citizen, of which $395 went for military spending and only 91¢ went for cancer research. Write a letter to your congressman either defending or attacking this distribution of national priorities.

4. This exercise is a group project. As students living in the area where your college is located, you are probably aware of some local problems. For example, there may be a slum area or a rural shantytown. There may be a large industry which is actively engaged in polluting the air or water, but which provides a high percentage of local jobs. There may be a "town versus gown" controversy. There may be an inadequate airport or hospital or other service institution. Choose some one of these problems and research it. Obtain as many facts, figures, and statistics as you can in the time allowed. Remember that a research project of this kind done in *depth* would take months instead of the few days you will have to spend. Then, as a group, prepare a detailed report on your findings.

5. In exercise 4 you will probably have used the structural techniques of exposition and description. Now see if you can propose a solution for the problem and use the technique of argument to defend your proposal. Try to present at least three well-motivated points to support your idea.

6. Choose one problem identified in exercise 4 and write a brief article, not more than five paragraphs, presenting the problem. Write the article first in traditional journalistic style, then in the New Journalism You-Are-There style. Pay careful attention to your use of language in both cases. Then compare your two articles and decide which would be most effective *on a long-term basis* for rallying people to the cause.

7. Many charitable organizations advertise in magazines for help to needy people, particularly children. A typical advertisement shows a beautiful, but pathetically thin child, dressed in rags, and is captioned "the average dog in America eats better than this child." Write a letter to the editor, of about 300 words in length, taking one of the following positions:

   a. Since there is little anyone can do about the starving people in this world, it is cruel to torment those of us who are not starving with this sort of thing.

   b. There is more than enough for the average American citizen to worry about without adding this ration of gloom and misery.

c.   The money spent for such ads would be far better spent for the starving children pictured.

d.   It is impossible for anyone to enjoy a magazine where full-color advertisements for electric pencil sharpeners are flanked by ads for help to destitute children, and the magazine is going to lose your subscription if it does not stop this illogical behavior.

8.   Write a letter of reply to the letter you wrote in exercise 6, from an editor attempting to defend his or her practice.

9.   What's wrong with your English class? Interview some members of the class on this question and write up your interview, editing carefully to present the best possible organization of the material

10.   A great controversy arose in the early 1970s over the claims made by nutritionist Adelle Davis that many, if not most, of American health problems could be solved by proper diet and doses of vitamins. The U.S. medical profession responded by attacking Ms. Davis's claims, which, if true, would mean that Americans are wasting millions of dollars on unnecssary medical care. Check out any one of Ms. Davis's claims—for example, application of Vitamin E to burns will stop pain, speed healing, and prevent scarring—by locating the medical sources she cites as references, and writing a report on the results of your research.

11.   Here is a paragraph from Marshall McLuhan's book, *Gutenberg Galaxy:*

> There can be no doubt that one of the essential reasons for the custom of dictation finds its explanation in the fact that, before the era of printing, schools and scholars had no adequate supply of texts. A manuscript book cost too much; the simplest way of getting them was for the teacher to dictate his text to his pupils. . . . The manual was necessary to the student, not only so far as it served for his university courses, but also because it would be useful in his future career. . . . Moreover, the university required that students present themselves at their courses furnished with books they had made, and if not that at least there be a book shared among every three students. . . . Finally, in presenting himself for his candidature for a degree, the student was required to present the books which belonged to him. In the liberal careers, it was the corps of the profession in question that examined the candidates for a post in order to see in what measure they were furnished with books.

If you were required to write your own texts in this way, what effect would it have on your decision about which courses to take? Explain your answer in 500 words.

12.   Choose an activity that you do well and that others might be interested in performing, and write a how-to-do-it article on the subject. Do not use more than 2000 words, but be sure that your article is clear and that the reader has sufficient information. If illustrations will be needed, provide either drawings or photographs.

13.   A sizeable percentage of nonfiction is written about *other* nonfiction, in the form of book reviews. Look at the following excerpt from a review by Lloyd Linford of Susan Berman's *The Underground Guide to the College of Your Choice.*

> For years, students at Harvard and Berkeley have been putting out "underground" guides to campus survival, insufficient and often unfair, and most particularly concentrating on what classes and professors to take or avoid, as if classes had anything to do with going to college. Now, thanks to Susan Berman and friends, we have an accurate, amusing and relevant guide to almost every major college and university in the U.S.A., a guide that focuses not so much on curriculum as environment.
>
> Covering more than 200 campuses, *The Underground Guide* examines tuition costs, town-gown problems, tribal sex mores (and the lack of them), the dope scene—in short, the real scam on going to college.

Do you agree with Mr. Linford's opinion as to what a student really needs to know about a college? (Assuming that he is serious, of course.) Do you agree with his assessment of past student guides to colleges? Write a paper of 500 words explaining your position on one of these two questions.

14.   Do one of the following, with another student:

    a.   Spend the hours from 2 A.M. to 6 A.M. in a Greyhound Bus terminal.

    b.   Take a trip—it can be a short one—on a Greyhound bus, and pay attention to what people are *saying*. (This writer once heard a serviceman in the back seat of such a bus tell his buddies that "sure, the Navy teaches you to kill, but in the Marines you learn to kill with *class*.")

Write a thousand words in the New Journalism style about your experience. Compare your paper with that of the friend who accompanied you—do your perceptions agree, or are they surprisingly different?

15.   You are a middle-aged homeowner in a suburb. To your horror, you discover that the young couple who bought the house next door to you has brought in half a dozen of their friends and has in fact created a commune. When you call your lawyer to find out what legal action you can take, you find that as long as the neighbor couple claims that their friends are only visiting, there is nothing you can do at all. Write a letter to the editor of your local paper protesting this scandalous situation.

16.   Choose ten square feet of ground, anywhere you like, and write a 1000-word description of those ten square feet. Your aim is to make it possible for anyone, whether he has seen the area or not, to unmistakably identify the ten feet in question. If you can also make your description interesting, you will have accomplished something unusual.

A Song of San Francisco Bay

MALVINA REYNOLDS

.The highway is laid as smooth as glass
For miles and miles and the cars can pass.
But the ant and the bee and the bush and the tree
Whose home it was are now exiles.
And the cars rush by for miles and miles,
To find a place where they can see
A plant, a bush, and a blade of grass,
And a ladybug, and a bee.*

Of the 270-odd miles of shoreline of San Francisco's great bay, some—not much, but some—is still in its natural state: grassy or lightly wooded hills leading down to a rocky border; marsh and tidelands green with reeds and salt grass, still alive with sea and shore birds and the infinite smaller creatures who populate such places. And if you wanted to see something like this, you might take a thirty-mile drive along the bay's northern shore—say on Highway 37—between Vallejo and San Rafael, with no towns between. If you'd been there before, a few years ago, you would remember a long stretch of secondary road a few feet

* From "The Highway," words and music by Malvina Reynolds. Copyright © 1965 by Schroder Music Co., ASCAP.

above tideland level, with open marsh or farmland on both sides and the bay itself stretching to the south.

But now on that route you would find no bay, no marshes, not even farms for miles beyond Vallejo. Just the usual decorations of the modern highway—auto junkyards, hamburger stands, motels, small factories, billboards, gas stations—and the bay not even in sight. So you might take one of the unnamed roads that heads south to where the bay should be, and you could find yourself in the enormous grounds of the Kaiser Steel plant. Driving into the grounds you'd go over a bumpy road through an expanse of raw ocher earth, with a lonely bunch of reeds in a small pool at a culvert showing what had been here before the steel mill took over. As far as the eye can see, lines of flatcars on the spur track carry monster steel pipe probably destined to provide drainage for the new highways that are being laid everywhere you look.

This isn't what you were looking for, so you bump back on the branch road to 37, into the roaring raceway of cars, heading westward again. It is ten miles or more before you finally reach open fields and then the marshes, with reeds and salt grass and, for the first time this trip, the cool wind that blows from the bay and across the flats.

After a while you want to stop, but it isn't easy to turn off, with the heavy traffic averaging 50 miles an hour, and some people might wonder why anyone would want to stop here anyway. No garage, no hot dogs, no bar—the cars all tearing by, headed some place. But it happens there are white herons feeding not far from the road, and you hope to get them with your camera. They have become accustomed to the heavy trucks roaring by and the endless line of cars. But you have to come up easy with the camera—they are not accustomed to people on foot.

The Veil: a darkness at noon

L. F.

It comes in smoke-thin chiffon or opaque black crepe, gaily printed cotton or heavy blood-red linen, stiff with gold embroidery and silver ornaments that flash a shield-shape in the sun. It obscures all the face from forehead to neck, shadows it no more than a breath of dark air or covers brow and nose like a mask. A hundred forms, one function: it separates the women who wear it from the outside world as surely as a wall.

The veil—always associated in the West with Islam—actually

preceded Islam in Arabia, but until the 10th century was not the rule, even among the aristocracy. More typical was the learned and witty Aisha bint Talha, an aristocratic beauty who, when her husband suggested that she veil herself, returned a reply that seems, historically, to have gone unanswered. "Since God, may He be exalted, has put upon me the stamp of beauty, it is my wish that all view this beauty and recognise His grace to them. On no account, therefore, will I veil myself."

Of all aspects of women's subordinate status in the Arab world, the veil—to both West and educated East—seemed the most glaring, a symbol of all the others. Some of the more self-righteous of the 19th-century western missionaries, in denigrating their sister faith, chose the veil as a symbol of woman's oppression (ignoring the indisputable fact that to girls with little knowledge of the world the veil did provide at least psychological protection).

The more educated men and women in countries where veiling is still common exhibit a similar attitude today. A popular opinion on the Arabian Peninsula is that the veil is something foreign—introduced to the Arabs by either the Persians or the Turks. Many men and women equally point out that in the time of the Prophet, that is when Islam was at its strongest as a religious force, there was little veiling. One foreign journalist taking pictures of Bahrain's 50th anniversary of education celebrations a few years ago provoked an unexpected reaction when he trained his camera on a group of veiled women onlookers: they immediately took the veils off.

Some premature efforts to lift the veil were indeed met by repression. When in 1911 the noted poet Jamil Khawi, in Iraq, made a frontal attack on the custom with a speech urging that the veil be "torn away," he was imprisoned for sedition. Some 10 years later when one woman in Beirut attempted, not to unveil, but to modify the color and form of the covering, she had vitriol thrown at her. Even in the mid-30's when a large group of Syrian women appeared unveiled in Damascus they found no safety in numbers: opposition bordering on violence forced them to resume their veils.

Reformers in Muslim countries have often taken first aim at the veil, none more strongly than Turkey's Kemal Ataturk two years after he became president. "I see women throwing a cloth or a towel or something of the sort over their heads covering their faces and their eyes . . ." he said. . . . "It makes the nation look ridiculous; it must be rectified immediately!" Shortly after, Iran's Shah Reza Pahlevi ordered schoolteachers and schoolgirls to unveil, then progressively forbade veiled women to use public conveyances or be treated at a government clinic. In the Arab countries, women themselves, took the initiative. By the 1930's a few upper-class women in Egypt, Lebanon, Syria, Palestine, Transjordan and Iraq had begun to unveil, and the practice had thoroughly taken hold in these countries among the young and in the cities by the 1950's. Few women now veil in Lebanon, Jordan, Egypt and Bahrain and the veil is being discarded slowly in Kuwait. In Saudi Arabia, the veil is legally mandatory but is often of fine chiffon, sometimes totally nonfunctional as far as concealment goes, and is often dropped in cars or inside shops. Veiling also decreases progressively as one enters the countryside—since it hampers peasant and Bedouin women in their chores—and women in southwest Arabia do not veil at all.

Somewhat surprisingly, the custom of veiling also remains strong in the Mediterranean countries of North Africa where unveiling didn't begin until independence in the 50's and 60's and is still confined to the young and the educated in the cities. Arab Tunisia's Bourguiba echoed Ataturk's remark of four decades earlier when he commented. "It is intolerable . . ." The former King of Morocco, Muhammad V, encouraged the just-beginning trend by making a point of sending his reform-minded daughter Princess Lalla Aicha—unveiled—to public meetings.

The women of the conservative countries who have totally unveiled seem to accept it as a matter of course; those who have not unveiled, accept it as a convention. Women's feelings towards the veil, in other words, are not at a reforming pitch. Among the men, the more educated seem anxious to have the veil disappear; the slightly less educated agree, with the provision that their own female relatives not be the first to discard it.

Today, however—even in the countries where it has long lain heaviest—the veil, like a dark storm cloud, is lifting. When the last vestiges of the veil have disappeared, those who regret its passing will, I think, be few, symbolizing, as it does, the shadow of a time when women from the lowest to the highest, the most educated to the illiterate, were begrudged not only freedom of marriage, of association, of movement, but even the light of day.

GM, You Can Relax Now

If anyone thinks that a return to the horse and buggy
will save us from pollution, read on

DON H. BERKEBILE

Deep within the breast of many crusaders for a better environment lies the thought that the automobile is the true root of all our evils, that its invention in the first place was the devil's own work and that our enslavement by it has opened the way to our destruction. Back to the horse and buggy, we sometimes murmur, as we choke for oxygen on a jammed city street. Back to the days of breathable air, when a person not only could cross a street safely and with a measure of dignity but also could park his horse and carriage within mere feet of his destination.

Yet a cool appraisal of horse-and-buggy days casts doubts on the ecological value of the old gray mare. Consider pollution: London, in 1875, had to get 1,000 tons of horse manure off its streets *daily.* American cities with a population of 12,000 horses (New York had more than ten times as many at the turn of the century) had to remove, daily, a 130-ton hill of manure.

Of course, it was excellent fertilizer, but it was not always usable. Manure gathered from the streets of a small city could be sold to nearby farmers, but if the city was large, neighboring farms couldn't absorb all of it. It was unprofitable to transport it farther than the local farms—the cost of conveying it was higher than the value of the manure itself. In such instances, manure was simply dumped somewhere. New York City deposited it on an island in the Hudson.

Manure waiting to be cleaned up from the streets bred billions of flies, which carried at least 30 diseases, some of them quite serious. And the horse disease called glanders, for example, could be severe enough to cripple urban transportation. It was also communicable to humans.

In addition to flies, birds followed the horses, and although they eat harmful insects, some may carry in their own droppings certain disease organisms that can affect man.

The urine from the horses couldn't be collected. It added to the filth and stench of the streets and made them dangerously slippery, not only for humans but for horses as well. The animals sometimes fell, injuring themselves so badly they had to be destroyed. Footing for the animals was better if the streets were laid of small stone blocks or bricks. But then the filth collected in the cracks. Use of asphalt or concrete made cleaning easier, but slipping increased.

Dead horses, of course, presented another problem. Wherever there was a huge horse population, there were sure to be huge numbers of corpses that had to be dragged away, at great effort and expense. In New York and Chicago around 1900, as many as 15,000 horses a year had to be hauled off.

Carriages, with their high center of gravity and uncertain means of locomotion, were accident-prone. Late in the nineteenth century, Paris could count 700 deaths and 5,000 injuries a year from carriage accidents. Innumerable accounts of serious accidents can be found in contemporary newspapers, diaries and journals. Runaway horses and capsized coaches were all too common.

As for parking a horse and carriage, remember that the smallest horse-drawn vehicle (four-wheeled) filled a space of roughly 6 by 16 feet, including the horse. Many such buggies could only carry two people. Compare that to today's automobile—6 by 17 or 18 feet—which carries six people. The horse could not be parked on the street all night. It required housing—also constant care and feeding whether it was in use or not. If a horse kept outside the urban was to be driven into the heart of the city, its owner had to allow for an average speed of about ten miles an hour on a level road.

The costs and problems of horse transport in cities during the early years of this century were so great that many of our forebears looked upon the automobile as their only salvation from urban ills and limitations. If we brought back the horse in sufficient numbers to accommodate our population, an even worse situation would be created.

Obviously we must alter our present trend in urban transportation—and inevitably we will. But *not* in the direction of the horse and buggy.

THE LANGUAGE AND STRUCTURE OF FOLKLORE

4

You are stranded on a small island with nine children ranging from three to seven years of age. The island is definitely not a tropical paradise; you have giant cacti, a kind of shrub with small blue flowers, huge tortoises, seagulls, and some friendly dolphins. There are also grasshoppers.

There is no hope of rescue any time in the immediate future, so that any education these children receive will have to come directly from their environment or from you.

Make up a bedtime story to tell the children, using as characters only the plants and animals of your small island world. Try not to exceed one thousand words, and keep in mind that if the children enjoy the story, you will probably have to tell it hundreds and hundreds of times over the next ten years.

DEFINING FOLKLORE

Definitions of folkore are probably as numerous as folklorists. Archer Taylor's definition is one of the best and most clear:

Folklore is the material that is handed on by tradition, either by word of mouth or by custom and practice. It may be folksongs, folktales, riddles, proverbs, or other materials preserved in words. It may be traditional tools and physical objects like fences or knots, hot cross buns, or Easter eggs; traditional ornamentation like the

Walls of Troy; or traditional symbols like the swastika. It may be traditional procedures like throwing salt over one's shoulder or knocking on wood. It may be traditional beliefs like the notion that elder is good for ailments of the eye. All of these are folklore.

Folklore is ordinarily associated with a particular group, large or small, and it serves as a force to unify that group and to give it a sense of community. Thus we find folklore of particular nationalities, like the folktales and folksongs of the Mexican people; folklore of particular occupational groups, such as the cowboy, the lumberjack, or the truck driver; folklore of religious groups, such as the Jewish or the Christian faith; and folklore of groups that crosscut these categories, such as the jump-rope rhymes of children. Even a very small and transient group may develop its own folklore; we are all familiar with the "in" joke that only the half-dozen members of our own circle of friends will understand.

AUTOGRAPH RHYME

First comes love,
Then comes marriage,
Then comes _____
With a baby carriage!

JUMP-ROPE RHYME

"Mother, Mother,
I am ill,
Send for the doctor
from over the hill!"
In comes the doctor,
In comes the nurse,
In comes the lady
With the alligator purse.

"Measles!" says the doctor.
"Measles!" says the nurse.
"Measles!" says the lady
With the alligator purse.

Folklore is a living force in human society. William R. Bascom lists a number of its functions, among them:

a.   Entertainment, amusement

b.   Transmission of culture from one generation to another

c.   Education (particularly in nonliterate societies)

d.   Social pressure on members of the group who seem disinclined to follow group standards

e.   Reinforcement of established beliefs and attitudes of the group

This is a simplified representation of the Orb of the World. The old conception of the Earth was that it is divided thus. The centre of the World was Jerusalem, the place where salvation came to mankind. The upper half of the Orb is Asia. The vertical line represents the Mediterranean Sea, on the right and left of which lie Africa and Europe respectively. In Early Christian Art the Lord was shown carrying this Orb in his hand; in later times this was altered to a ball with a Cross upon it.

Two signs used to exorcise evil spirits. In the case of both these signs, as with the pentagram and the octogram, it is worthy of note that they call for a certain dexterity, and that a clumsy person would be unable to draw them.

Rudolph Koch, The Book of Signs

Alan Dundes points out that "one of the most important functions of folklore is its service as a vehicle for social protest."

The language of folklore is special, with a heavy emphasis on the sort of structure that makes it readily memorable. Just as a speech must be so organized that it can be remembered without time for the leisurely examination given to printed material, so must folklore, because it is transmitted primarily orally. When a group of folktales is set down in a book for reading, their language still clearly reveals that they are meant to be heard rather than seen.

Even graffiti, perhaps the briefest of folk-language items, have a clearly definable structure. Paul D. McGlynn points out that an example of graffiti is "a pronouncement, an utterance, a proclamation," saying, "they are rhetorically removed from the obligations of debate, the abrasions of conversation, and the circumscription of social personality." We remember graffiti like "Jesus saves; Moses invests" or "Free the Watergate 500";—even, perhaps, when we would like to forget them.

Speaking "Carnie"

PATRICK C. EASTO and MARCELLO TRUZZI

The folklore of some groups may go so far as to develop a special in-group way of talking, as when children talk Pig Latin. Even more elaborate is the language style of carnival workers. Here are some rules for "Carnie."

1. Separate the word into syllables.
2. Add a long "ee" sound after the consonant beginning the syllable (or "ee" alone if there is no consonant.)
3. Insert a short sound like "u" in "tug."
4. Now insert a "z" before the rest of the syllable.
5. Move to the next syllable.

cat	*becomes*	kee-uh-zat
dog	*becomes*	dee-uh-zog
eat	*becomes*	ee-uh-zeet
people	*becomes*	pee-uh-zeep, ee-uh-zul

In fast speech these words may be condensed even farther. For example, "sucker" should be "see-uh-zuk, kee-uh-zer" but it becomes "see-uh-zucker."

Today we have portable graffiti too—the pin-on button and the bumper sticker.

STRUCTURE OF THE FOLKTALE

In this unit we will concentrate on a particular type of folklore, the short folktale, and try to isolate the characteristics that make it possible for us to recognize such a folktale. We will begin with an example that is probably familiar to everyone, the story of the Three Billy Goats Gruff.

Once upon a time there were Three Billy Goats Gruff, who wanted to go up on the mountain and eat grass. To do so they had to cross a bridge over a stream, and underneath that bridge there lived a wicked old troll.

One morning the first and smallest Billy Goat Gruff started across the bridge on his way up the mountain to eat grass. "Trip-trop, trip-trop," went his feet. When the troll heard that, he shouted, "Who is that trip-tropping over my bridge?"

"It's only me, the littlest Billy Goat Gruff!" said the little goat.

"I'm coming up there and eat you up!"

"Oh, don't do that," said the first Billy Goat Gruff. "I'm so small I wouldn't even make a mouthful. Wait for my brother, the middle-sized Billy Goat Gruff, he's much bigger and fatter than I am!"

"Oh, all right," grumbled the troll, and the first Billy Goat Gruff went on up the mountain to eat grass.

Then along came the second Billy Goat Gruff. "TRIP-TROP, TRIP-TROP," went his feet. When the troll heard that, he shouted, "Who is that TRIP-TROPPING over my bridge?"

"It's only me, the middle-sized Billy Goat Gruff!" said the second goat.

"I'm coming up there and eat you up!"

"Oh, don't do that," said the second Billy Goat Gruff. "I'm so small I'd only make one mouthful. Wait for my brother, the biggest Billy Goat Gruff, he's much bigger and fatter than I am!"

"Oh, all right," grumbled the troll, and the second Billy Goat Gruff went on up the mountain to eat grass.

Then along came the third Billy Goat Gruff. "TRIP-TROP, TRIP-TROP," went his feet. When the troll heard that, he shouted, "Who is that TRIP-TROPPING over my bridge?"

"It's only me, the biggest Billy Goat Gruff!" said the big goat.

"I'm coming up there and eat you up!"

"Come ahead!" said the biggest Billy Goat Gruff, and when the ugly old troll leaped up on the bridge the goat lowered his head and butted him into the stream, where he turned into a rock and was never heard from again. And the biggest Billy Goat Gruff went on up the mountain to eat grass.

And that is the end of the story of the Three Billy Goats Gruff.

All of us recognize this story as a folktale, but what are the characteristics that allow us to do so? It begins with the phrase "once upon a time," but that can't be all there is to it. If you were to take a brief story from your morning newspaper and start it with the words "once upon a time," that wouldn't make it look like a folktale to you.

The folklorist Axel Olrik has proposed that there is a set of laws that specify the characteristics a sequence of language must have in order to qualify as a folktale. A number of these proposed "laws" can be summarized as follows:

1. THE LAW OF OPENING
   The opening of a folktale is not sudden; it does not begin with direct action.

2. THE LAW OF CLOSING
   A folktale does not end suddenly.

3. THE LAW OF REPETITION
   A folktale will include many instances of repetition, both of events and of language.

4. THE LAW OF THREE
   Folktales have a strong tendency to group things in sets of three.

5. THE LAW OF TWO TO A SCENE
   There will never be more than two characters directly involved in any scene in a folktale.

6. THE LAW OF CONTRASTS
   We will always find contrasting pairs in a folktale. If there is a rich man, there will be a poor man, if there is a beautiful sister, there will be an ugly sister.

7. THE LAW OF THE SINGLE STRAND
   A folktale will not have subplots, which detract from the main story line.

8. THE LAW OF THE USE OF TABLEAUX
   Each scene in a folktale is presented as a separate unit.

9. THE LAW OF FOLKLORE LOGIC

The sequence of events in a folktale must have *internal* plausibility. That is, although they may be impossible, they must make sense within the frame of the story.

10. THE LAW OF CONCENTRATION ON A LEADING CHARACTER

In a folktale we often find that a single character holds the stage throughout the entire narrative—for example, Silly Jack or Cinderella.

11. THE LAW OF UNITY OF PLOT

In a folktale every element introduced must work toward an event that the listener could have foreseen from the very beginning.

Looking again at the Billy Goats Gruff story, do we see that these laws apply? We do, of course. The tale does not open or close with a goat crossing the bridge. Instead, there are separate introductory and closing sequences. There are three goats, three crossings of the bridge, three challenges from the troll to the goat, and three replies. In each scene we see only one goat and the troll—just two characters—interacting. There are no subplots; we hear nothing about the activities of either the troll or the goats outside the single story line of the trip up the mountain to eat grass. There is a three-way contrast, with a small goat, a middle-sized goat, and a big goat. Each bridge crossing is presented as a single scene. And from the very beginning we have been able to anticipate that somehow the biggest goat would get the better of the troll. Both the events in the story and the language itself are highly repetitive. Because this is a folktale, we are willing to accept this repetition, and we enjoy it. Finally, everything that happens in the story makes sense within its frame of reference.

We could set up a simple schema for this story:

I. Opening Sequence
  A. First scene
  B. Second scene
  C. Third scene
II. Closing Sequence

You will recognize that this pattern parallels the basic model for compositions presented in unit 1. The introductory paragraph presenting the main idea of the composition is here replaced by an introductory sequence setting the scene for the folktale. The closing sequences show the same parallel. Instead of three support-ing points of an argument which develop the main idea of a com-position, we find three scenes that develop the story line.

Many folktales, particularly the English folktales that most of us hear as children, are written on this pattern or expansions of it. The Three Little Pigs, The Three Bears, Rumpelstilskin (an ex-ample of the pattern doubled), and numerous others are good ex-amples. This structure has a certain predictability which makes the listener or reader feel secure; if the boy goes to the well for water once, we know he will go twice more; if he is defeated twice, we know that on the third attempt he will win; if the first two knights who try to win the beautiful princess in marriage fail, we know the third will manage. Knowing that nothing bad can happen—except to the bad who deserve it—we can relax and enjoy the pattern of the story.

Until recently the same kind of security was incorporated in the Western movie, where we knew that the good guys would al-ways win, no matter how bad it looked in the middle, and this is still true for such contemporary folk-heroes as Superman and Bat-man. It isn't that we don't like real suspense, or that we cannot appreciate tragedy, but neither seems appropriate to us within the folklore context.

Often a particular folktale is found all over the world, in countries totally unrelated in culture and widely separated geo-graphically. There are said to be nearly a thousand different ver-sions of the Cinderella story; it turns up in India, Africa, the state of Missouri, Canada, Brazil, Indonesia, and the Philippines. Folk-lorist Stith Thompson collected a Cinderella story from the Zuñi Indians of North America. In this story the Indian Cinderella lives in a hovel in Utah, wearing ragged dirty clothing, and she is forced to raise turkeys for a living. When she hears that there is going to be a Zuñi festival, to which she has not been invited, she begins to cry. A turkey gobbler tells her that the turkeys will help her, but that she must not forget them during the celebration. The turkeys dress her up, fix her hair, and give her jewelled necklaces and ear-rings to wear. She is the hit of the dance and has such a good time dancing with the young chiefs that she almost forgets the turkeys; when she remembers, the sun is setting and she has to run. The turkeys are angry and they disappear singing sad songs. Mean-while the turkey girl finds herself once again dressed in filth and rags.

Because of the apparent universality of elements in folklore, a number of books are devoted to the classification of these elements. These books are called type and motif indexes. The *Type and Motif Index of the Folktales of England and North America*, prepared by Ernest W. Baughman, contains entries like these:

| page 17 | 751A | *The Peasant Woman is Changed into a Woodpecker.* |
| page 64 | 2025 | *The Fleeing Pancake. A woman makes a pancake which flees. Various animals try in vain to stop it. Finally the fox eats it up.* |

A "fleeing pancake," no matter in what story it turned up, would be recognized as an example of Type #2025.

TEACHER. Ferrabeau, can you define the folktale?
FERRABEAU. Sure. A folktale is a ridiculous story told out loud.
TEACHER. Like your excuses for not doing your homework.
FERRABEAU. Yeah. You might say that.

Some folktales have a curious habit of turning up all over a large area and representing themselves as true stories. An excellent example of this phenomenon is the famous story of the ghost hitch-hiker, in which a man driving along a lonely road late at night sees a young woman in formal evening dress standing on a bridge. When he picks her up she sits in the back seat of the car and he drives her home. They arrive at her house, but when the driver turns around to let his passenger out he finds nobody there. Puzzled, he goes up to the house and tells his story, only to be told by a sad elderly woman that this happens all the time, that people are continually bringing the girl home, but that she really was killed in an automobile accident on that bridge many years before.

This story is so persistently presented as truth that it has been reported in newspapers all over the United States as a real occurrence, and this writer has heard it told as "a true story that happened to somebody I know" from three different sources in three different states. It would be very easy to retell this story in a standard folktale pattern. For instance:

OPENING

Once there was a man who had to drive home from work each night along a lonely road that crossed a bridge over a river.

FIRST SCENE

One night as he was just coming to the bridge he saw a young girl standing beside the road, dressed in an evening gown. "Kids!" he said, as he passed her by.

SECOND SCENE

The next night he saw her standing there again, and again he said "Kids!" as he passed her by.

THIRD SCENE

The next night he saw her again, but this time he picked her up, saw her settled in the back seat of the car, and headed for her house as she gave him directions. But when he reached her house and turned around she had disappeared.

CLOSING

He went into the house to tell her family, and her mother told him sadly that the girl had been killed in an accident on that bridge almost thirty years ago. After that the man always found another way home.

Notice that in such a telling of this story, even if we were to expand it greatly, we would not add any information about the phantom girl's activities before the accident or any information about the man's life outside the actual events of the tale. To add this type of information would lead us beyond the limits of the folktale and into the area of the short story, just as eliminating the pattern and keeping only the bare facts would make the sequence a news story. Let's try writing the first paragraph of this story in all three modes:

FOLKTALE

Once there was a man who had to drive home from work each night along a lonely road that crossed a bridge over a river.

NEWSPAPER STORY

Jack Smith, engineer at Psycho-Filbernetics, Inc., drives home from work each night via Burton Road and the old Pelletier Bridge.

SHORT STORY

He had never really felt comfortable about that bridge, or about the road either. It had always seemed to him that there was something eery about the place, something almost unclean. He shivered and gripped the wheel more tightly.

You see how clearly the difference shows up in the language? People in newspaper stories do not say "abracadabra" or repeat the same speech three times in a row. They are identified by name and occupation: the *facts* are given. On the other hand, neither the folktale nor the newspaper story is concerned with the thoughts and feelings of the characters. In the short story, although like the folktale it may not stress names and places and dates, the character cannot be just "a man" but must be developed, made vivid and real to the reader. We will take up these differences in more detail in the next unit.

Now do you feel that the narrative you wrote for the children stranded with you on the island could be recognized as a folktale? If not, revise it, including what you have learned from this unit.

EXERCISES

1. All of the following are American folklore "objects." Choose one and write a 500-word essay explaining *why* it is folklore. Which of the folklore functions mentioned in this unit does it fill?

 a. Banjo
 b. Autograph book
 c. Easter egg
 d. Charm bracelet
 e. Rabbit's foot
 f. Dulcimer
 g. Bumper sticker
 h. "Mother" pillow
 i. Piggybank (are they always pigs?)
 j. Hope chest

2. Make up a similar folklore object list from another culture. Write a brief essay about one of the items on your list, as in exercise 1.

3. One kind of folklore is the joke made to a particular pattern. In the 30's we had Knock-Knock Jokes; in the 40's an especially repulsive variety called Little Moron Jokes; in the 50's there were Beatnik Jokes. More recently we have had Elephant Jokes, Grape Jokes, Pickle Jokes, Wind-Up Doll Jokes and Good News/

Bad News Jokes. Collect at least ten examples from one of these categories and write an analysis of no more than 1000 words. (A good source for the older forms is the *Journal of American Folklore* or older people you know.)

Explain what you feel are the defining characteristics of the chosen joke-type, why people feel that these jokes are funny, how they relate to the era and culture in which they appear, and any other relevant information that seems appropriate to you.

4.   The paper doll is an American folklore object; it is probably impossible for a female child to grow up in this country without getting involved with paper dolls. Write a brief research paper (perhaps 1000 words maximum) on one of the following topics or a similar topic of your choice:

    a.   The History of the Paper Doll

    b.   The First American Paper Doll

    c.   The Function of the Paper Doll in American Childhood

    d.   Types of Paper Dolls

Does a male child or an adult have any reason to use paper dolls? Can you think of ways that paper dolls *could* be used by adults? Who draws paper dolls and designs their clothes? Have you ever met anyone who worked in the paper doll industry? Where do paper dolls come from? Notice that there appear to be only mainstream, "establishment" paper dolls? Why?

5.   It is interesting that the same folklore types turn up in folktales all over the world. But what about the structure? Do the laws proposed by Olrik apply to all cultures or only to Western societies? Investigate the folktales of some other culture. For example, look at African folktales, or the folktales of Australia, or Chinese folktales. Or look at the folktales of an American Indian tribe, which fall outside the Anglo culture. Do Olrik's laws apply to these stories? Write a brief paper supporting your position. If you see any laws that do not occur in Olrik's set, mention them.

6.   An element of American folklore which has persisted and seems likely to go on forever is the *zipper* song. In a zipper song there is a four-line verse, the last line of which is known as the *tag* and is always the same for every verse. The first three lines are always a single line repeated three times. The name *zipper* comes from the fact that after the person leading the song sings a verse or two, anybody can "zip" in a new verse. Here is a typical example:

Goin' down the road feelin' bad,
Goin' down the road feelin' bad,
Goin' down the road feelin' bad, Lord, Lord,
I ain't gonna be treated thisaway.

Goin' where the water tastes like wine,
Goin' where the water tastes like wine,
Goin' where the water tastes like wine, Lord, Lord,
I ain't gonna be treated thisaway.

GOING DOWN THE ROAD

I'm goin' where them dust storms never blow,
I'm goin' where them dust storms never blow,
I'm goin' where them dust storms never
Blow, Lord, Lord,
And I ain't gonna be treated this a-way.

You can see how a zipper song could be a useful vehicle for the folklore function Dundes calls "social protest." For example,

> English teachers drive me up the wall,
> English teachers drive me up the wall,
> English teachers drive me up the wall, Lord, Lord,
> I ain't gonna be treated thisaway.

Write a new zipper song of your own, to a tune you know or a tune you compose.

7. Sometimes we can obtain a different perspective on a particular language sequence by looking at it from an entirely different point of view. For instance, can you tell "The Three Billy Goats Gruff" as a comic strip? Can you tell it with pictures only? How many frames (separate pictures) do you need to tell the story? Do they correlate exactly with the separate episodes or scenes in the language version of the story? Can you do the same thing with "Rumpelstilskin"? Try it and see what you find out.

8. One of the most famous American folklore elements, and one we owe to black culture, is the music called the *blues*. Write a 1000-word essay on the blues, using one of the following topics or a similar topic of your own choice:

  a. The Function of the Blues as Social Protest
  b. The "Talking" Blues
  c. A Famous Blues Singer and His/Her Work
  d. The Language of the Blues

I Can Make My Own Songs

SON HOUSE

People wonder a lot about where the blues came from. Well, when I was coming up, people did more singing in the fields than they did anywhere else. Time they got to the field, they'd start singing some kind of old song. Tell his ol' mule, "Giddup there!", and he'd go off behind the mule, start plowing and start a song. Sang to the mule or anybody. Didn't make any difference. We'd call them old corn songs, old long meter songs. They'd make it sound good, too. You could hear them a half-a-mile off, they'd be singing so loud. Especially just before sundown.

They sure would go a long ways. Then they called themselves, "got the blues." That's what they called the blues. Them old long meter songs. You'd hear them talking and one would say, "You know ol' so-and-so really can sing the blues!" They didn't use any instruments. Just natural voice. They could make them rhyme, though, just like the blues do now, but it would just be longer meter. Holler longer before they say the word. They'd sing about their girl friend or about almost anything—mule—anything. They'd make a song out of it just to be hollering.

The way I figured it out after that, after I started, I got the idea that the blues come from a person having a dissatisfied mind and he wants to do something about it. There's some kind of sorrowness in his heart about being misused by somebody. That's what I figured the blues is based on.

---

9. A common complaint about much folklore is that it uses a kind of language that is not up to the standard set by the prestige dialect in a given area. Assume that you are the parent of a high-school student who is in a folklore course where sequences like the following (quoted by Ozark folklorist Vance Randolph) keep turning up in the class materials: "I ain't never done no dirt of no kind to nobody," Or the classic hillbilly musician joke—"Can you read music?" "Not enough to hurt my playin.'" Write a letter to the editor of the local paper, of about 300 words, objecting to the use of such materials in the education of your child. Then take the opposite side of the question and write a reply to the protesting letter, either from a student in the class or from a parent who thinks the protestor is wrong.

10. Proverbs are a common item in folklore of all cultures. Often a proverb in one culture turns up looking quite different in another culture, but both clearly transmit the same information. For example, we have the proverb "When in Rome do as the Romans do." John C. Messenger tells us that this turns up in Nigeria as "If you visit the home of the toads, stoop." Do some research and find at least five more such pairs. Can you find some examples of three or more versions of a single proverb?

11. Folklore can function as a form of social protest. The protest song probably comes first to mind as an example; what other kinds of folklore offer opportunity for protest in our culture today? Write 500 words explaining one of these.

12. We mentioned that folklore can serve as a unifying factor for certain ethnic, national, professional, or age groups. The ex-

amples mentioned in the text were traditional ones. What about some newer groups—has there been time for a folklore to emerge from them? Answer this question for one of the following in about 600 words.

    a. Radical activists

    b. Hippies

    c. Astronauts

    d. Commune people

    e. Computer programmers

    f. American acupuncture practitioners

    g. Futurists

13. Every major holiday has its own folklore in the form of songs, special greetings, customs, and particular foods. Invent a new holiday that you feel is needed, describe it, and provide it with at least three of the folklore items just mentioned.

14. The folk hero is a major element of folklore. Consider Pecos Bill, Paul Bunyan, and Davy Crockett. These heroes have certain common characteristics. The manner of their birth and death is often very unusual; they frequently have been abandoned or lost as children and are then raised by animals. They travel widely, performing amazing exploits. See if you can prepare a set of laws for the characterizing of a folk hero, either in Western Anglo culture or in another culture about which you have special knowledge.

15. Are there any female folk heroes? If so, do they follow the laws you found in exercise 14? Write an essay of not more than 1000 words stating your position.

Women's Songs

MEREDITH TAX

Ballads

Hard is the fortune of all womankind,
She's always controlled, she's always confined
Controlled by her parents until she's a wife,
Then a slave to her husband the rest of her life.

Women's fortunes have always been hard. The history of most women, of ordinary women through the ages, is unwritten. The vast majority of women who have lived never learned to read or write, and nobody else bothered to record their opinions or deeds for them, because nobody thought them important enough.

Women's culture, for that reason, has been largely oral—passed down from mother to daughter in the form of songs, "old wives' tales" (which you might call popular science), and proverbs. Songs are one of the few ways we have of finding out how our remote ancestresses felt about their lives.

Ballads may begin by recording some version of actual events, but these events are soon mythologized as the song is passed around. The events find their most economical, memorable, and satisfying shape in the process of transmission. This shape is art—which is just a way of talking about the issues of real life in a form that gives you images to act as handles for your experience.

> Queen Jane lay in labor for six weeks and some more;
> Her women grew weary and the midwife gave o'er.
>
> Oh, women,-kind women, as I know you to be,
> Pray cut my side open and save my baby.

Now no woman—even one who needed a Caesarian—ever lay in labor for over 6 weeks. It'd kill her. But to women who had gone through many a difficult birth, this wasn't an exaggeration—it was real life taken to the extreme so that no one could miss the point.

> Queen Jane she turned over and fell in a swound,
> They cut her side open, the baby was found . . .
>
> The baby was christened the very next day;
> His mother's poor body lay mouldering away.

Women didn't live through Caesarians in the days before doctors sterilized their knives.

A lot of the focus in songs about women's lives was death. Death for the mother, for the baby, for the lovers, for the runaway daughter, for the unfaithful wife, for the deserted maiden or the one who gets pregnant and becomes a problem to her lover. We live at a pretty high level of material comfort, health, and refinement; our oppression as women is measured in subtler ways. Death was the measure for centuries of women in harder circumstances; the power your father or husband had over you was the power to kill you, swiftly or by degrees. Pioneer husbands in America often wore out three or four wives, between childbirth and hard work. Nineteenth century women were lucky to see half their children live to grow up—look at the tiny graves in any old grave-yard. Children still die like that in "underdeveloped" (and exploited) areas; Aunt Molly Jackson tells it:

> The rich and mighty capitalists,
> They dress in jewels and silk;
> But my darling blue-eyed baby,
> She starved to death for milk.

Most ballads are not about such everyday kinds of murder. The lives of most women have been relatively uneventful—housework, husband, childbirth, poverty, loneliness, death—these aren't events. Maybe a war or two. It's not this pattern but the violent variations from it that ballads are about—the same things that drugstore romantic thrillers are about now. Ballads are the escape fiction of women who can't read. The characters in them act out, in simplified and bloody fashion, themes born in escape fantasy and wish fulfillment and guilt. Some are pure escape with no ending:

> Yes I'll forsake my house and home,
> My husband and my ladies;
> I'll forsake my new born babe
> To ride with the Black Jack Davy.

More often the escape fantasy is overtaken by that of guilt; women are not supposed to even think about running away from their husband and kids:

> They were not gone but about three weeks,
> I'm sure it was not four,
> When the ship sprang a leak and began to sink
> And it sank to rise no more.

Ballads are rituals of rejection; of recognition and reunion after long separation; of haunting, thwarted love and despairing suicide; of bloody revenge; of incest, infanticide, and murder. They satisfy the imagination while containing the terror of the events they describe in the regularity of their form: the repetitive tune, the rhyme, the conventional imagery that recurs in ballad after ballad.

They are the songs of generations of women who accepted their hard lot and dreamed of wild poetry; who did not band together to struggle, and who died young.

Complaints

Another kind of women's song complains more directly about the oppression of daily life:

> When I was single, marryin's all I craved,
> Now that I'm married, Lord, I'm troubled to my grave,
> Wish I was a single girl again.

The most complete of these is "The Housewife's Lament" found in the diary of a 19th century Illinois pioneer woman, who had 7 children and outlived them all. It is a complete catalog of housework, ending with the housewife's total defeat by her environment:

> There's too much of worriment goes to a bonnet,
> There's too much of ironing goes to a shirt,
> There's nothing that pays for the time you waste on it,
> There's nothing that lasts us but trouble and dirt.

> **CHORUS**
> Oh, life is a toil and love is a trouble,
> Beauty will fade and riches will flee,
> Pleasures they dwindle and prices they double,
> And nothing is as I would wish it to be.

> In March it is mud, it is slush in December,
> The midsummer breezes are loaded with dust,
> In fall the leaves litter, in muddy September
> The wallpaper rots and the candlesticks rust . . .

> With grease and with grime from corner to center,
> Forever at war and forever alert,
> No rest for the day lest the enemy enter,
> I spend my whole life in struggle with dirt.

> Last night in my dreams I was stationed forever
> On a far little rock in the midst of the sea,
> My one chance of life was a ceaseless endeavor
> To sweep off the waves as they swept over me.

> Alas! 'Twas no dream; ahead I behold it,
> I see I am helpless my fate to avert.
> She lay down her broom, her apron she folded,
> She lay down and died and was buried in dirt.

Other songs pit husband against wife in a contest over who can do the most work, or do the other's work best. The wife always wins hands down.

Women's Liberation Songs

The women's liberation movement has been going strong for almost two years now, and from the beginning made building its own culture an essential part of its politics. That included writing songs. People say when I tell them about it, "Do you mean we're going to be a singing movement again?"; which bugs me because it makes it sound like something that's out of their control. It seems to me that what makes a singing movement is just for a lot of movement people to start singing, and that's something that's within their power to control.

I guess people in the radical movement stopped singing some time ago. Maybe it was when whites got kicked out of SNCC. Maybe it has something to do with rock culture. There's a lot of rock music that's great, and some that's really political; and people can participate in it by dancing. But it's not music that most people can make for themselves. You need a together group, for one thing. Then you need a lot of equipment, all of which costs money and takes some expertise. It's not very mobile either—and the kind of demonstrations we have these days, you wouldn't want to bring anything more expensive or bigger than a kazoo along. All these factors limit the usefulness of rock as a political weapon.

It seems crucial to me that we build a culture which includes music that people can and do make for themselves. We're fighting a system in which everything is made for us—beginning with all our decisions. Our entertainers, our culture, our selves, all get turned into commodities by the system's media. We have to have our own ways of communicating which don't involve these media. The most reliable one is still word of mouth, person to person. It's the one least likely to get distorted in transmission. So I think that everybody who feels the need of political music should start learning how to make and sing it.

Of course that's not the whole story. Unless you are part of a political movement that is alive, your songs might still turn out private or academic or irrelevant. One reason that so many songs are beginning to come out of the women's liberation movement now is that it's the most alive white movement going. Its politics come right out of the experience of each of us. That makes for good songs, too—ones that aren't just head trips. Women's liberation makes everyday life political.

Maybe another reason songs are coming out of the women's liberation movement has to do with the fact that, in white urban American culture, being expressive has always been the province of women. It's a compensation for our lack of power—we are allowed to sing, dance, giggle, cry, and wear bright clothes. We're even encouraged to do these things as part of our role in society—what good is a bird in a gilded cage if it doesn't sing?

Look At My Life (Tune: Traditional)

Look at my life — what have I done? — J learned to walk — but not to run, — J learned to walk — but not to fly, when they tied my wings — J be-gan to die.

I was first a daughter, and then a wife
Belongin' to somebody else all my life
I never learned what I need to know
And I started to die when I started to grow. (Cho.)

Oh, if I'd had a daughter, I'd've killed her at birth
'Cause I'd've known what her life was worth
Born of a slave, tied down with a rope
Married to a slave, livin' without hope. (Cho.)

Look at the mirror upon the wall
Is that a toy, girl, is that a doll?
Is there anybody there behind the mask?
What's the answer? Are you scared to ask? (Cho.)

Oh, when I die and go to hell
They'll keep me doin' the things I learned to do well
I'll be cookin' and sewin', standin' by the sink
Have to die at least twice to get time to think. (Cho.)

Words by Meredith Tax. © *1970 by Meredith Tax. Used with permission.*

So when we get together to struggle for equal power and for liberation, it comes naturally to express this struggle in song.

We need songs—all political movements do. Songs catch our political understanding of our everyday experiences and make it memorable; songs put experience into a form that sums it all up and that everybody can share. They provide images that we can use as we continue to struggle. In doing that they become weapons with which we can arm the people. Power to the sisters and their music!

THE LANGUAGE AND STRUCTURE OF PROSE FICTION

5

A new law has been passed in the United States making it compulsory for all American citizens under twenty-five years of age to attend four years of college at government expense. Choose a character from the following list and write a short story of about two thousand words describing the effect of this new law on the character's life and his or her way of dealing with the situation.

a. You are a nineteen-year-old man doing well in a job that you like with a future that appeals to you.

b. You are a twenty-year-old woman living on a small farm with your baby son.

c. You are a twenty-year-old man, married, traveling around the country with your wife in a camper.

d. You are a twenty-one-year-old woman running a small business that has weathered two rough years and is finally holding its own.

DEFINING THE SHORT STORY

There is no problem about the recognition of prose fiction. We recognize it because it is clearly labeled as such, saying at the beginning, "The Frumious Baldersnatch, a story/novel by Jane Q. Writer," and because it is a narrative.*

* There was a day when the line between the fictional and the nonfic-

Stories, or short narratives, have been around as long as we have had recorded writing, and probably existed thousands of years before there were any such records. The earliest recorded story we have is an Egyptian example called "The Two Brothers," which dates from about 3200 B.C. Fables, parables, and folktales we have always had in abundance, but the short story, as we understand the term today, dates roughly from the year 1800. The question, then, is how we distinguish the short story from the earlier short forms such as the folktale and the fable.

STRUCTURE OF THE SHORT STORY

First, there is no set of fixed "laws" for the short story corresponding to that for the folktale. A short story is not likely to show heavy dependence on groups of three, nor are its scenes restricted to some specific number of characters. A short story may contain numerous subplots, and a writer may devote much attention to minor characters. The short story appears in such infinite variety that laws like "The Law of Two to a Scene" would be impossible.

Fiction is not restricted to a special vocabulary in the way that technical or scientific writing may be. It does not have ritualized phrases like the "once upon a time" of folklore or the "Dearly Beloved" of religion. It cannot be characterized by rhetorical devices like parallelism and antithesis in the political speech, or by formal devices like rhyme and meter in poetry.

Certain structural characteristics are, however, common to most short stories. We can say that a short story, with a few exceptions made for experimental work, must have the following elements:

1. PLOT: What happens
2. CRISIS: The high point of the plot
3. SETTING: Where it happens

---

tional narrative was so sharp that there could be no confusion, label or not, but this situation no longer exists. Given two unlabeled narrative structures, one by a short story writer and the other by a New Journalist like Truman Capote, it is unlikely that today one would be able to say for sure which was fiction and which nonfiction. This ambiguity results because the techniques of fiction, as well as the techniques of film, have been appropriated by the nonfiction writer.

4. CHARACTERIZATION: Who it happens to and who makes it happen

5. THEME: Why we should care what happens

Some of these elements appear in earlier narrative forms. Folktales have plot and crisis, but they tell us nothing about the country where the heroine lives or the manner in which she passes her days. We learn nothing about her appearance except that she is beautiful and, perhaps, has long golden hair. In parables and fables the whole characterization is summed up by labels such as "the sly fox," "the greedy rich man," or "the handsome and courageous prince." Setting and characterization, as elements of the narrative, do not occur except incidentally until the modern short story; the parable and fable were almost entirely based on theme.

Much contemporary nonfiction uses *setting*, and it is usual for speeches and sermons to have *theme* as a prominent element. *Characterization* is used in nonfiction articles about people. Newspaper stories can be said to have a *plot*. But only in fiction do we find all five elements blended together into a unified whole.

We will examine one short story in this unit to see how the five key elements are presented and use specific paragraphs as examples. The story is science fiction written by Clifford D. Simak and is entitled "A Death in the House."

There is a good reason why a science fiction story, rather than an adventure story, a love story, or some other type, was chosen as the example for this unit. A primary characteristic of our times is the incredible speed with which our society is subjected to change. The book *Future Shock* is devoted entirely to a description of the effect of this rapid change on the people who have to live with it. We wake up in the morning knowing that something could have happened while we were asleep that will profoundly change the quality of our lives.

All of us live nowadays with a lot of WHAT-IFS running around in our heads. What if they're right and there is going to be a worldwide famine? What if there is really intelligent life on Mars and it turns out to be more powerful than we are? What if somebody goofs and a bomb gets dropped by mistake? What if the gasoline reserves are exhausted and we can't use our cars any more? What if. . . ? Science fiction stories offer us painless answers to those questions, painless in the sense that we can explore them without penalty because they are not real. This makes science fic-

Jim Muldowney

"I get plenty of ideas . . . but I just can't seem to get them on paper."

tion part of the survival equipment, and worth knowing something about.

Let's look at that story now.

PLOT AND CRISIS

Simak starts with this sentence:

> Old Mose Abrams was out hunting cows when he found the alien.

The sentence tells us a lot. It tells us that this story is going to be about the following WHAT-IF: What if you found a wounded creature from outer space on your property? It tells us that the event takes place on a farm, and that it's probably a small farm, because people don't go out alone hunting cows on great agribusiness operations run by conglomerates.

Mose Abrams takes the creature home, because it is hurt; he tries to take care of it, but it dies. When he tries to give it a decent burial, nobody wants to cooperate, so he buries it on his farm in the garden and hides its birdcage-like spaceship in his machine shed. A strange plant grows out of the grave. And then:

> Farm life went on as usual, with the corn laid by and the haying started and out in the garden the strange plant kept on growing and now was taking shape. Old Mose couldn't believe his eyes when he saw the sort of shape it took. . . .
>
> The morning came when he found the plant standing at the door and waiting for him.

Mose has been lonely, and so he makes the plant a kind of pet. Then one day the two of them come across the spaceship in the shed, and the plant so clearly wants to repair it that Mose gives it a try. But it's no use.

> Mose showed it iron and steel; he dug into a carton where he kept bolts and clamps and bushings and scraps of metal and other odds and ends, finding brass and copper and even some aluminum, but it wasn't any of these.
>
> And Mose was glad—a bit ashamed for feeling glad, but glad all the same.

The old man thinks he has his new friend safely earthbound, until by accident it sees a silver dollar, and "Mose knew, with a sinking heart, that it had been silver the critter had been hunting." With his life savings, a hoard of silver dollars, Mose repairs the ship and the alien leaves, handing Mose a little ball of crystal just before he takes off.

Here is the ending of the story:

> It was dark and lonely and unending in the depths of space with no Companion. It might be long before another was obtainable.
>
> It was perhaps a foolish thing to do, but the old creature had been such a kind savage, so fumbling and so pitiful and eager to help. And one who travels far and fast must likewise travel light. There had been nothing else to give.

Now we can sum up this plot very quickly:

1. A farmer finds an injured alien on his farm.

2. When the alien dies despite his attempts to help, he buries it in his garden.

3. A new alien, a mobile plant, grows from the grave and becomes a kind of companion for the farmer.

4. Using his hoard of silver dollars, the farmer repairs the alien's ship so that he can leave.

5. The alien leaves his own companion behind as a gift—a small crystal ball.

A summary like that is not very interesting. E. M. Forster once said that "The King died and then the Queen died" is not a plot. To have a plot you must have "The King died and then the Queen died of grief." That is, a plot has to be more than a recital of the fact that X happened and then Y happened. The writer has to make us wonder what is going to happen next. To do this, he adds (among other things) the element of *crisis*.

Simak does this very skillfully:

> The critter still was standing across the table from him, stacking and restacking the pile of silver dollars. And now it showed him with a hand held above the stacks, that it needed more of them. This many stacks it showed him, and each stack so high.
>
> Mose sat stricken, with a spoon full of oatmeal to his mouth. He thought of all those other dollars, the iron kettle packed with them,

underneath the floor boards in the living room. And he couldn't do it; they were the only thing he had—except the critter now. And he could not give them up so the critter could go and leave him too.

It's at a point like this that the old radio serial used to end. There would be a few bars of organ music, and then a sepulchral voice would say what everyone was thinking: "Will Old Mose sacrifice his life savings to help his alien friend? Will he go back to his old lonely life, condemned to that loneliness by his own hand? Tune in tomorrow. . . ." This is crisis. The writer builds the events of the story until he achieves a point where the reader desperately wants to find out what will happen next.

CHARACTERIZATION

If the reader knows how the crisis will be resolved, it won't work. In the Billy Goats Gruff, for example, you know from the beginning that the biggest goat will get the best of the troll, and the crisis is trivial. In a story like "A Death in the House," if the person who found the alien was someone totally selfish and egotistical the crisis would be equally trivial, because the reader would be almost certain he wouldn't help the alien. But Simak has used characterization from the beginning to make the crisis logical. For example,

> He didn't know it was an alien, but it was alive and it was in a lot of trouble and Old Mose, despite everything the neighbors said about him, was not the kind of man who could bear to leave a sick thing out there in the woods.

This tells us a lot about our character. He is an old man, hence possibly alone and free of interference. He is not overly concerned with the opinions of his neighbors, hence he is likely to be stubborn, independent, and a loner. He is a compassionate man.

Simak backs this up by presenting some additional information:

> Ever since his wife had died almost ten years before, he had lived alone on his untidy farm and the housekeeping that he did was the scandal of all the neighbor women. Once a year, if he got around to it, he sort of shoveled out the house, but the rest of the year he just let things accumulate.

Mose was a stubborn man. One had to be stubborn to run a runty farm like this. Stubborn and insensitive in a lot of ways. But not insensitive, of course, to a thing in pain.

We now have a good picture of our man, and it is important that we see him this way, as a stubborn old man who does things *differently from everybody else*. This is especially important, because we must believe that this man just happens to have a hoard of silver dollars handy when the alien needs them to repair the ship. Simak brings in the silver early in the story, when he has Old Mose call a doctor to try to help the injured "critter."

Mose went to the cupboard and got the cigar box almost full of silver dollars and paid the doctor. The doctor put the dollars in his pocket, joshing Mose about his eccentricity.

But Mose was stubborn about his silver dollars. "Paper money don't seem legal, somehow," he declared. "I like the feel of silver and the way it clinks. It's got authority."

And once more:

The doctor thought, like all the rest of them, that the only silver Mose had was in the cigar box in the cupboard. There wasn't one of them who knew about the old iron kettle piled plumb full of them, hidden underneath the floor boards of the living room. He chuckled at the thought of how he had them fooled.

We see the character of Mose through the things Simak, as author, says about him directly; we see it through the things Mose does; and we see it in his speech. For example, the remark about paper money and silver, and the following longer speech:

"I tell you, Sheriff," said Mose. "This thing came here from somewhere and it died. I don't know where it came from and I don't know what it was and I don't hanker none to know. To me it was just a living thing that needed help real bad. It was alive and it had its dignity and in death it commanded some respect. When the rest of you refused it decent burial, I did the best I could. And that is all there is to it."

Notice that although these are the words of a plain man, they are not the words of a stupid one. Simak is nudging us a little; from time to time someone in the story mentions the nearby university, and we are made to realize that if an educated man had found the alien it would probably have ended up in a jar of formaldehyde with scientists measuring it, weighing it, and slicing at it.

We learn very little in this story about the character of the alien—which is not surprising. It is after all just that, *alien,* and we, like Old Mose, have trouble understanding it. Except for the statement Mose makes that "in death it commanded some respect," we know almost nothing about it until the final paragraph in which its gift to Mose is described, and we learn that it saw Old Mose as "a kind savage." We know a good deal about its looks, however; Simak tells us

> It hadn't any face. It had an enlargement at the top of it, like a flower on top of a stalk, although its body wasn't any stalk, and there was a fringe around this enlargement that wiggled like a can of worms.

It is important that Simak has made it clear to us what kind of man Mose is, since a lesser man might have fled from such a creature, called the police, or perhaps killed it in hysterical terror.

SETTING

A writer's use of setting may vary from the meticulous practice of Dickens, where every setting is described in such detail that an artist could easily paint each scene from the written description, to the contemporary work of people such as John O'Hara who may use almost no setting at all. It is difficult for a writer today to include great chunks of description without boring the reader.

TEACHER.   Ferrabeau, how can you tell what word is the subject of a sentence?

FERRABEAU.   Nothing to it. If it's not the first word, it'll be the second one.

If it seems to you that describing a setting should be easy—after all, you just write down "what everything looks like"—you might try one of the elementary tasks of the technical writer.* Try to describe a familiar object, like a pencil, so that it would be im-

* A technical writer must be able to describe tools and machines, and their parts with such exact precision that the descriptions are almost like blueprints of the object.

mediately recognizable to an individual who had never seen such an object before. Or stand in front of a mirror and stick your tongue out as far as you can, look at it carefully, and then describe it in such detail that someone reading your description would know that you were describing a tongue. You'll find that it isn't easy at all. Which details *must* you mention, in order to ensure recognition? Which ones can you afford to leave out? Which ones can the reader fill in for herself or himself?

A writer may have to do little more than include a sentence like "it was a typical middle-class Midwestern suburb" to set the scene. Most of us can fill in the details sufficiently well in such a case, and we would be bored if the writer persisted in saying things like "all the houses looked exactly alike, except that for some the garage was on the left side and for others it was on the right." We already know that. In a science fiction story a single sentence like "the mobile flowers spun gracefully on the hearth, giving off silver sparks and humming serenely to themselves" may be enough to wrench the reader out of reality and into an imagined universe. The writer must decide for himself (a) how much setting is necessary to the story, and (b) how much detail is required to make that setting clear to the reader. Simak abandons straight description altogether in "A Death in the House" and instead allows us to get all our information about setting indirectly.

You will remember the statement that Mose cleaned only once a year by shoveling out the house; this tells us something about what the place must look like. Here are some other scraps of setting:

> He went up the woods path with it, heading back for home, and it seemed to him the smell of it was less.
>
> He took it into the house and laid it on what he called a bed, next to the kitchen stove. He got it straightened out all neat and orderly and pulled a dirty blanket over it, and then went to the stove and stirred up the fire until there was some flame.
>
> He got the lantern down off the peg and lit it and went stumping out the door. The night was as black as a stack of cats and the lantern light was feeble, but that made not a bit of difference, for Mose knew this farm of his like the back of his hand.
>
> He went down the path into the woods. It was a spooky place, but it took more than woods at night to spook Old Mose.

And finally, a word or two about the setting that the alien has to deal with:

As he lay in bed that night, strange thoughts came creeping in upon him—the thought of an even greater loneliness than he had ever known upon this runty farm, the terrible, devastating loneliness of the empty wastes that lay between the stars, a driven loneliness while one hunted for a place or person that remained a misty thought one could not define, but which it was most important one should find.

THEME

To talk about theme properly, we need to consider what the motive behind a story may be. The story is ordinarily intended to entertain us. It attempts to arouse in us the kind of emotions that are aroused by real people in real situations of joy, or trouble. In addition, it may try to get across to us a message that is very important to the writer, and this message is most often the theme of the story.

Nobody can tell you precisely what the theme of a story is, except perhaps the writer himself. Sometimes, as in John Steinbeck's *The Grapes of Wrath*, the theme is so powerfully presented that no one could overlook it, but only a very skillful writer can get away with laying it on so heavily. If we, as readers, start to feel that we are being preached at, that the writer is using the story as a kind of sleight-of-mouth to slip over a message, we will balk and put it down, and so it is usually necessary that the theme be hidden. One reader may see a theme that another reader will not see, or a theme that the writer did not realize was there.

If the question of the main theme of "A Death in the House" had to be answered by this writer, it would be by saying that it is "As ye sow, so shall ye reap." With two subsidiary themes right up there beside the big one—that wisdom is not necessarily confined to scientists and experts; and that, with love, communication is always possible. You may not agree with this, and that is quite all right. Simak may not agree with it, for that matter. Robin Scott Wilson, in "Theme: To Mean Intensely," sums it up this way:

> Put formally, *theme* is the writer's vision of life interpreted in terms of his own personality; it is a series of perceptions which the writer believes to be accurate and significant and which he communicates in the system of values and sentiments and incidents that is the story. It is the sum of plot, and character, and setting.
>
> Isolating *the* theme of a story—call it intellectual concept, message, meaning, intention, moral (as in Aesop) or ontology—is a slippery business.

Now look again at the story you wrote as a preliminary exercise for this unit. Can you improve it? Does it contain sufficient material on the setting so that the reader can visualize the surroundings where the action takes place? Are your characters real people, so that the reader cares what happens to them? Is there a real plot to your story, with a genuine crisis, or is it just a tepid listing of one event after another? Are the things that happen in your story *logical*—that is, once you have made your characters known to your reader, do the things they say and do follow logically from their characterization? Revise your story carefully, trying to make it so good that a reader would find it difficult to put it down once he has begun reading it. You may have to increase the length, but be sure that the words you add are necessary improvements and not just padding. It is probably accurate to say that the shorter a short story is, the harder it is to write—remember that it must contain no *waste* words. Stay as close to the two-thousand-word total as you can without sacrificing your story.

EXERCISES

1.   One of the concepts discussed in this unit is the difference between the folktale or other early narrative forms and the short story as we know it today. Choose a folktale, a parable, or a fable that you particularly like and *rewrite* it as a short story.

2.   Would it be as easy to convert a short story into a fable, a parable or a folktale as it was to do the converse? Why or why not? Write 300 words explaining your answer.

3.   One very important factor in writing fiction that we did not take up in this unit is the writer's *point of view*. There are several common choices: the story told completely in the first person, from the point of view of a single character in the third person, or from various points of view alternating from character to character, in the first person. Also common is the *omniscient author* viewpoint, in which the author presents everything from any convenient viewpoint, including his or her own. Find a brief story that you like and rewrite a portion of it, perhaps 1000 words, from a different point of view. Does this change the story radically? Can you explain why?

4.   Someone once said that an underground paper is always founded by three dedicated people, and that inevitably two of them will fire the third person because his way of showing up on time and meeting deadlines is "bourgeois" and/or "capitalistic."

Write the scene of the firing as a brief short story. Compare your version with several others in the class. Do differing points of view result in widely different stories?

5. Here is a paragraph from the *Saturday Review* for June 5, 1971:

> Remember the story about the San Francisco hippie who put a dime in a parking meter and lay down for an hour's sleep in the little plot of land he had just rented from the city. Imagine the result in Manhattan if 1,000 anti-freeway partisans arrived one morning at 7:30 with folding chairs and "rented" all the available parking space on several major streets for two hours.

After you "imagine the result" of this anti-freeway action, write a short story about it.

6. The following paragraph by Norman Martien is a good source of ideas for short story plots. Read it carefully and make a list of the stories you could write using it as springboard; try to list at least three.

> An inept teacher who has got hold of some piece of a truth will shove it at his students in the classroom; he will confront them with exams and grades to insure that they have accepted his lesson. Both he and his students will remain in possession of some brittle and useless fragment of knowledge. Mostly, he and they will have learned to distrust each other. So when students find a truth of their own, they shove it at their elders with signs and slogans, and when these seem to fail they confront them with the destruction and occupation of buildings. The tools are more obvious, and so they seem crude, but their methods are learned from the very teachers who denounce them.

7. Using this same paragraph as a source, write a short story about a student protest from the point of view of a teacher like the one Martien describes.

8. Here is the market description for *Scholastic Scope:*

> *Scholastic Scope* 4th-6th grade reading level; 15–18 age level; subject matter: interests of urban students, relationships between people (inter-racial, adult–teen-age, employer-employee, etc.) in family, job, and school situations. Urban settings. Strive for directness, realism and action, perhaps carried through dialogue rather

than exposition. Try for depth of characterization in at least one character. Realistic stories, written from viewpoint of a member of one of our minority peoples, not necessarily focusing on race relations, would be helpful. Avoid too many coincidences and random happenings. Even though *Scope* wants action stories, this is not a market for crime fiction. Story lengths from 500–1,500 words. Plays up to 3,000 words.

Read the description through carefully; it tells you exactly what the editor of this publication wants. Then try to write a short story tailored to the market description.

9.   In an interview in *Writer's Yearbook*, Kurt Vonnegut says that "anytime the reader fails to get the message, it's the writer's fault." Is Vonnegut right? Defend your position in 500 words.

10.   The sculptor Yehiel Shemi has made the following statement about kibbutz life:

One of the most crucial problems in the world, not only in the kibbutzim, is the amalgamation of intellectual work with physical work. And to live together, to do together, is one of the main ideas of the kibbutz. But in day-to-day life, one man goes out into the fields, and in the fields are flies and snakes and it's hot and it's not extremely interesting every moment of the day.

And his friend who came to the kibbutz with him is an intellectual type. He goes to a room with a lot of shade and he sits and opens a book and starts working. And he becomes a lecturer at the university, let's say, and he's a very respected man.

In day-to-day life there is a gap. Actually the one who works in the field has to be broadminded enough. He has to feel that he *gains* because he has a friend, a sculptor, who lives here. That's all. From the *fact* that there is an intellectual here. And this is very difficult. He asks, "What does he give me? Nothing." And I say he gives a lot, but you have to be built to absorb it and not everybody's built this way.

Use this statement as the basis for a brief short story, 1500–2000 words, written from the point of view of (a) the intellectual or (b) the man doing physical work. Use an American commune for the setting if you don't feel comfortable with the kibbutz locale.

11.   You are a young writer of short stories who resents the way they have been disappearing from contemporary magazines. Write a letter to the editor of a magazine of your choice protesting

the situation and explaining why you feel the proportion of short stories should be greater. Don't go beyond about 300 words. Then write a letter of the same length, from the editor, in reply.

12. In the San Francisco Greyhound Bus Station there are rows of TV chairs; they look much like high-school desks, since they have one arm for the television set. People sit in these chairs, brace an elbow on the chair arm, lean their chins on their hands, and pretend to be watching television. There is a policeman on duty there who goes his rounds inside the terminal. If he sees anyone sleeping instead of actually watching TV he knocks their elbows off the chair arm so that they crack their chins on the chair. It is forbidden to go to sleep in the bus station. Can you use this as a basis for a short story? Try to keep it under 3000 words.

Final Exam

It was a solemn occasion. The fact that the sun shone brilliant and blue through the windows, clearly signalling joy, was no help. If anything, it made it worse, setting off the grim faces of the Administrators in sharp relief, burning their frowns on their foreheads like Ritual-Markings for the spring festivals. Kelah would have welcomed rain, a dismal weather to match the dismal weather of his mind.

Beside him his father sat stiff and nervous in the formal robes of his Profession, trying to explain the situation to the other seven men.

"My son refuses," he said in the dead voice that Kelah had grown miserably familiar with lately, "he just refuses. He says flatly that he will not enter the competitions for any of the Professions."

"Hmmmmm," said the Senior Administrator.

"I have brought him up according to every dictate of our culture. I have given him everything a boy could want. He has been provided with the finest schools, the most brilliant tutors, the best of—"

The Senior Administrator cut him off. "Yes, yes, Lawyer ban-Tressix," he said, "we understand all that. The reputation of your household is secure, and you need not belabor us with a recitation of all the things you have done for this unfortunate and ungrateful young man."

The Lawyer flushed, mumbling, "I beg your pardon, Citizen Administrator," and Kelah sighed at the thought of the penalty he himself would undoubtedly pay for this public humiliation of his father.

The Administrator-Advocate began, then, to ask him the set of questions he had been expecting.

"Do you understand, Kelah ban-Tressix," he demanded, fumbling in the pockets of his robes for the drug to which he was addicted, "do you understand the consequences of your decision?"

"I do."

"Are you sure of that?"

"I am."

"You understand that you will be an outcast from your society?"

"Yes."

"You realize that every credit disc issued to a citizen of this planet is issued on the basis of membership in one of the Twelve Professions? You realize that without a credit disc there is no way to buy or sell, to obtain even the minimum necessities of life?"

"I know that, Citizen Administrator," Kelah said doggedly.

"Light's Beard, young man!" the Senior Administrator put in. "Don't you know you'll be no better off than a woman?"

"He'll be worse off," said the Administrator-Advocate, spitting the words out like seeds from between his teeth. "A woman at least *exists,* by virtue of her association with a man who does belong to a Profession."

"You will literally have no rights at all, Kelah," said one of the others. "You will simply not . . ."

Not exist at all," the Senior Administrator finished it off.

Kelah nodded. He knew it all. Had he not heard it from his father and from his teachers, over and over again all these years until he was physically sick at the sound of it? He bowed his head and let it all flow over him again, unresisting, since it had long since ceased to be anything but noise. The disgrace to his family. The pain he would cause the males of his household. The fact that he could never marry, that he could not have a household of his own. The fact that should he find some unattached woman desperate enough to ally herself with him and then have difficulties with her, none of the facilities of the Women's Discipline Unit would be available to him. The fact that he could not be buried, since all burials were in Profession Plots. On and on and on . . .

He didn't care. He knew it all by heart and he didn't care. He would not, he would *not* be shoved into a slot for the rest of his life, his every move and every word from his mouth until he died prescribed for him by the Regulations Manual of his Profession! Better any kind of existence than that, better a free outcast than a comfortable slave! He did not even care if they saw all that on his face. There was nothing more that they could do to him now.

"Are you convinced?" said his father at last, rigid beside him, his voice almost trembling. "Do you see that it is hopeless?"

The Senior Administrator looked around him, taking a count of the heads nodding an affirmative, and said, "Indeed we do." And he pushed a set of studs on the comset at his side.

CONGRATULATIONS! the comset caroled, red and yellow lights flashing, bells ringing, and a jet of perfume of dorka-flowers rising slowly into the air from a rear orifice. CONGRATULATIONS, CITI-ZEN BAN-TRESSIX, YOU HAVE PASSED ALL THE TESTS FOR AD-MISSION INTO YOUR PROFESSION! IF YOU WILL JUST STEP INTO THE ROBING ROOM, CITIZEN, YOU WILL BE ISSUED YOUR ROBES AND YOUR CREDIT DISC! CONGRATULATIONS! CON-GRATULATIONS!

Kelah was almost too stunned to ask for an explanation. "What . . ." he stammered. "What is it . . ." He saw that now they had, one and all, smiles to match the sunshine.

The Senior Administrator pushed another stud and the wall at his left went suddenly translucent. On it, lifesize, was a three-dimensional projection of a young man whose robe—unlike all the others Kelah had ever seen, with their solid color and single contrasting stripe—was a rainbow of colors, a mingled and melting absolute riot of color. Around his neck hung a string of tiny haffa-bells, with a credit disc pendant from the center bell. And beside his head was the printed legend

AUTHORIZED COSTUME OF THE PROFESSION OF REVOLUTIONARY

"Oh, no," Kelah breathed. "Oh, please, no . . ."

The Senior Administrator cleared his throat.

"This," he said gravely, "is the Thirteenth Profession. You will understand, I am sure, why it is not publicized . . . we could not have every young man, in the first flush of adolescent rebellion, thinking that he was suited for Revolution, now could we?"

Kelah forgot his manners and grabbed his father's arm.

"It's a joke, Father?" he pleaded. "Surely this has got to be a joke?"

Lawyer ban-Tressix shook his head. "No, my son," he said happily, "it is as true as that you are my very dear son. My only fear was that they would not be convinced and that you would not pass the test. Con-gratulation, Kelah! Your mother will rejoice, there will be feasting and dancing in the Women's Quarters tonight. The Light bless you, my son, you have made me a happy man!"

The Administrators filed out of the room, one at a time according to their rank, and his father with them. They would go off together now to drink wine and talk about this, leaving him behind as befitted one who was not of their Profession.

Kelah gripped his hair with both hands, laid his head down on the table, and beat his forehead against the syntho-wood. "No," he said, over and over and over. "No. No. No." When the fedrobots came to take him to the Robing Room he was still saying it.

They paid no attention to him at all.

POLITICAL LANGUAGE AND ITS STRUCTURE

6

You are the leader of a band of revolutionaries who have just taken over a small country, deposing a vicious and brutal dictator. The people support you, but because of the dictator's long years of exploitation your country is in serious difficulties, and you know it will be years before there is adequate food, housing, medical care, and education. You go on television and give a speech to your people; your purpose is to win their loyalty so completely that they will support you through the rough years ahead.

One of the most important parts of a political speech is its closing paragraph in which the speaker tries to leave his hearers with something to remember. Sketch roughly the content of the speech you make—listing the points in three or four words will be sufficient —and then write your closing paragraph in full. Remember that it must be memorable, that it must be speakable, and that it must rally your people round you for the long, difficult time ahead.

Political language has a broad and varied range, including the daily debates on the floor of Congress, campaign speeches for local, state, and national offices, and the carefully chosen words of diplomats representing their country. We will select as typical of this language the political speech presented by the speaker as a self-contained unit and intended to be heard rather than read. We will examine portions of such speeches in detail and try to learn some essential facts about the way that they are constructed. As in previous units, we will concentrate our efforts upon examination of these materials as *examples of language.*

DEFINING THE POLITICAL SPEECH

Parrish and Hochmuth have defined a speech, in general, as "an utterance meant to be heard and intended to exert an influence of some kind on those who hear it." The definition should be applicable to political speeches as well, as a subclass of all speeches; the *subjects* of political speeches, however, will be a restricted class. Such speeches are not likely to be about tennis, advertising, welding, washing machines, rock music, or the best method for teaching French to college students. They will instead deal with political campaigns, the working of government, and with important issues of the day.

With this definition in mind, we can now look at some examples. We will begin with the closing paragraphs or closing lines of a number of Inaugural Addresses, by presidents of the United States. Each of these addresses would have been intended to achieve roughly the same purpose: to set the tone for the coming administration; to win the loyalty and support of the people of the United States for the term of that administration; and perhaps to state personal goals and principles of the incoming presidents.

The first example is from Abraham Lincoln's First Inaugural, delivered on March 5, 1861.

> I am loath to close. We are not enemies, but friends. We must not be enemies. Though passion may have strained, it must not break our bonds of affection. The mystic chords of memory, stretching from every battlefield, and patriot grave, to every living heart and hearth-stone, all over this broad land, will yet swell the chorus of the Union, when again touched, as surely they will be, by the better angels of our own nature.

Here is the final paragraph from Lincoln's Second Inaugural, March 4, 1865.

> With malice toward none; with charity for all; with firmness in the right, as God gives us to see the right, let us strive on to finish the work we are in; to bind up the nation's wounds; to care for him who shall have borne the battle, and for his widow, and his orphan—to do all which may achieve and cherish a just and lasting peace, among ourselves, and with all nations.

Teddy Roosevelt, on March 4, 1905, said:

We know that self-government is difficult. We know that no people needs such high traits of character as that people which seeks to govern its affairs aright through the freely expressed will of the freemen who compose it. But we have faith that we shall not prove false to the memories of the men of the mighty past. They did their work, they left us the splendid heritage we now enjoy. We in our turn have an assured confidence that we shall be able to leave this heritage unwasted and enlarged to our children and our children's children. To do so we must show, not merely in great crises, but in everyday affairs of life, the qualities of practical intelligence, of courage, of hardihood, and endurance, and above all the power of devotion to a lofty ideal, which made great the men who founded this Republic in the days of Washington, which made great the men who preserved this Republic in the days of Abraham Lincoln.

On March 4, 1913, Woodrow Wilson ended his First Inaugural with the following paragraph:

This is not a day of triumph; it is a day of dedication. Here muster not the forces of party, but the forces of humanity. Men's hearts wait upon us; men's lives hang in the balance; men's hopes call upon us to say what we will do. Who shall live up to the great trust? Who dares fail to try? I summon all honest men, all patriotic, all forward-looking men, to my side. God helping me, I will not fail them, if they will but counsel and sustain me.

Here is President Harry Truman, speaking to the nation on January 20, 1949:

But I say to all men, what we have achieved in liberty, we will surpass in greater liberty.

Steadfast in our faith in the Almighty, we will advance toward a world where man's freedom is secure.

To that end we will devote our strength, our resources, and our firmness of resolve. With God's help, the future of mankind will be assured in a world of justice, harmony, and peace.

And finally, here is the closing paragraph of Richard Nixon's address delivered on January 20, 1969.

Our destiny offers not the cup of despair, but the chalice of opportunity. So let us seize it, not in fear, but in gladness—and "riders on the earth together," let us go forward, firm in our faith, steadfast in our purpose, cautious of the dangers; but sustained by our confidence in the will of God and the promise of man.

Our earlier definition of a political speech said that a political speech is language meant to be heard, intended to have an effect on those who hear it, and restricted to the general class of political subjects. The six examples above meet this definition adequately, but is the definition itself adequate?

Consider the following example:

All right, everybody. I'm President now. Things are going to be very different around here. I want you to know that anybody who steps out of line is going to be in big trouble. If you don't understand what I mean by that, you can see my Cabinet members. They'll explain. Remember what I told you and everything will be fine from now on.

Or, at a somewhat different level of government:

I've told you people in the back row to stop eating celery in these meetings so many times that I can't even remember the total, and I'm sick of it. I want you to quit, right now. It's stupid behavior.

Or a nonthreatening example:

Everybody here who follows the guidelines written down in this paper will be given a substantial bonus. I want you to be happy. Happiness is not possible unless incomes are adequate. This program is new and I want you to like it. There's no reason for you to worry anymore.

Are these last three examples political speeches? They are on political subjects, they are intended to be heard, and they certainly are intended to have an effect on the individuals who are listening. Except for the subject matter, this is true of "Everybody put your hands up or I'll blow your heads off!", but nobody would call such an utterance a *speech*, political or otherwise. The question is, then, where does the difference lie? How do we immediately identify the sequences from the inaugural addresses as political speeches and quickly eliminate the constructed examples?

"I pledge myself to work for closer ties and better understanding between
my country and that funny little place I've been appointed ambassador
to."

Perhaps the difference lies in the vocabulary. The first six
examples are pretty fancy in their choice of words, and the last
three are not. We can test this thesis by constructing an example
in very ordinary speech, as follows:

We aren't here to play; we're here to work. We've played long
enough, and we've fooled around, and we've wasted our time.

And where did it ever get us? What good did it ever do us? Now it's time to do something else. Something we can be proud of. Something we can put our backs into. Something we can go home and talk to our friends and our families about. The only way we'll get a chance to play is by grabbing our chance to work. Now let's get started.

What about this example? There's not a fancy word in it, but it is clearly a political speech, and we recognize it as such. That recognition has to have some principled basis.

THE STRUCTURE OF RHETORICAL DEVICES

Let's take a careful look at some sentences from these examples.

1. We are not enemies, but friends.
2. Here muster not the forces of party, but the forces of humanity.
3. Our destiny offers not the cup of despair, but the chalice of opportunity.

The structure of these sentences is very clear: *Not X, but Y*. What about the following examples?

4. This is not a day of triumph; it is a day of decision.
5. We aren't here to play; we are here to work.

Sentences 4 and 5 appear slightly different from the first three examples, but their underlying structure is the same. We understand them in the same way and could paraphrase them to eliminate the difference, as follows:

6. This is not a day of triumph, but a day of dedication.
7. We are here not to play, but to work.

In every case, we understand these sequences to mean *Not X, but (on the contrary) Y*.

This structure is called *antithesis,* and is one of the oldest devices of speech-making. It occurs not only as *Not X but Y*, but also as *X but not Y*—for example, Shakespeare's famous "I come to bury

Caesar, not to praise him." (Redo that one: "I come not to praise Caesar, but to bury him.")

The point of antithesis is to set up two alternatives which contrast and to indicate your choice between them. The contrast should be apparent, and the choice must matter. Look at the following example. Would it be likely to have much effect on the listener?

> **8.** I am here not to stare at you, but to gaze at you.

This sentence has the structure of antithesis, but it fails; there is no real contrast between "stare" and "gaze," and it's impossible to believe that the choice would matter.

"Ferrabeau," said the teacher, "how do you find the subject of a sentence?"

"Oh," said Ferrabeau, "I find it pretty useless, by and large."

Remember that the political speaker always has to speak in a double context: the context of events and the context of the culture he and his listeners share. (If the second context is *not* shared, his problems are very different.)

Look at the following examples:

> **9.** I bring you not hamburgers, but hot dogs.
> **10.** I bring you not hamburgers, but cough drops.
> **11.** I bring you not hamburgers, but sirloin steaks.

In the context of American culture, the first example is silly, because both hamburgers and hot dogs are inexpensive foods intended for informal occasions. The second example is senseless, because there is no way to contrast a hamburger with cough drops. It is only the third example, which contrasts the inexpensive and informal hamburger with the expensive and formal steak, that would work as an example of antithesis.

Now let's examine another set of sequences from the various examples at the beginning of this unit and look for additional characteristics that can be isolated and defined.

> **12.** With malice toward none; with charity for all; with firmness in the right . . .

13. Let us strive on to finish the work we are in; to bind up the nation's wounds; to care for him who shall have borne the battle . . .

14. . . . which made great the men who founded this Republic in the days of Washington, which made great the men who preserved this Republic in the days of Abraham Lincoln . . .

15. Men's hearts wait upon us; men's lives hang in the balance; men's hopes call upon us to say what we will do.

16. . . all honest men, all patriotic, all forward-looking men . . .

17. To that end we will devote our strength, our resources, and our firmness of resolve.

18. . . . firm in our faith, steadfast in our purpose, cautious of the dangers . . .

19. Something we can be proud of. Something we can put our backs into. Something we can go home and talk to our friends and our families about.

What are we looking at in these examples? Not antithesis, certainly. Here is a famous example of the same phenomenon, from Winston Churchill's speech to the British people before the Battle of Britain:

> We shall fight on the beaches, we shall fight on the landing grounds, we shall fight in the fields and in the streets, we shall fight in the hills, we shall never surrender.

Ferrabeau handed in an essay on "What I Did Last Summer."

"Ferrabeau," said the teacher crossly, "Why on earth is this essay just one sentence two pages long?"

"Sorry about that," said Ferrabeau, "but I couldn't remember the rule for the use of the period."

Nor does this technique have to be confined to the space of a single sentence or two. Consider a section from John F. Kennedy's Inaugural Address:

> Let both sides explore what problems unite us instead of laboring those problems which divide us.
>
> Let both sides, for the first time, formulate serious and precise pro-

posals for the inspection and control of arms—and bring the absolute power to destroy other nations under the absolute control of
all nations.

Let both sides seek to invoke the wonders of science instead of its
terrors. . . .

Let both sides unite to heed in all corners of the earth the command of Isaiah—to "undo the heavy burdens and let the oppressed
go free."

There is a similarity between this and antithesis, in that both
offer us at least X and Y. But where antithesis offers X in *contrast* to Y, this technique offers X as a *parallel* to Y. It's called
parallelism and, like antithesis, is a classical rhetorical device.

One of the easiest ways to understand how parallelism works
is to hack a good example of it to pieces. For instance, compare
the original Churchill example with the mutilation of it that follows:

20. We shall fight on the beaches.
    We shall fight on the landing grounds.
    We shall fight in the fields and in the streets.
    We shall fight in the hills.
    We shall never surrender.

21. We shall fight on the beaches.
    We'll fight on the landing grounds.
    In the fields and streets we'll fight.
    We're going to struggle up in the hills, too.
    Surrender is out.

Notice that there is nothing fancy about Churchill's vocabulary. Churchill, like Franklin D. Roosevelt, used plain speech with
tremendous effectiveness.

What elements in addition to antithesis and parallelism set
these speeches off from ordinary speech?

22. Who shall live up to the great trust? Who dares fail to
try?

23. And where did it ever get us? What good did it ever do us?

When Patrick Henry gave his famous speech attempting to convince his fellow Americans to undertake a revolution against the British oppressors, he used this same technique, saying:

24. Why stand we here idle? What is it that gentlemen wish? What would they have? Is life so dear, or peace so sweet, as to be purchased at the price of chains or slavery?

These examples are all questions, but they differ from the ordinary questions because no answer is expected or desired. They are called *rhetorical questions,* and the speaker ordinarily answers them himself. If someone in Patrick Henry's audience, hearing "Why stand we here idle?" had taken him literally and broken in with an explanation—"Well, you see, Pat, the reason we're just standing here idle is that we're listening to you."—everyone in the audience would have been outraged, and Patrick Henry would never have had the chance to finish his speech.

Now we must decide whether antithesis, parallelism, and rhetorical questions are unrelated, or whether there is some common characteristic that underlies the language of political speeches, and that we can use to modify slightly the otherwise accurate definition proposed at the beginning of this unit.

Remember, to begin with, how a speech is *encountered* by those listening to it. It's not like an essay or a short story or a set of directions for building a boat, because first and foremost it isn't written down. Think what this has to mean—it means that although the listener is supposed to understand what is being said and to remember it so well that it will have a lasting effect upon him, he has only one chance at the language. There is no opportunity to review what has been said, as there would be if it were written down and could be looked at again and again at leisure. A speech must be constructed in such a way that the listener is given every possible aid in following and remembering it.

This is not unique to political speeches; it is the classic problem of literary language in a culture which does not have a written language, for instance. The strategy for getting around the problem is simply to provide so symmetrical, so balanced a structure, that the listener is able to use that structure as a kind of set of pigeonholes to file away the content in. All three of the rhetorical devices discussed above lead to the attainment of that sort of balanced, symmetrical structure.

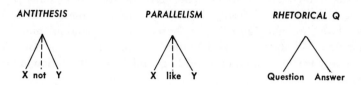

ANTITHESIS	PARALLELISM	RHETORICAL Q
X not Y	X like Y	Question Answer

Although content is an important part of these rhetorical devices, they are primarily devices of *form*. The three devices listed are by no means an exhaustive list. If you are interested in reading about other ways of achieving structural balance, the place to look is a standard handbook of rhetoric.

RHETORICAL DEVICES OF CONTENT

We are now going to examine some of the characteristics of political language which are based more on content than on rhetorical form.*
First, consider the following sets of sentences.

25. (a) The army destroyed the village at dawn.
(b) The army's destruction of the village happened at dawn.
26. (a) The ideas of student radicals have corrupted our society, and that is tragic.
(b) The corruption of our society by the ideas of student radicals is tragic.

You will notice that both pairs of sentences have the same basic content, so that they can be termed *synonymous* pairs. A political

---

* There has been a great deal of fuss made in recent years about the advisability of separating "form" from "content." There are many scholars who feel that such a separation is a grave mistake and should never be attempted. Their point of view is that the form and content create a whole, and that one is inextricably a part of the other.

It is important to remember that it takes *both* form and content to achieve meaningful language. Thus, nominalization—which significantly alters *content*—does so only because of its grammatical form. It is possible, however, to discuss form and content separately without losing sight of their essential oneness.

speech, however, is intended to influence those listening to it, and the effect of the *b* sentences is very different from the *a*.

English has many related pairs of nouns and verbs like those in the two sentences above. The verb "destroy" is matched by the noun "destruction," the verb "corrupt" by the noun "corruption." Similarly, we find "agree" and "agreement," "abandon" and "abandonment," "introduce" and "introduction." It is also possible to turn any verb into a noun by adding "-ing," as in the following pairs.

> **27.** (a) The trees burned.
> (b) The burning of the trees. . . .
> **28.** (a) The army burned the fence.
> (b) The army's burning of the fence. . . .

This process of making nouns from verbs has a number of names; we will use the term *nominalization* here. What is important is not its name, but what it accomplishes. If you look at sentence 25(a) you will see that it makes a claim that the army destroyed the village. This claim is unsupported, and the responsibility of the speaker, called "the burden of proof," is to provide that support. In sentence 25(b), however, no such proof is called for. The destruction has become something that can be taken for granted, and the only real question is whether it happened at dawn or not.

"Ferrabeau," said the teacher, "define the verb."

"Easy," said Ferrabeau. "The verb is an *action* word. Like typhoon. Like circus. Like earthquake. Like . . ."

Similarly, in 26(a), the claim is made that the ideas of student radicals have corrupted society. In 26(b) this corruption is mentioned, in nominal form, as if there were no question at all about its existence, and the only proof required is that this corruption is tragic.

The technique of nominalization is very clever indeed. A listener *might* respond to 25(b) by shouting "*What* destruction of the village?" But it's unlikely, because a speech goes by rapidly, without opportunity for review, and the unsupported nominalizations tend to slip past the hearers unnoticed.

Patrick Henry, in the speech mentioned earlier, used the technique of nominalization as a way of forestalling any claim from his listeners that he doubted that they were patriotic. He began his speech with the following sentence:

> **Mr. President: No man thinks more highly than I do of the patriotism, as well as abilities, of the very worthy gentlemen who have just addressed the house.**

The effect of the nominalization is to establish that there can be no question about the individuals' patriotism—which of course Patrick Henry goes on to question at some length. It makes it awkward for the gentlemen being criticized to leap to their feet and demand to be told whether their patriotism is at issue. Its existence has already been stated, by Patrick Henry himself.

We are all so familiar with this nominalizing device that we would have no difficulty in producing fifty more examples. For instance:

29. The unreasonable demands of the workers
    (for "the workers' demands are unreasonable")
30. The cooperation of the defendants
    (for "the defendants are cooperating")
31. The defilement of our sacred institutions by these traitors
    (for "these traitors have defiled our sacred institutions")

The device is somewhat less dangerous if we are aware of it.

The second device related more to content than to form in political language is that of carefully choosing words which bear a heavy cultural load. These words have special connotations, a special weight of meanings in addition to their simple dictionary meanings, that are part of the cultural tradition of the listeners. Here are some examples from the inaugural speeches:

32. . . . from every *battlefield* and *patriot grave*, to every living *heart* and *hearthstone* . . .
33. We in our turn have an assured confidence that we shall be able to leave this *heritage* unwasted and enlarged to *our children* and *our children's children*.
34. . . . a day of *triumph* . . . a day of *dedication* . . .
35. With God's help, the future of *mankind* will be assured in a world of *justice, harmony* and *peace*.
36. Our *destiny* offers not the cup of *despair*, but the chalice of *opportunity*.

There are certain words, like those underlined above, to which the speaker has the right to assume that listeners will react in a special way. The mere presence of such words in a political speech is reassuring, lulling, and in a very real sense contributes to the recognition of the speech as coming from "one of the good guys."

The choice of such words is not always simple. It is not just mother, home, the flag, and apple pie that is involved here. In the essays, "President Kennedy's Inaugural Address," Burnham Carter, Jr., makes the following statement:

> . . . one notices right away that Mr. Kennedy uses the word *pledge* seven times in a row (the last two with slight variations to avoid monotony.) *Promise* would never do here, for "promises, promises, always promises" has become a cant phrase for us.

Then, too, it is possible to use culturally weighed words not to reassure the listeners, but to provoke them. There is a particular highly rhythmic four-syllable word which is as characteristic of the speeches of radical activists as quotations from the King James Bible are characteristic of the speeches of mainstream politicians. The simple presence of this word is sufficient to enrage establishment audiences, and is therefore an excellent way of getting their attention.

The paragraph below, taken from John Kennedy's inaugural speech, is a typical example of the use of culturally weighted words; they are italicized.

> To our *sister republics* south of our border, we offer a special *pledge*—to convert our good words into *good deeds,* in a new *alliance* for *progress,* to assist *free men* and free governments in casting off *the chains of poverty.* But this *peaceful revolution* of *hope* cannot become the prey of *hostile powers.* Let all of our *neighbors* know that we shall join them to oppose *aggression* or *subversion* anywhere in the Americas. And let every other power know that this hemisphere intends to remain *the master of its own house.*

Another device of political language that fits into this category is the *oxymoron*. It combines contradictory elements, such as "silent noise" or "light darkness." Its effect is frequently much the same as the effect of combining a positive number 6 with a negative number 6; that is, the net result is zero.

We see the oxymoron so frequently today that it is extremely important to be aware of its existence. The expression "a clean bomb" is an oxymoron, as is the "cold war."

Finally, the speaker may use the device of renaming a particular thing because its original name has become heavily loaded with negative significance. This last technique, the coining of *euphemisms,* may be the most dangerous of all. Neil Postman has said that "the semantic environment is polluted when language obscures from people what they are doing and why they are doing it," and the euphemism is probably the Super-Polluter.

For example, the reaction to the statement that a child is starving is predictably negative. By saying that the child is "suffering from a nutritional deficiency" that reaction can be cooled down considerably. To refer to the destruction of a town by bombs as an "incident" is to lessen the emotional effect of that act. To avoid saying that something is "wrong," which a speaker knows cannot be very helpful in bolstering his or her cause, the something can be called "inappropriate." To disguise the fact that the job of a garbage collector is unpleasant and dirty, it can be renamed "sanitary engineer."

Our semantic environment is so cluttered with euphemisms these days that it is indeed hard at times to know what we are doing and why we are doing it. The only way to deal with euphemisms is to become sharply aware that such verbal animals exist, to watch carefully for them, and to replace every single one of them we encounter with the original word it is doing sneaky duty for.

FINAL DEFINITION

We can now summarize our examination of political language, as typified by the political speech, and say that it has at least the following characteristics:

1.   It is intended to be heard;
2.   It is intended to influence those who hear it;
3.   It takes advantage of such strategies as euphemisms and nominalizations, and the use of culturally loaded words, in order to increase that influence;
4.   It deals with political subjects, such as current affairs and the workings of government;

   5. It has a balanced structure, achieved by the use of such
rhetorical devices as parallelism and antithesis, so that it can
be easily followed and remembered.

   You will see at once that a familiarity with these characteristics makes it extremely easy to parody the language of the political
speech. Great skill is thus required in the preparation of political
language, since the line between *conforming* to the set of listed
characteristics and *parodying* them is bound to be very narrow and
is easy to cross inadvertently. John F. Kennedy, whose speeches
were classic examples of political language, was well aware of
this danger, as shown by the parody he gave of his own inaugural
address at a subsequent dinner party. He began by saying "We
observe tonight not a celebration of freedom but a victory of party,
for we have sworn to pay off the same party debt our forebears
ran up nearly a year and three months ago." His original address
began, "We observe today not a victory of party but a celebration
of freedom. . . . For I have sworn before you and Almighty God
the same solemn oath our forebears prescribed nearly a century
and three quarters ago."

   There are many more characteristics of political language,
even when our sample of that language is confined to the area of
political speeches, that we have not examined here. For example,
we have paid no attention to the skillful use of patterns of sound,
as in Lincoln's "mystic chords of memory," "heart and hearthstone,"
or Kennedy's "for the first time, formulate." We have not discussed
the device of *paradox,* which we see in Kennedy's "bring the absolute power to destroy other nations under the absolute control of
all nations." To deal with all the devices of political language, even
briefly, would go far beyond the scope of this brief introduction.

   But it is perhaps now clear that the whole strategy of political
language is to use language itself, *systematically,* in such a way as
to influence those who hear and to make them remember what the
speaker wants to have remembered.

   Now, look once again at the paragraph you wrote at the beginning of this unit, the final paragraph of a revolutionary leader's
speech. Is it immediately identifiable as part of a political speech?
Does it employ the language strategies discussed in this chapter?
Are you satisfied with it as you originally wrote it? If not, rewrite
it using the information you have found in this chapter to improve
it as an example of the language of politics.

The Right to Write

HON. MORRIS K. UDALL

Surprisingly few people ever write their Congressman. Perhaps 90 percent of our citizens live and die without ever taking pen in hand and expressing a single opinion to the man who represents them in Congress —a man whose vote may decide what price they will pay for the acts of government, either in dollars or in human lives.

Mail to a modern-day Congressman is more important than ever before. In the days of Calhoun, Clay, Webster and Lincoln, Congressmen lived among their people for perhaps nine months of the year. Through daily contacts in a constitutency of less than 50,000 people (I represent ten times that many) they could feel rather completely informed on their constituents' beliefs and feelings. Today, with the staggering problems of government and increasingly long sessions, I must not only vote on many more issues than early-day Congressmen but I rarely get to spend more than 60 days of a year in Arizona. Thus my mailbag is my best "hot line" to the people back home.

Some suggestions that apply to all congressional mail:

1. *Address it properly.* "Hon. _____ _____, House Office Building, Washington, D.C. 20515," or "Senator _____ _____, Senate Office Building, Washington, D.C. 20510.

2. *Identify the bill or issue.* About 20,000 bills are introduced into each Congress so it is important to be specific. If you write about a bill, try to give the bill number or describe it by a popular title ("truth in lending," "minimum wage," etc.).

3. *The letter should be timely.* Sometimes a bill is out of committee or has passed the House before a helpful letter arrives. Inform your Congressman while there is still time to take action.

4. *Concentrate on your own delegation.* All letters written by residents of my district to other Congressmen will simply be referred to me for reply, and vice versa.

5. *Be reasonably brief.* Every working day the mailman leaves some 150 or more pieces of mail at my office. It is not necessary that letters be typed—only that they be legible—and the form, phraseology and grammar are completely unimportant.

6. *Student letters are welcome.* Their opinions are important to me.

Some DO's:

7. *Write your own views—not someone else's.* A personal letter is far better than a form letter or signature on a petition. I usually know what the major lobbying groups are saying, but I don't often know of your experiences and observations, or what the proposed bill will do to and for you.

8. *Give your reasons for taking a stand.* I may not know all the effects of the bill and what it may mean to an important segment of my constituency.

9. *Be constructive.* If a bill deals with a problem you admit exists, but you believe the bill is the wrong approach, tell me what the right approach is.

10. *If you have an expert knowledge share it with your Congressman.* I can't possibly be an expert in all fields; many of my constituents are experts in some of them. I welcome their advice and counsel.

11. *Say "well done" when it's deserved.* Congressmen are human too, and they appreciate an occasional "well done" from people who believe they have done the right thing. I know I do. But even if you think I went wrong on an issue, I would welcome a letter telling me you disagreed; it may help me on another issue later.

Some DONT's:

1. Don't make threats or promises.

2. Don't berate your Congressman.

3. Don't pretend to wield vast political influence.

4. Don't try to instruct your Congressman on every issue that comes up. Don't be a pen pal.

In conclusion . . .

During the two-year life of this Congress, the House clerk will record my votes on more than 250 issues. But in a very real sense these will not be my votes, they will be yours too.

EXERCISES

1. Identify the rhetorical devices used in the following selections from famous speeches; underline the culturally loaded words.

Is this the part of wise men, engaged in a great and arduous struggle for liberty? Are we disposed to be of the number of those, who, having eyes, see not, and having ears, hear not, the things which so nearly concern their temporal salvation? For my part, whatever anguish of spirit it may cost, I am willing to know the whole truth; to know the worst, and to provide for it.

PATRICK HENRY

For this is what America is all about. It is the uncrossed desert and the unclimbed ridge. It is the star that is not reached and the harvest that's sleeping in the unplowed ground.

Is our world gone? We say farewell. Is a new world coming? We welcome it—and we will bend it to the hopes of man.

LYNDON JOHNSON, INAUGURAL ADDRESS

The time has come for us to leave the valley of despair and climb the mountain so that we may see the glory of the dawn, a new day for America, a new dawn for peace and freedom to the world.

RICHARD NIXON, ACCEPTANCE SPEECH

2. Select one of the example paragraphs in this unit or in the exercises and write a parody of it, staying as close to the original in structure and style as possible.

3. Would students learn more if college professors used the devices of political language in their lectures? Write a brief defense of your answer.

4. Assume that the following lines are taken from political speeches. Complete them in your own words.

    a. Not every man can become President, but _____

    b. To our friends we offer our trust, because they are our friends; to our enemies, _____

    c. If we are to win this struggle, if we are to triumph over this _____

    d. You ask me why I stand here before you today; I _____

    e. At last we have come to the end of this terrible conflict; now _____

    f. If we had only known, fifty years ago, what we know today, if we had only _____

5. Locate a collection of speeches, or go to the bound volumes of *Vital Speeches of the Day* at your library. Find ten ex-

amples of one of the political language strategies discussed in this unit and demonstrate how the examples are constructed.

6. The following selection is from a speech by Seattle, a Dwamish Indian chief, before Isaac Stevens, Governor of Washington Territory, in 1854. Study it carefully and write an analysis of the speech, paying particular attention to its characteristics as an example of political language.

> Every part of this soil is sacred in the estimation of my people. Every hillside, every valley, every plain and grove, has been hallowed by some sad or happy event in days long vanished. The very dust upon which you now stand responds more lovingly to their footsteps than to yours, because it is rich with the blood of our ancestors and our bare feet are conscious of the sympathetic touch. Even the little children who lived here and rejoiced here for a brief season will love these somber solitudes and at eventide they greet shadowy returning spirits. And when the last Red Man shall have perished, and the memory of my tribe shall have become a myth among the White Men, these shores will swarm with the invisible dead of my tribe; and when your children's children think themselves alone in the field, the store, the shop, upon the highway, or in the silence of the pathless woods, they will not be alone. At night when the streets of your cities and villages are silent and you think them deserted, they will throng with the returning hosts that once filled and still love this beautiful land. The White Man will never be alone.
>
> Let him be just and deal kindly with my people, for the dead are not powerless. Dead, did I say? There is no death, only a change of worlds.

7. Do any of the portions of speeches presented in this unit or in the exercises seem to have gone over the line into parodies of political language? Which ones? Defend your choice, but remember that a phrase considered a cliche today may have been vivid and new when it was first used.

8. You have just heard a political speech by a young radical activist who used words ordinarily considered obscene. You are furious about this, for one of the following reasons:

    a. Women and children were present;

    b. The audience reacted so violently to the obscenities that you couldn't hear the rest of the speech;

    c. The speaker's obscenities made a bad impression that detracted from the rest of the content of the speech.

Write a letter to the editor of your local paper, not more than 300 words long, presenting your position based on one of the reasons offered above.

9. Write an angry letter to the editor attacking the letter you wrote as part of exercise 8.

10. It is possible to regard political language as an abuse of language, preying upon the susceptibilities of listeners by hiding real problems and partial untruths behind a smoke screen of rhetoric. Write a one-page defense of this position; now write a one-page attack on the same position.

11. Write an analysis of the following portion of the inaugural address of President Calvin Coolidge, given on March 4, 1925. Discuss both form and content and compare this speech with the closing paragraphs of any of the other inaugural examples in this unit. Which speech is better? Why?

> We should not let the much that is to do obscure the much which has been done. The past and present show faith and hope and courage fully justified. Here stands our country, an example of tranquillity at home, a patron of tranquillity abroad. Here stands its Government, aware of its might but obedient to its conscience. Here it will continue to stand, seeking peace and prosperity, solicitous for the welfare of the wage earner, promoting enterprise, developing waterways and natural resources, attentive to the intuitive counsel of womanhood, encouraging education, desiring the advancement of religion, supporting the cause of justice and honor among the nations. America seeks no earthly empire built on blood and force. No ambition, no temptation, lures her to thought of foreign dominions. The legions which she sends forth are armed, not with the sword, but with the cross. The higher state to which she seeks the allegiance of all mankind is not of human, but of divine origin. She cherishes no purpose save to merit the favor of Almighty God.

12. Assume that the speech quoted in exercise 11 was given at the inauguration of the most recent United States president, and that the inauguration took place within the past six months. Would the speech have been appropriate? Why or why not? Write a brief essay of approximately 500 words defending your position.

13. Write the missing lines for this hypothetical dialogue:

FATHER. All you kids, yelling about being adults, and civil rights, and the mess we've made of your world, and now just look at you—

give you the right to vote and what do you do? You *don't* vote, that's what.

SON.   The reason I didn't vote is that it would be useless if I did.

FATHER.   Now that just goes to show that the voting privilege should be reserved for people who have some capacity for mature judgment. You don't even make any sense!

SON. _____

14. A commonplace tactic of American radical rhetoric is the comparison of present-day radicals with the Americans who took part in the Revolution that liberated us from England. Is the comparison justified, or is it a false analogy? Write a 10-minute speech on either of these positions.

15. In his book, *Message Ends,* David Craig describes an interesting technique called *reverse propaganda.* In this technique, words that have been proven to produce negative reactions in the reader or listener are salted systematically through a sequence of language to produce a negative response to the entire sequence. Thus, a two-page article whose surface content urged the readers to support a local tax bill would contain a number of these negative words, allowing the writer to prevent the passage of the bill while at the same time giving the appearance of supporting it. One example of this reversal effect—obviously unintentional—is the refusal of a number of people to buy any product whose commercials include the words "bathroom bowl" or "kills germs." It makes no difference what else the commercial may say, the presence of those two expressions is sufficient to annoy the listeners.

Can you think of more examples of this inadvertent reversal phenomenon in your life? Describe as many as you can.

Do you think this reverse propaganda technique could be a dangerous mechanism for influencing people? Write a brief essay stating why this technique is or is not potentially dangerous.

Mad's Guaranteed Effective All-Occasion Non-Slanderous Political Smear Speech

BILL GARVIN

My fellow citizens, it is an honor and a pleasure to be here today. My opponent has openly admitted he feels an affinity toward your city, but I happen to *like* this area. It might be a salubrious place to him, but to me it is one of the nation's most delightful garden spots.

When I embarked upon this political campaign I hoped that it could be conducted on a high level and that my opponent would be willing to stick to the issues. Unfortunately, he has decided to be tractable instead—to indulge in unequivocal language, to eschew the use of outright lies in his speeches, and even to make repeated veracious statements about me.

At first I tried to ignore these scrupulous, unvarnished fidelities. Now I do so no longer. *If my opponent wants a fight, he's going to get one!*

It might be instructive to start with his background. My friends, have you ever accidentally dislodged a rock on the ground and seen what was underneath? Well, exploring my opponent's background is dissimilar. All the slime and filth and corruption you can possibly imagine, even in your wildest dreams, are glaringly nonexistent in this man's life. And even during his childhood!

Let us take a very quick look at that childhood: It is a known fact that, on a number of occasions, he emulated older boys at a certain playground. It is also known that his parents not only permitted him to masticate excessively in their presence, but even urged him to do so. Most explicable of all, this man who poses as a paragon of virtue exacerbated his own sister when they were both teenagers!

I ask you, my fellow Americans: is this the kind of person we want in public office to set an example for our youth?

Of course, it's not surprising that he should have such a typically pristine background—no, not when you consider the other members of his family:

His female relatives put on a constant pose of purity and innocence, and claim they are inscrutable, yet every one of them has taken part in hortatory activities.

The men in the family are likewise completely amenable to moral suasion.

My opponent's second cousin is a Mormon.

His uncle was a flagrant heterosexual.

His sister, who has always been obsessed by sects, once worked as a proselyte outside a church.

His father was secretly chagrined at least a dozen times by matters of a pecuniary nature.

His youngest brother wrote an essay extolling the virtues of being a homo sapiens.

His great-aunt expired from a degenerative disease.

His nephew subscribes to a phonographic magazine.

His wife was a thespian before their marriage and even performed the act in front of paying customers.

And his own mother had to resign from a woman's organization in her later years because she was an admitted sexagenerian.

Now what shall we say of the man himself?

I can tell you in solemn truth that he is the very antithesis of political radicalism, economic irresponsibility and personal depravity. His own record *proves* that he has frequently discountenanced treasonable, un-American philosophies and has perpetrated many overt acts as well.

He perambulated his infant son on the street.

He practiced nepotism with his uncle and first cousin.

He attempted to interest a 13-year-old girl in philately.

He participated in a seance at a private residence where, among other odd goings-on, there was incense.

He has declared himself in favor of more homogeneity on college campuses.

He has advocated social intercourse in mixed company—and has taken part in such gatherings himself.

He has been deliberately averse to crime in our streets.

He has urged our Protestant and Jewish citizens to develop more catholic tastes.

Last summer he committed a piscatorial act on a boat that was flying the American flag.

Finally, at a time when we must be on our guard against all foreign isms, he has coolly announced his belief in altruism—and his fervent hope that some day this entire nation will be altruistic!

I beg you, my friends, to oppose this man whose life and work and ideas are so openly and avowedly compatible with our American way of life. A vote for him would be a vote for the perpetuation of everything we hold dear.

The facts are clear; the record speaks for itself.

Do your duty.

For Revolution

JOHN D. ROCKEFELLER 3RD

Today, just as 200 years ago, we are at a turning point. Our society is in ferment. We face difficult unresolved problems, a crisis of confidence, an uncertain future. There is as much divisiveness and fear and alienation today as there was then. The profound currents of social change in motion in our society now are concerned with the same humanistic ideals and values that motivated the men and women of colonial America—freedom and justice and truth and the "quality of life," which is the modern translation of Jefferson's immortal phrase "the pursuit of happiness."

The remarkable fact is that although we have been far from perfect, we persist. Our founding values have been preserved even if most of us take them for granted and some have access to them only with great difficulty. In many ways we have matured rapidly as a society in recent decades. We have outlived some of our myths, the myth of our invincibility, for example, or the idea that a melting pot will mold everyone into some standard and comfortable notion of what an American should be. We are questioning the soundness of perpetual growth. We are increasingly able to look at our past more honestly than was possible even a decade ago.

And, more importantly, we are a society on the move. We are in the early stages of the Second American Revolution. What began in part as the black revolution and the youth revolution has spread to some extent through all elements of our society. And so we have Women's Liberation, the consumerism movement, the concern for our environment, a new interest in corporate responsibility, a new consciousness among native Americans, a growing concern over the nature of work, increasing involvement in political life, a new directness and ease in human relations.

The common thread running through all of these and similar phenomena is a reconsideration of the values by which we order our lives and our society. This is the core of the Second American Revolution, whose purposes are to improve the quality of life for all our citizens and to bring finally into fruition, for all, the great humanistic values of the first American Revolution. It is thus a revolution of fulfillment rather than overthrow, a peaceful movement toward a higher level of human existence.

This growing concern for what life is all about, so characteristic of our time, is made possible in very large measure by the advanced state of the American economy. We are moving into what economists refer to as a postindustrial society. Industrialization is not an end in itself but is a preparation for the next and higher stage of human development. The chief purpose of an industrial society is industrial production. The chief purpose of the new society—a humanistic society—is human growth, the creating of conditions that provide genuine opportunity for each member to develop his full potential.

The central task of the Second American Revolution is to reconcile our dominant materialistic values with our enduring humanistic values— to preserve the benefits of economic and technical progress but to order them within the context of a society that is increasingly humanistic and person centered.

I see the Second American Revolution as a positive and promising social force. To me this is every bit as challenging and exciting a time to be alive as was the era of the first American Revolution. But today, just as then, there is nothing automatic or preordained about the outcome of the social movement that is underway. We need only think of international tensions, the growing disparity between haves and have-nots, the terrible complexity of many of our problems. The Second American Revolution could become distorted. It could degenerate into violence. Only the understanding and involvement of growing numbers of Americans can assure its course, can fulfill its promise of a better and brighter future for all of us.

I am basically optimistic. Virtually everything is wide open for change. I look upon this positively, for to me it means that wide-ranging progress is possible. It means that all individuals have as never before the opportunity to influence the course of events in however large or small a way. And it also means that the opportunity for personal growth was never greater.

I am optimistic also because I believe that understanding and involvement are increasing—particularly among the "moderates," the vast American center that includes so many millions of people of goodwill, who wish only the best for their country and their fellow citizens. And, to the extent that this happens, the bedrock strength of our democratic values and ideals will be working for us in full force—the strength of free men and women making free choices.

We are a very fortunate people, and we have a great deal to celebrate. But how do we move beyond celebration for its own sake to a Bicentennial that serves our best purposes in this time of ferment and change? It seems to me that there are three major requirements. The first is that we must see and understand and use the inspirational quality of the Bicentennial to its fullest power. The second is to conceive of the Bicentennial primarily as a time for achievement, for coming together and doing what must be done if we are to move this great nation forward. And third, we must set a proper time span for the Bicentennial within which inspiration and achievement can have full play. My proposal is that we reject the notion of the Bicentennial as only a national birthday party on July 4th, 1976, or even as a one-year anniversary in the year 1976. Rather, we should see it as covering a substantial period of time, as a Bicentennial Era.

The founding of our nation did not begin and end with the signing of the Declaration of Independence in 1776. The Revolutionary War began more than a year earlier, and it dragged on for years and was very nearly lost. It was not until the climactic Battle of Yorktown in 1781 that victory was assured. It was not until the Treaty of Paris in 1783 that the war was formally ended. The Constitution was not drafted until

1787. And finally, it was not until 1789 that the Constitution came into force and the Union truly began—with the first Congress, the first sitting of the Supreme Court and the inauguration of the first president. It took 13 years—from 1776 to 1789—to move from independence to union. I propose that the Bicentennial cover a similar period of time, that it be conceived as an era lasting from 1976 through 1989, based on the two great pillars: the Declaration of Independence and the Constitution.

A Bicentennial Era will have several advantages. It will help us avoid dissipating patriotic fervor in a one-year anniversary and suddenly relapsing to business as usual. It will include more than one presidential administration, thus helping the Bicentennial to be as free as possible of political partisanship. It will relieve us of the pressure to try to get everything ready by 1976—and fortunately so, since it is too late to do that anyway.

We need time to concern ourselves with the deeper meaning of what our country is all about, what our unfinished agenda is and what we want to become in the years ahead. The Bicentennial offers us an opportunity to rediscover our roots and sense of identity. It offers us common ground, a chance to unite in common purpose if we will but take it and make the most of it.

There is a tremendous range of opportunities for achievement. The one I believe to be the most important and at the same time the least developed is the instituting of new methods of planning and goal setting, at both the national and local levels.

How can we make our cities more livable? How can we better draw on rural America? How can we best protect and enhance our environment? How can we establish and assure the rights of all our citizens? What should be the nature of our economic system? What should be the role of government in the years ahead? We need to assemble our best talent to consider these and other difficult questions. And we need to create goal-setting processes that allow for wide citizen participation in making choices for the future.

Some may feel that dealing with such issues and creating such mechanisms is not relevant to the Bicentennial. I say this is what the Bicentennial should be all about. This is what renewal and rededication are all about. Two hundred years ago our forebears lived through a period of crisis, of commitment, of planning, of achievement. I submit to you that we can do no less in our time.

RELIGIOUS LANGUAGE AND ITS STRUCTURE

7

At last Earth has been visited by a group of extraterrestrial beings who are willing to stick around for a while. They are touring the planet, studying the culture and lifeforms. We don't know a great deal about the way these aliens look, because they are wearing their life-support systems, but we do know that they are reptiles, that they are black from head to navel and white from navel to feet, that they are hairless, that they are unisexual, and that they reproduce by budding.

As professor of comparative religion at a large university, you have been assigned the task of explaining Earth religions to these visitors. As a first step you have decided to explain to them the primary moral principles of the religion that is your specialty.

Choose one such principle and write an essay of about 500 words that will explain the chosen principle to the alien visitors.

DEFINING RELIGIOUS LANGUAGE

There are many different kinds of religious language, some of them distinguishable from other kinds of language only by the subject which is their content. Look at this brief example from a sermon by Martin Luther King:

I have a dream that one day every valley shall be exalted, every hill and mountain shall be made low, the rough places will be made plain and the crooked places will be made straight, and the glory of the Lord shall be revealed, and all flesh shall see it together.

This is our hope. This is the faith that I go back to the South with. With this faith we will be able to hew out of the mountain of despair a stone of hope. With this faith we will be able to transform the jangling discords of our nation into a beautiful symphony of brotherhood. With this faith we will be able to work together, to pray together, to struggle together, to go to jail together, to stand up for freedom together, knowing that we will be free one day.

We recognize this language sequence as religious because it mentions prayer and faith, and because it includes Biblical language, not because of its distinctive structure. The structural characteristics that we see here are the same as those of the political speech: parallelism, culturally loaded words, and speech which is patterned in sound, rhythm, and syntax for the purpose of memorable form.

Religious language, however, contains in addition ritual elements from the sacred scriptures of a given religion as well as archaic words and phrases which do not occur in other kinds of language. For example, the use of a quotation from the Bible, the Koran, the Bhagavad-Gita, or any other sacred work, will often mark a sequence of language as religious. It is only in a religious context that people are addressed as "brethren," or that we hear the phrase "we are gathered together" or find ourselves referred to as "beloved." It is only in a religious context that we hear the form "let's" expanded to "let us" as in "let us now turn to page one hundred and seventy-three." If we heard a factory foreman say "let us now begin production of this sub-assembly," we would be much surprised.

Another type of religious language deals with *ethics*, the question of how man should behave. For example:

It is doubtful if any act is right "in itself." Every act is a link in a chain of causes and effects. It cannot be said that it is wrong to take away a man's possessions against his will, for that would condemn all taxation—or the removal of a revolver from a homicidal maniac; neither of these is stealing—which is always wrong. . . . The rightness of an act, then, nearly always and perhaps always, depends on the way in which the act is related to circumstances; this is what is meant by calling it relatively right; but this does not in the least imply that it is only doubtfully right. It may be, in those circumstances, certainly and absolutely right.—William Temple.

This passage can be termed religious language, but it is indistinguishable from the language of any philosopher writing on the same subject. We can identify it as religious language only if we know it is contained within a book with a religious subject.

A third kind of religious language, however, seems to differ more specifically. Of such language Neil Postman says:

> At its purest, the language of religion has as its main purpose the construction of metaphors which give concrete form to humanity's most profound fears and exaltations. It serves to minimize fear, to increase freedom, and to provide a sense of continuity and oneness.

We cannot simply call such language *mystical*, although much of it has been written by mystics, because it occurs outside the mystical context as well. For example, the following quotation from Alan Watts is an almost perfect example of this kind of speech.

> Holiness is very hard to describe, but quite unmistakable when met with in the flesh; a wise innocence, a relaxed intensity, a humorous humility, a supernatural naturalness, an unsentimental devotion—all wrapped up in an atmosphere which is vaguely scary. For the holy man is numinous; he radiates something of the *shekinah*, the light of glory, the presence of the Most High.

Here is another example, from William James, *Varieties of Religious Experience:*

> Among other things, I did not merely come to believe, but I saw that the universe is not composed of dead matter, but is, on the contrary, a living Presence; I became conscious in myself of eternal life. It was not a conviction that I would have eternal life, but a consciousness that I possessed eternal life then; I saw that all men are immortal; that the cosmic order is such that without any peradventure all things work together for the good of each and all; that the foundation principle of the world, of all the worlds, is what we call love, and that the happiness of each and all is *in the long run* absolutely certain. The vision lasted a few seconds and was gone; but the memory of it and the sense of the reality of what it taught has remained during the quarter of a century which has since elapsed.

Spiritual Community Guide for North America. Artist: Fatima Jablonski

The last example is from the book *The Caravan*, by Stephen:

Religion in general is groups of folks. Now I think that when we were in the place that I called a communion earlier, I don't think there was anybody here who was not enlightened at that time. Does everybody understand that? . . . Don't think of enlightenment as you go along this road for years and years and years and years and then there's a great big golden gate and you go in and they put a thing around your neck and say, "Zap, you're enlightened!" It's that every once in a while you have flashes of sanity and they get closer together, till pretty soon you got a straight string of it and you say, "Far out, this is it!"

What is your reaction to this sort of language? If you find it

incomprehensible, you are not alone. Here is the famous philosopher
A. J. Ayer, talking about this problem:

> We do not deny *a priori* that the mystic is able to discover truths
> by his own special methods. We wait to hear what are the propo-
> sitions which embody his discoveries, in order to see whether they
> are verified or confuted by our empirical observations. But the
> mystic, so far from producing propositions which are empirically
> verified, is unable to produce any intelligible propositions at all.

Notice that this reaction is not to the *content* of the statements
made by the mystic, but rather to the *language,* which is claimed to
be unintelligible.

The question then is whether we can look at this sort of language and determine what characteristics it has that provoke such
terms as "unintelligible." Look at the following sequence:

up whistle cork polysynthetic the witch Moriarty off

That sequence of words is certainly unintelligible. Compare it with
the three examples by Watts, Temple, and Stephen, and you can
readily see that this is not the same *kind* of unintelligibility.

Let's look at the Watts example again to see if we can identify the source of difficulty. First, we can list some of the phrases
he uses:

1. wise innocence
2. relaxed intensity
3. supernatural naturalness

These phrases, like the rhetorical device of the oxymoron which was
discussed in the unit on political language, reverberate in one's
mind. They are structurally comparable to pairs like the following:

4. admirable courage
5. devoted kindness
6. tender love

Notice that you do not react to them as you reacted to the truly
unintelligible and meaningless string of words. A classic sentence
used in linguistics classes is "I saw a square circle." You know it
can't mean anything, and yet you have this uncanny feeling that

you know *exactly* what it means; it is this reaction that is provoked by a phrase like "a supernatural naturalness."

The problem here seems to be squarely in the language itself. Those who produce mystical language, or even nonmystical religious language of the kind we have been discussing, complain that words cannot express what they want to say. And those who encounter such language justly complain that they cannot understand the linguistic result of trying to say what cannot be said. There appear to be two major areas of difficulty—a kind of deficiency of vocabulary and grammar, and an apparent disregard for the laws of logic. We can perhaps understand this problem more clearly if we look at it in another way.

Imagine that you were assigned the task of writing a novel of the scope of *War and Peace,* but that you were restricted arbitrarily to using the vocabulary list taken from the back of a third grade reading text. This would be a straightforward vocabulary problem, similar to the difficulty Israeli writers experienced when they first tried to write about airplanes, rockets, lasers, synthetics, and vaccines in Biblical Hebrew.

Or imagine the following situation:

> You have seen Bill hit Hermione, with your own eyes. You know exactly what happened. But in your native language there is no mechanism for indicating that one noun is the direct object of a verb's action.*

In this situation, it would make no difference how clearly you had seen Bill hit Hermione, nor how well you understood and remembered the incident—there would be no way you could communicate the experience.

If you had to manage *both* these situations, and if you nonetheless made a gallant effort to express the inexpressible, you would find yourself in the classic writing dilemma of the religious mystic. On a less extreme scale, you would have the everyday problems of the writer of theological language.

The second facet of this problem (and perhaps one resulting from the first) is that the laws of logic frequently appear to be suspended in such language. In ordinary language you can expect that attention will be given to these laws of logic. You would

---

* You should be aware that there is no human language which actually has this characteristic. In every language the direct object of the verb is marked either by word order, by some special piece attached to the verb itself, or by some other device.

be outraged, and rightly so, if you were expected to take the following paragraph seriously:

> The Brentworth Zoo has so many animals now that caring for them is becoming increasingly difficult. Space is limited, and the animals are being subjected to unhealthy crowding. We have only one veterinarian, and there is just no way for him to attend to the medical needs of the animals, even when he works long hours. It costs very little, of course, to feed such a small number of animals. We are asking you, therefore, to dig deeply into your pocket at this holiday season and to give whatever you can spare, in order to help us put an end to this very serious situation.

The difficulty here is with the fourth sentence, which ought to be the third supporting point. That sentence does not agree with the rest of the paragraph; if there are so many animals that it is impossible to provide them with adequate space, shelter, or medical care, then it cannot be true that there is no difficulty in providing them with food. The only possible reaction to the paragraph is to throw the plea for funds away in disgust.

TEACHER. Ferrabeau, what's the difference between the direct object and the indirect object?

FERRABEAU. That's hard, but I can handle it. The direct object gets right to the point, but the indirect object is a lot more subtle about the whole thing.

What we expect, then, is *system*. We expect the various parts of a sequence of language to hang together and to have a relationship, one to the other. If we ask someone, "Who broke the window?" and they answer us by saying "Four people will fit in the back of a Volkswagen," our sense of the logic of communication is outraged. We expect one thing to follow from another, in language as in any other area of our daily life.

If we see that people die, and the mystic tells us that they are immortal, or if we see misery all about us and we read that evil does not exist, it is just like the Volkswagen answer to the question about the window. In all communication there is a content that is not overtly present in its surface shape. Remember the concept of *presupposition* in unit 1? The knowledge that we have when we hear a sentence like "Even Bill could solve this prob-

lem"—that Bill is not very smart and the problem is an easy one—
is something we can count on every English-speaking person sharing, even though it is not overtly present in that sentence. In the
same way, we feel that we should be able to count on certain
shared common knowledge about the real world, facts such as
"people die," "not everyone has enough to eat," and "sugar melts
in water." These elements of common knowledge are also a kind
of presupposition, in that all of us living in the same world share
them and take them for granted in framing our speech and writing.
In much religious language, however, these real-world presuppositions do not seem to be included.

We can summarize by saying that we recognize religious language by the following characteristics:

1. It deals with a set of topics understood to be specifically
religious.
2. It contains archaic and/or ritual linguistic elements.
3. It frequently contains apparent logical paradox.

This unit is not the place to try to solve the problems of religious language. In the first place, that is a job for people who
are experts on the subject and have a great deal of time to spend
working on it. In the second place, it is far from certain that the
problem is solvable.

We can, however, try to shed a little more light on the situation by turning to the last of the three questions we have been
posing about language: what is it for?

Sermons and ethical discussions are intended to teach, to inform, and to persuade. The language that we find in such materials
is suitable for their purpose. But what about the third kind of religious language, mystical language? It may well be that the source
of much of the problem we have with such language lies in a *mis-
understanding* of "what it is for." Look at the following passage:

On numerous occasions when I have found myself occupying approximately the same physical space that you were occupying at
that time, I have noticed a significant degree of alteration in such
physiological measures as the rate of my pulse and respiration,
the temperature of my body, and the adrenalin content of my
blood. This leads me to believe that, all things considered, my
further association with you in geographic terms would be highly
desirable and its achievement of maximum importance to my continued well-being.

Cartoon courtesy Better Homes and Gardens. © *Meredith Corporation, 1973. All rights reserved.*

"Heal the sick. Solace the lonely. Comfort the bereaved. Placate the ripped-off. Console the mugged. Unwind the uptight . . ."

The reason that this sequence, as compared with "When I'm near you I go wild—don't leave me," seems so ridiculous is that it is not appropriate to use the language of the sciences for communication about love for another person. Similarly, it may be that the various language modes that we are familiar with—the language of politics, philosophy, education, science, business, and law are not suitable for communication about the mystic experience. It may well be that no language mode now available to us *is* suitable for that purpose, and that until such a mode is discovered or developed, language will continue to seem inadequate. The purpose behind this kind of religious language seems to be an attempt by the writer to communicate something vitally important about a personal experience. We can appreciate that purpose, and evaluate the language in the light of our knowledge of that purpose, even if the communication fails.

One of the more powerful taboo mechanisms is simply not providing a vocabulary for the experience to be tabooed. In this case, you are forced into surrogate vocabularies that can be categorized as mystical or nutty, and easily dismissed, leaving you shamed and doubtful that you really had the experience after all. How many contemporary films, plays or novels can you bring to mind that deal with unadulterated ecstasy? Positive, unconditional joy may, as a matter of fact, turn out to be the real pornography of these transition years—strange, embarrassing, titillating.—George B. Leonard.

One of the most curious things about religious language is the usual American reaction to it, which resembles a seven-year-old boy's reaction to the language of romantic love. Faced with religious language out of its "proper place"—that is, outside the walls of a religious building—the American is embarrassed and changes the subject with all possible speed. It is because of this cultural trait that the problem given at the beginning of this unit avoided the real question. That is, it did not ask you to actually produce religious language, in the form of a sermon or a prayer or a meditation, but let you off with a kind of talking *about* religious language. Nonetheless, the work you have done in this chapter may have made it possible for you to improve on your original work.

EXERCISES

1. It is sometimes possible for a really skillful person to produce a kind of religious language that does not seem to suffer from any of the usual handicaps. For example, Stephen, the author of *Monday Night Class* and *The Caravan,* says that karma "can sometimes be partially expressed as taking a full swing at a golf ball in a tile bathroom. You know it's going to get you."

Choose three key words from any religious doctrine with which you are familiar and try to redefine them so that the resulting definition is as vivid as this one.

2.   Alan Watts has something to say about the current difficulty of Western society in dealing with religion and religious expression:

> Western cultures have bred a type of human being who feels strongly alienated from everything which is not his own consciousness. He is a stranger both to the external world and to his own body, and in this sense he has lost his connection with the surrounding universe. He does not know that the "ultimate inside" of himself is the same as the "ultimate inside" of the cosmos, or that, in other words, his sensation of being "I" is a glimmering intimation of what the universe itself feels like on the inside. He has been taught to regard everything outside human skins as so much witless mechanism which has nothing whatsover in common with human feelings and values. This style of man must therefore see himself as the ghastly and tragic accident of sensitive and intelligent tissue caught up in the cosmic toils like a mouse in a cotton gin.

Is Watts's analysis correct? Does it make sense? Explain your position in a brief essay of about 600 words.

3.   The parable, a brief story told for purposes of moral instruction, was not discussed in this unit because its *language* is not distinct from other languages. For example, many folktales would make excellent parables. However, there is a special kind of parable which requires you to think very hard; here is a Sufi example.

> Nasrudin lost a beautiful and costly turban.
>
> "Are you not despondent, Mulla?" someone asked him.
>
> "No, I am confident. You see, I have offered a reward of half a silver piece.
>
> "But the finder will surely never part with the turban, worth a hundred times as much, for such a reward!"
>
> "I have already thought of that. I have announced that it was a dirty old turban, quite different from the *real* one."

Read this parable carefully and write a brief answer to the question: "what is the parable intended to teach?"

4. In the New Testament, Jesus says that we are to sell everything we have and give it to the poor, and that we are to live like the lilies of the field, not worrying about what we will eat or drink tomorrow or where we will live. Write an essay about the effects on American society if this instruction were taken seriously by all American Christians.

5. Alistair MacIntyre has said that "mystical writers tend to say what cannot be said at somewhat inordinate length." Do you agree with this statement? What would cause mystical writers to explain things at inordinate length? Write a brief statement explaining your position.

6. The following quotation is from *The Caravan:*

The moral code is simple and obvious and everybody really knows what it is and the children know what it is. Kids can go along and they can argue about how many balls you're supposed to use in three-cornered catch or anything like that, but there's always a place where all the kids will agree and will say, "Hey, that ain't fair," and they'll all agree on that. And everybody knows what's fair, everybody knows what's just, it's really simple. It's been put down in words for thousands of years. . . . I was reading a local quote hip unquote newspaper which was talking about how it was cool to rip off, how so long as it's only General Motors you can go ahead and steal from them because it doesn't matter. It may not matter to General Motors—General Motors may be able to write it off in taxes, and it may not matter to them a bit—but it matters terrible to your soul to do the action, never mind who you do it to.

Is this religious language? Is it a sermon? How can you tell? What is the moral principle being presented? Rewrite this passage in a more traditional religious style that will meet the standards of the average composition class. Compare the two versions; is one more effective than the other? Why? Write a 300-word statement defending your position.

7. In a *Psychology Today* interview, Robert Nisbet suggests that the American presidency may be acquiring a pomp and majesty more royal than democratic because "the sacred has in large measure been jettisoned by American churches." Do you agree? Write a brief paper of no more than 600 words explaining your position.

8. Here is another example from *The Caravan.*

Now out here in the limitless universe is God, who peeks in through a peephole, and that peephole is "I." That's the peephole that God peeks into the universe through, is capital "I," first pronoun—also e-y-e, an eyeball eye. Well, this is a metaphor, eyeball eye at this point, because that means this is the ego, which has got to be included because that's another word for "I." Same stuff.

Rewrite the example as either (a) a conventional religious prose paragraph, (b) a poem, or (c) a comic strip.

9. Octavio Paz makes the following statement:

Christianity suppressed the orgiastic character of religion, and the decadence of Christianity is provoking the resurrection of bacchanals and orgies, in the ancient religious sense of those two words. In all these youthful movements one can see a thirst for religion, a nostalgia for ritual. These movements aren't truly religious, but prereligious. And they are not religious because they lack the essential ingredient of ritual, the repetition of the sacred days. Also they lack revelation, a doctrine, prophets and martyrs. The youth movement betrays our deficiencies, it shows that there is a vacuum at the heart of contemporary society, which neither philosophy, nor politics, nor science, nor art have succeeded in filling. But the youth movement is not the answer we are hoping for, it is an explosion of despair.

Do you agree with Paz's statement that the current religious movements of youth are only "prereligious" and are an "explosion of despair"? Are his reasons valid? State your position as clearly as you can.

10. Interview a local minister, priest, rabbi, or other religious official on the subject of the paragraph in exercise 10. Write a brief interview about his or her opinions.

11. Herman Kahn says that "the earth didn't come with an instruction book." We can't argue with that—but if it had, what would the instructions have been? Write the table of contents for such an instruction book.

12. The Navajo artist Carl Gorman has written:

It has been said by some researchers into Navajo religion, that we have no Supreme God, because He is not named. This is not so. The Supreme Being is not named because He is unknowable. He is simply the Unknown Power. We worship him through His creation.

We feel too insignificant to approach directly in prayer that Great Power that is incomprehensible to man. Nature feeds our soul's inspiration and so we approach Him through that part of Him which is close to us and within the reach of human understanding. We believe that this great unknown power is everything in His creation. The various forms of creation have some of this spirit within them. . . . As every form has some of the intelligent spirit of the Creator, we cannot but reverence all parts of the creation.

What is your reaction to this statement? Write a brief essay of perhaps 500 words stating your feelings on this subject.

13. An exception to the statement about the language of sermons lacking special characteristics is found in the spontaneous rural sermons of some American preachers, particularly in the South. Here is an excerpt from a sermon by the Reverend D. J. McDowell; analyze it and see if you can list specific devices of language that set it off both from the standard "city" sermon and from other speeches. Does it seem to be poetry or prose? Why? (In his article, "The Formulaic Quality of Spontaneous Sermons," Bruce A. Rosenberg quotes this sermon and says that it is metric language, chanted rhythmically by the preacher, with audience participation expected and encouraged.)

> Keep your hand in God's hand
> And your eyes on the starposts in glory
> Lord said he would fight your battles
> If you'd only be still
>
> You may not be a florist
> Am I right about it?
> But you must tell them, that He's the Rose of Sharon
> I know that's right
> You may not be a geologist
> But you must tell them, that He's the Rock of Ages
> I know that's right
> You may not be a physician
> But you must tell them, that He's the great Physician
> You may not be a baker,
> But you must tell them, that He's the Bread of Life
> Am I right about it?
> You must tell them
> That He's a friend
> That stick close t'his brother

He said, "I'll not cast ya out
In the sixth hour, and in the seventh hour
I didn't know I was turnin' ya out"
If y'keep your hand in God's hand.

From Notes on The Transformation

GEORGE B. LEONARD

I sit on a bare knoll westward of Mt. Tamalpais' west peak watching the stars fade. Now and then I glance at the faint emanation of pale gold along the eastern horizon. The ground is hard and dry, for the rains are overdue. Though it is cool now, the clarity of the sky promises another hot day. Just to the west of me there is a clump of California oaks, and a forest of firs 75 yards downhill to the south. If I am still enough, I can sense the soft respiration of the trees. I toy with the idea of sharing a tree's existence—foliage spread out to receive the sun, trunk thrusting downward in sexual union with the earth, roots feeling their way toward moisture. I focus my attention on one of the gnarled oaks to the west, a silhouette against the grasses beyond. I try to enter its double life of light and darkness, air and earth.

For a brief moment I experience the tree's being, then I am thrust back firmly to my separate existence, capable of seeing the tree at a distance, touching it, cutting it down, analyzing it. I have been given names for each of its constituent parts, terms for its processes and ways for relating it with the other elements of the biosphere. But I have been made incapable of entering its being and sharing its life. The dryads have long since been banished from the forests, and metaphor itself is suspect; the pathetic fallacy is, after all, a fallacy. I am left with logic and separateness, and can bring to mind no myth-heroes of the woods except Paul Bunyan and Smokey the Bear.

But something is wrong with this mode of perceiving and being, even in strictly scientific terms. The physicists have taught me that the tree, so substantial and impenetrable, actually is mostly "empty space," if we conceive the subatomic elements of which it is made as particles. It is certainly quite transparent to radiation of wavelengths longer than one meter (including all radio waves) and shorter than one angstrom (including X rays and gamma rays). Only a conspiracy of my genes makes the tree opaque to me. In the experience of the living beings from which I am descended, electromagnetic radiation within the narrow band we call visible has proved to be useful for guidance and survival in a particular terrestrial mode of existence. Through long evolution we have developed eyes sensitive only to the radiation vibrating between 10^{14} and 10^{15} times a second. Therefore the tree appears impenetrable to my sight just as it would be impenetrable to my physical body, a handy correspondence. Its opacity, however, is operational, not ultimate. Physics and mathematics have provided us a respectable way of acknowledging what primitive peoples have always known: the tree is not really solid. There is room in it for spirits.

But this too—the idea of the tree as composed of empty space between tiny particles—is obviously an oversimplification. Bertrand Russell once defined matter as whatever satisfies the equations of physics. Ever since the early 1920's, it has become increasingly clear that the elementary particles can be treated mathematically and experimentally as energy waves. Even earlier, light waves and other forms of radiation were shown quite clearly to consist of particles. All discussion on whether photons and the basic stuff of matter are "waves" or "particles," however, simply demonstrates the limitation of human language and the bankruptcy of the conceptual framework upon which language is based. Both "object" and "space" are constructs. The constituent stuff of what we call matter exists entirely apart from "visible" and "invisible," far beyond conventional concepts of "real."

The dark dome of sky above me on this mountain morning is transparent. Beyond the darkness, layer upon layer of luminosity. Of what is the world made? Surely we need no concrete building blocks, however infinitesimal, to explain substance. We know that matter is pent-up energy. Surely we need no concept of tiny bodies to bind this immense energy. What may seem to be small moving bodies constituting matter— the "particles" of physics—can be conceived, in Einstein's words, as "pulselike concentrations of fields, which would stick together stably." Indeed, we may go on to imagine the elementary particles as resonant centers of vibrancy, which can combine with others to create new centers of vibrancy, which may combine again in varying pitch and pattern. The interplay of all this vibrancy manifests itself in the spangled diversity of common experience.

Of what is the world made? Underlying everything, forming itself into what we now call electrons, protons, neutrons and all the rest, obliterating basic distinctions between matter and energy, substance and spirit, joining all manifestations in common origin and cause, there is the elemental vibrancy. Let us say that substance is vibrancy tending toward transformation. All existence—whether mountain, sky, star, shaft of sunlight, thought, song or self—is vibrancy. And the oak tree (if only I had eyes to see) is a particular arrangement of vibrant energy. The oak tree (if only I had ears to hear) is a consummation of its constituent vibrations, thus a perfectly harmonious strain of music. The oak tree (if only I had ways to learn) is available for me to enter and experience fully.

But I have been taught that it is a "thing," solid and separate from me. The perceptual mode bequeathed me by my particular culture denies me identity with the tree and insists that it and I remain forever walled off from one another. In the same way, I and all of us who live and breathe and take our psychic sustenance from this culture are convinced that we are solid and separate, forever walled off from our wives and lovers, brothers, fathers, friends and children, sisters and mothers; forever alone and alienated; locked for life in the prisons of our skins.

THE LANGUAGE AND STRUCTURE OF POETRY

8

Here is an example of a poem that could be looked upon as relatively "modern." Study the poem carefully and decide what it means to you. Then write another poem of your own, in any form you choose, that says the same thing the example poem says.

CLUSTER CODE

some things tangle

    (I have seen the roses begin
    to rain gold is a natural thing
    at this level where)
some things tangle

there is no way to avoid
    (what we have flung across feels
    the winds use us for rigging
    at this level where)
there is no way to avoid

if I knew how to give
    (more of me is twined beneath
    the earth of how we double sharing
    at this level where)
if I knew how to give
I would, more
and more

you are not to think, ever,
that nets are made of
knots

DEFINING THE POEM

How do we identify poetry? This is one of the hardest questions to answer that we have yet examined, and mysteriously so. Mysteriously, because every one of us knows a poem when we see it or hear it, but no one has yet come up with a *definition* of a poem that really works.

The Second College Edition of *Webster's New World Dictionary* defines the poem as follows:

> 1. an arrangement of words written or spoken, traditionally a rhythmical composition, sometimes rhymed, expressing experiences, ideas, or emotions in a style more concentrated, imaginative, and powerful than that of ordinary speech or prose; some poems are in meter, some in free verse;
>
> 2. anything suggesting a poem in its effect.

Even if we restrict ourselves to the first part and ignore the impossibly vague second one, there is no way to apply this definition accurately. The item *poem* can't be eliminated from a large class of other items all meeting the same definition. For example, consider the following advertisement:

> Beneath the steam, under the butter
> below the milk,
> someplace inside that great-tasting oatmeal
> there's more protein than any other whole grain cereal
> QUAKER
> Oatmeal
> The more they eat the better you feel.

Is this a poem? No? Why not? Let's examine the definition and compare it carefully with the ad.

> a. An arrangement of words written or spoken—The Quaker Oats ad fits.
> b. Traditionally a rhythmical composition, sometimes rhymed (some poems are in meter, some in free verse)—This is rhythmical language, although not in meter or rhyme.
> c. Expressing experiences, ideas, or emotions in a style more concentrated (check!), imaginative (check!), and powerful

BENEATH THE STEAM, UNDER THE BUTTER, BELOW THE MILK,

someplace inside that great-tasting oatmeal there's more protein than any other whole grain cereal.

Quaker Oatmeal

The more they eat the better you feel.

1972 THE QUAKER OATS COMPANY

© *1972 The Quaker Oats Company.*

(check!) than that of ordinary speech or prose—The ad meets this description.

To make it even more clear, let's try a minor experiment. First, let's rewrite the Quaker ad so it *looks* like a poem, as follows:

QUAKER AD

beneath the steam
under the butter
below the milk

someplace inside that great-tasting
oatmeal
there's more protein
than any other
whole grain cereal

Quaker Oatmeal
the more they eat the better you
feel

And secondly, let's rewrite the information contained in the ad in what the dictionary calls "ordinary speech or prose."

There is more protein in Quaker Oats than in any other whole grain cereal, although it may be necessary to look for it under the milk, steam, and butter. You will therefore feel better about your family's well-being in direct proportion to the amount of Quaker Oats that they eat.

Certainly there is no question that the ad, compared with the example of ordinary prose, is more "concentrated, imaginative, and powerful." But is the ad a poem?

No. In the sense we ordinarily think of poems, it's not, but the only way we know *that* is because we recognize it as an ad, right? That is, because this particular sequence of language has an identifiable membership in another category of language tokens, we can eliminate it from the category we call *poem*. And only because of that. And even then we will probably have to admit our confusion by saying that it is a very "poetic" ad—which throws us squarely into the middle of Webster's second definition: "anything suggesting a poem in its effect." (Its effect on what? or on whom?)

TEACHER.   Ferrabeau, can you tell me the difference between twentieth-century poetry and eighteenth-century poetry?

FERRABEAU.   Sure. In the eighteenth century, poets knew where to put their punctuation marks.

This is a real problem. We can look at a living creature and say, "Aha—it's got two legs, it has feathers, it lays eggs, it's cold-blooded, it's got a beak, and on top of that it builds a nest, it flies, and it sings its head off—that, for sure, is a *bird!*" There is no way we can do this kind of checklisting for the creature we call a "poem."

It might be interesting to take a look at what some poets, presumably experts on poems, have said when *they* were trying to define the poem. Here is a sampling.

WILLIAM DICKEY
A poem is a house in the mind.

JOHN CIARDI
Poetry is a way of meaning more than one thing at a time.

JOHN HALL WHEELOCK
So simple a thing as a word, by general consent symbolizes, or stands for, an indefinitely manifold, infinitely complex, item

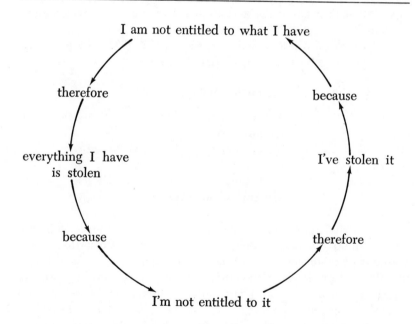

R. D. LAING
Knots

of experience. A poem is a constellation of such symbols, representing a poet's re-discovery of some phase of reality.

ROBERT FROST

A poem is a momentary stay against confusion. Each poem clarifies something. . . . A poem is an arrest of disorder.

And then there was Emily Dickinson, who stated that she could recognize a thing as a poem if she felt physically as if the top of her head had been taken off.

These definitions perhaps bring us closer to what we all think we mean by the word "poem" than *Webster's* did, but they are still subject to difficulties. The Stan Kenton song title, "Celery Stalks at Midnight," meets Ciardi's definition, but it isn't a poem. The definitions provided by Dickey and Dickinson are impossible to judge—that is, nobody can tell anything about the kind of internal reaction specified in those two definitions. Robert Frost's definition is equally subjective; there is no way an independent observer can, for example, take a look at *Hiawatha* and say "Aha! It's a momentary stay against confusion and an arrest of disorder. It's definitely a poem!"

And all of these definitions, except Ciardi's, will probably only apply to *good* poems. Consider the following:

CURIOUS GREEN LINES

A frog
sat on a log
beside a dog
in a bog
in the fog . . .
Ah, Spring! Ah, April!

Nobody is going to call that a house—even a disorderly house —in the mind. Nobody is going to call it an arrest of disorder. Upon seeing it you will *not* feel that the top of your head has been taken off. But unfortunately, although the only appropriate response to the thing is nausea, it *is* a poem, and any literate native speaker of English recognizes it as one. It is just a very bad poem indeed.

This brings us to that last and most difficult question in the task of evaluating language. Is it beautiful? That decision is a matter for esthetics. What is beautiful to one reader is utter garbage to another, one generation's masterpiece is another generation's hackwork, and who is ultimately to judge? There is no objective standard against which the reader or listener can measure a sequence of language to find out how "beautiful" it may be. It is for this reason that the distinction often made between poetry and verse is not really much help. To say that one sequence is a poem and the other a verse is no more than to say that the first is a better poem than the second.

Basically, we recognize poems by certain conventions established by our culture, and by which we have all agreed to abide. Let's say that a sequence of language has the following set of characteristics:

1. It is set in the middle of a page and surrounded by white space.

2. It has a title printed immediately above it.

3. The lines of words do not stretch regularly from the left margin to the right margin, but are chopped off in either patterned or irregular lengths.

4. The content does not appear inconsistent with our idea of poetic content—that is, it cannot be immediately recognized as an announcement of an auction or something of that kind.

Given these four characteristics, we can say that "Curious Green Lines" is almost certainly a poem. Because this sequence meets these conditions, we must accept it as a (horrible) poem, and it is because the rewritten Quaker Oats ad has been deliberately set up to meet them that it looks like a poem to us.

This definition in terms of four physical characteristics does all sorts of violence to our usual conception of poetry. Nonetheless, it is as accurate a method of identifying a poem as any proposed to date, so far as this writer has been able to determine.

The problem lies in the tendency to confuse literary language with "literature." We are in some way demanding of all poems that they be *good* poems, although we have no accurate way of determining what a good poem is. It is essential to remember that simply because a sequence of language is *bad* poetry does not make it less a poem; it does not turn into a novel or a political speech or a business contract. It just stays a bad poem.

Poetry has always been a risky business, and in America writing poetry has never been a reliable way to make a living. The woman or man with a talent for rhythmic language, skillful use of words, and striking linguistic images generally can be expected to turn to the advertising business, where such skills are well rewarded, rather than to poetry. Poetry, like ballet and opera, has remained the pleasure of a few, and it is possible to exclude poetry from your life in a way that it is not possible to exclude prose. In America, then, we cannot argue that the understanding of poetry—much less its composition—is a survival skill, in the way that understanding the political speech and the newspaper are.

The chances are, though, that even if you feel that you dislike poetry, you like it when it is combined with music. For instance, consider the following:

CIRCLES IN THE SAND

For the masters there are the ashes and flames
Glorious games, pleasures that bring pain.
Seasons alter, my life stays just the same
Naked I came, naked I shall remain.
Open your hearts, hear what I have to say
Masters change with seasons
Seasons never change.*

CHARLES WATTS and PAUL STEIN

Certainly this is poetry. These lyrics and others like them have brought to the young people of the 60's and 70's an appreciation for poetic language that was not common in young people a generation earlier. The song lyrics of the previous generation, for example, included such lyrical masterpieces as "Cement Mixer, Putty, Putty," and "Mairsie Doats and Doasie Doats." We thrilled to lines like "R-A-G-G-M-O-P-P, Rag Mop!" instead of the lyrics of Dylan, Donovan, Cat Stevens, and Joni Mitchell. The difference is striking, and perhaps will lead to greater popularity for poetry-without-music in years to come.

CHARACTERISTICS OF POETRY

The structure of poetry is a vast subject bristling with technical terms like apocope and anapest and synecdoche, and this brief discussion is not the place to go into these devices.† Instead of attempting to select a few of the many characteristics of poetic structure, we will concentrate on the larger question of how poetry differs from the majority of prose works—excluding such obvious ex-

* © 1969 by Sufi Pipkin Music, P.O. Box 2389, Hollywood, California, 90028.
† See Babette Deutsch's *Poetry Handbook* if you are interested in detailed information on this subject.

ceptions as James Joyce's *Finnegan's Wake*. We will begin by looking at two brief poems about a simple subject, birds.

WHERE WE MUST LOOK FOR HELP

The dove returns; it found no restingplace;
It was in flight all night above the shaken seas;
Beneath ark eaves
The dove shall magnify the tiger's bed;
Give the dove peace.

The split-tail swallows leave the sill at dawn;
At dusk, blue swallows shall return.
On the third day the crow shall fly;
The crow, the crow, the spider-coloured crow,
The crow shall find new mud to walk upon.

ROBERT BLY

CORN

I am the corn quail.
What I do is quick.
You will know only
The Muffled clucking,
The scurry, the first
Shiver of feathers
And I will be up,
I will be in your
Head with no way out,
Wings beating at the
Air behind your eyes.

JAMES MC MICHAEL

If we look at these two examples carefully, we can identify them at once as poems simply by observing their physical appearance on the page. They are surrounded by white space, they are titled, and their lines do not run from margin to margin of a page or column as prose does. In addition, the first example has both rhyme and an obvious rhythmic pattern; the second, although it lacks rhyme, has a regularity of rhythm that is appropriate to poetry rather than to prose.

Even in the second poem, which has no rhyme, we find words paired by their sounds; for example, "quail" and "quick," "shiver" and "feather." In the first, in addition to the true rhymes like "dawn" and "upon," we find near rhymes—"seas" and "eaves," "place" and "peace." We find rhymes tucked within the lines rather than at the end, like "flight" and "night," "fly" and "magnify."

What we see in these two examples, then, is a characteristic that we have learned to look for in language sequences, systematic

---

IF THE OWL CALLS AGAIN

At dusk
from the island in the river,
and it's not too cold,

I'll wait for the moon
to rise,
then take wing and glide
to meet him.

We will not speak,
but hooded against the frost
soar above
the alder flats, searching
with tawny eyes.

And then we'll sit
in the shadowy spruce and
pick the bones
of careless mice,

while the long moon drifts
toward Asia
and the river mutters
in its icy bed.

And when morning climbs
the limbs
we'll part without a sound,
fulfilled, floating
homeward as
the cold world awakens.

JOHN HAINES

---

structure. Structure occurs in prose as well, and even in ordinary conversation, but it is not given the attention that it receives in poetry, where we know that the patterns are intended to matter. If you are sitting at the table and the person next to you says "Please pass the peas," you do not think to yourself, "Now there's a line containing four one-syllable words, three of which begin with the letter *p* and two of which rhyme." You just pass the vegetable requested. If that same person then went on to say "I'm achin' for the bacon" you would begin to have a nagging feeling that something odd was going on, and if he followed that up with "Buttered bread is what I dread" there'd be no doubt in your mind that you were being put on. That kind of patterning is totally inappropriate for dinner table conversation. When it happens accidentally, as in "please pass the peas," we don't notice. It takes grotesque exaggeration or a deliberate persistence to bring systematic sound patterns in conversation to the hearer's attention.

This is not true in poetry. By convention, the moment we have identified a sequence as poetry we know that we are expected to give close attention to all patterning within the sequence. This is very different from our processing of prose and of ordinary conversation.

You will remember from the unit on political language that one of the major purposes of patterning in language is to make the hearer or reader able to *remember* the sequence. In poetry, particularly rhymed and metered traditional poetry, this is especially true, so much so that we put pieces of information we have to memorize into poetic sequence, as in "Thirty days hath September, April, June, and November." In a society where the literature is not written down, and where there is no opportunity for the hearer to look at the poetry on a page and review it at his or her leisure, the device of repetition becomes necessary to emphasize the structure and to make remembering a simpler task.

What happens if we try to tamper with the patterning we find in a poem? It's easy to find out by rewriting our two example poems, keeping the obvious content as nearly the same as possible but eliminating the patterned structure.

1. The dove flew all night above the shaken seas and under the eaves of the ark, but it found no place where it could stop and rest. The dove shall magnify the tiger's bed. Give the dove peace. At dawn the split-tail swallows will leave the sill, and

the blue swallows will return at dusk. The crow, which is spider-coloured, will find new mud to walk on.

2. I am the corn quail. What I do is quick. The only thing you'll notice will be the muffled clucking and the scurry of my feathers in their first shivering. Then I will be up inside your head with no way to get out. My wings will beat at the air behind your eyes.

These passages are no longer poems, but prose. If you were reading them as prose, you would probably find it odd because of the sentences like "give the dove peace" and the corn quail's statement that he will fly into your head and be unable to get out. Nonetheless, you would recognize the sequences as prose.

What if we keep the poetic structure but substitute words having the same approximate meaning? This won't hurt a prose sentence—look at the following set, any one of which will do as well as another:

a. Pick up that basket and put it beside the chair.
b. Lift that basket off the ground and set it down by the chair.
c. See that chair over there? Would you set that basket down beside it, please.
d. Pick that basket up and put it down by the chair.

We cannot take this kind of liberties with a "sentence" of poetry.

a. It was in flight all night above the shaken seas.
b. It flew all night long over the shaken ocean.
c. It was in flight through the entire night over the disturbed ocean.
d. It flew from sundown to sunset above the shaken seas.

You can see that none of the alternative versions of the *a* line from Bly's poem will fit into the rest of the poem. This is because the patterning of a poetic line is as much a part of it as the content, and we cannot tamper with it without destroying it. The rhyme of "flight" and "night" and the hissing sound pattern of "shaken seas" are an integral part of the line. If you are a poet, you can take a particular poem and keep the content intact while altering the patterns to suit yourself, and the result may be as fine a poem as the one you worked from, but it will be a *different* poem. This is of course the basic problem in translating poems from one language to another, because the chances of maintaining both content and form are almost nonexistent. The translator is not likely to find a pair of rhyming monosyllables like "flight" and "night" in the other language; he will probably find that if he uses a pair of such words to maintain the structure he must alter the content slightly, while if he maintains the content unchanged he will have to use a different structure.

A third characteristic of poetry that makes it differ from other language is our tolerance as readers for sequences of language that we would not accept ordinarily, sequences that violate the grammar rules of our language. For example, we will accept lines like the following:

Sad in the corner sits the child.

This is a mild example which might appear in prose, but in conversation it would be unacceptable. Nobody talks like this; we say "Look at that poor kid sitting there in the corner. He looks miserable." How about the following line from e. e. cummings?

My father moved through theys of we.

There is no way this line could appear in conversation, nor could it occur in anything but the most experimental prose. Magazine articles, political speeches, sermons, cookbooks, biology texts, none of the other prose with which we commonly associate the word "prose," would contain any remarks about someone moving through theys of we. We understand it, and we know that it is structurally parallel to a line like "my father moved through drifts of snow," but it is too deviant for anything but poetry.

We have found, then, three basic characteristics of poetry that set it off from ordinary language and prose:

a. A significant amount of systematic structure in the form of patterns of sound and shape

b. A structure that cannot be tampered with because change destroys it

c. A deviance from the grammar rules of ordinary language

We are willing to accept these differences in return for the pleasure we receive from poetry. In fact, it is these differences that enable us to see things in a new way and feel them more intensely, because they joggle our minds and get past the barriers imposed by familiarity.

If you walk along a street every day and always pass a large oak tree, the time will come when you hardly see that tree at all. It is too familiar to you. But if one morning someone has painted that oak tree gold, you'll notice it. The poet goes around mentioning familiar things in an unfamiliar way, so that you will see them clearly again.

MOTIVE OF POETRY

The motive behind poetry is a little easier to state than the definition of poetry. Although there are poems that are intended to teach and to inform, they are unusual; basically a poem has only one purpose. The poet has had an experience, or has heard of or imagined an experience, and is trying to use words in such a way that those words will cause the reader to feel the same emotions that the experience evoked in the poet. The poet is an emotion-maker; whether his poem causes the reader to feel ecstasy or grief, tranquillity or nausea, a poem is intended to re-create an experience so vividly that the emotions accompanying that experience are re-created as well.

In the same way that we experience emotions as a result of the direct sensory input from the world around us, we experience emotions from the indirect sensory input the poet provides us with. A good poem is probably the most powerful language statement, in terms of its effect upon a reader or listener, that can be made.

We have spent very little time in this unit talking about the technical devices of poetry because our concern has been with general principles. Nonetheless, you may find that you can now improve the poem you wrote at the beginning of this unit. Try it and see.

EXERCISES

1.   Analyze one of the poems used as examples in this unit for patterns of sound and shape. Look for rhyme patterns, for groups of words that begin or end with the same sound, and for patterns of rhythm. Look also for patterns of syntax. For example, if a poet used a "for to" construction like "for Mary to leave" again

and again in a single poem, that would be an example of syntactic patterning. List as many examples of this patterned structure as you can.

2. Writing of Leningrad, Suzanne Massie makes the following statement:

> Someone once explained seriously to me that it was impossible to get the book of such and such a poet because the printing was only a 'tiny' 10,000 copies. In the U.S. a print order of 2,000 copies of a volume of verse is considered to be a rather daring risk.

Write a paper of no more than 1000 words, explaining why the U.S. has the indifferent attitude to poetry that makes 2000 copies of a book of poems a publishing risk.

3. In Ireland the value of poetry was once regarded highly enough that poets were given special tax advantages, like oil companies in America. Do you think such a practice would be justified? Write a brief essay explaining your position.

4. William Heyen has said that writing poetry is exhausting *physical* work. Is this true? Write either 500 words of prose or a poem of any length stating your opinion on this question.

5. The budget committee at your school has just appropriated $10,000 for the basketball team and turned down the creative writing department's request for $1000 for poetry readings. Write a letter to the editor of your school paper, 300 words in length, either protesting or approving this decision.

6. The following poem was written by Marie Borroff, using a computer.

> The river
> Winks
> And I am ravished.
>
> Dangerously, intensely, the music
> Sins and brightens
> And I am woven.

What is your opinion of this poem? Should we say that Ms. Borroff wrote it or that the computer wrote it? If a computer can write poetry, does that mean it is trying to evoke in the reader an emotion that the computer has felt? For that matter, *is* computer poetry really poetry? Write a paper of about 1000 words explaining your position on this matter.

7.   Do a research paper on computer poetry, not more than fifteen double-spaced pages in length. You should answer questions like the following:

a.   When did computer poetry start?

b.   Are there any famous computer poets?

c.   In producing a computer poem, what is the role of the computer and what is the role of the human being? Can a properly programmed computer produce poetry all by itself?

d.   What is the position of some critics and poets with regard to computer poetry?

8.   There are a few American colleges which have poetry teams, just as they have basketball teams, debating teams, and swimming teams. It is conceivable that if poetry became more fashionable in this country we might see the rise of a Poetry World Series, a Poetry Olympics, professional Poetry Leagues, and similar phenomena. Assume that you are a member of the National Poetry Board and write a set of rules for the conduct of a National Poetry Tournament. Be sure that you define clearly such concepts as the poetry "foul."

9.   In an article called "Getting Out of Schools," Norman Martien makes the following statements:

> There is no such thing as an Institution of Learning. Learning is a living process, our institutions are lifeless abstractions.
>
> The places we call schools are institutions where the power of the past dispossesses us of the present. This includes the power of abstraction, the power of ownership and inheritance, the power of destruction.
>
> This grasp upon men and things goes under several false names: viz., Learning, Tradition, Service.

Write a poem three stanzas long, one stanza for each of the three parts of Martien's claim above, restating what he has here said as prose. Never mind whether it's a "good" poem or not.

10.   There is an interesting hybrid form of poetry, very popular in France, called the "prose poem." A prose poem would read much like the prose rephrasings of the two example poems in this unit; that is, the form looks like prose but the content looks like poetry. Find an example of a prose poem, either an English translation or an original, and read it carefully. Then write an analysis

THE COMPUTER'S FIRST CHRISTMAS CARD

JOLLYMERRY
HOLLYBERRY
JOLLYBERRY
MERRYHOLLY
HAPPYJOLLY
JOLLYJELLY
JELLYBELLY
BELLYMERRY
HOLLYHEPPY
JOLLYHOLLY
MARRYJERRY
MERRYHARRY
HOPPYBARRY
HEPPYJARRY
ROPPYHEPPY
BERRYJORRY
JORRYJOLLY
MOPPYJELLY
MOLLYMERRY
JERRYJOLLY
BELLYBOPPY
JORRYHOPPY
HOLLYMOPPY
BARRYMERRY
JARRYHAPPY
HAPPYBOPPY
BOPPYJOLLY
JOLLYMERRY
MERRYMERRY
MERRYMERRY
MERRYCHRIS
AMMERRYASA
CHRISMERRY
ASMERRYCHR
YSANTHEMUM

EDWIN MORGAN

of no more than 1000 words stating why the sequence is a prose poem and not simply prose. (Or, alternatively, you may argue that you don't feel that it is a poem at all.) Be careful not to fall into the trap of saying that the sequence is simply "poetic" prose; this is just a way of escaping the difficult task of making a clear statement.

11. Complete the following dialogues:

FATHER. So you've finally decided what career you're going to follow, son! That's great, just great! What did you decide?
SON. I've decided to be a poet, Dad. A professional poet.
FATHER.

MOTHER. Now that you've finished college, I suppose you'll be going to work. Have you decided what you're going to do?
DAUGHTER. Sure. I thought I'd make my living writing poetry. How does that sound to you?
MOTHER.

HUSBAND. Mary, I've made up my mind about something, and I think we ought to talk about it.
WIFE. All right, love, what is it?
HUSBAND. I've decided to quit my job and write poetry for a living.
WIFE.

MAN. You say your friend's a writer? That's really interesting. What kind of stuff does he write?
WOMAN. He's a poet.
MAN. A poet? Oh, I thought you meant he was really a writer. You know.
WOMAN.

12. Education now strongly emphasizes practical skills and learning things that are relevant to the student's real-world functions. Assume that you are a professor of modern poetry and that your college's curriculum committee has decided to eliminate your course because it is a frivolous waste of the students' time. The committee has agreed to allow you to come to their next meeting and speak in defense of the course; they will give you fifteen minutes. Write your speech and present it to the class.

13. The definition of poetry in this unit, and the claim that we recognize a poem primarily by its physical characteristics, is not likely to be popular with everyone. It is, of course, a definition by default. Write a brief paper either (a) defending the definition in this unit, (b) proposing a new one of your own, or (c) defending a definition proposed by someone else with which you agree.

14. Why is poetry more agreeable to many people when it is accompanied by music? The words are the same in both cases, but when you take the words away from the music there is a radical change. Can you explain this? Write either a brief poem or a paper of no more than 500 words on this subject.

Poetry

JUDSON JEROME

One of the most ancient dicta about art is that the work inheres in the material, that the artist merely releases an innate form. The sculptor sees the statue imprisoned in the granite. The playwright or novelist listens to his characters: the play or story evolves as he lets them become and act out their destinies. The musician hears and sets down the potentialities of his instruments. The poet is an aeolian harp, passive and sensitive, letting the winds of inspiration play through him. This view is related to the traditional invocation of the muse, a kind of poetic prayer that inspiration come. *Inspiration,* of course, means to breathe in spirit, to draw upon the transcendent source of animation. Whether it is the figure in the stone or the wisdom of the gods which is the subject of art, the artist is the transmitter, the medium, whose greatest talent is responsiveness to the given.

Contrast that line of thought with one in which the artist is the manipulator, controlling his material and shaping it to his demands. Much of the advice to writers—in this column and this magazine generally as well as from other sources—is based on the assumption that the chief virtue of the artist is his mastery of techniques, his ability to whip something into shape, to exert power over rather than to receive and transmit. These views can, of course, be reconciled: having received inspiration the artist must have the skill to bring vision into expression. But there is a cultural bias against the view of the passive artist which we have to be aware of. Materialism and scientism prejudice us against beliefs which accept mystery or are premised upon spiritual reality. In general we tend to value individual initiative, action, and control—a reflection of the *machismo* mentality our articulate women are now protesting. Moreover, as we advise writers, it is natural that we should emphasize what they can do as opposed to what they should be. One can be instructed in techniques, but cannot be told how to become inspired.

It was only recently that I understood very clearly what it means to discover the art work in the material and to release it from its confines—as opposed to *using* the material to *make* a work of art. The lesson I learned was not in writing poetry, but in cutting flowerpots from chestnut oak on the bandsaw. Our commune is supporting itself with a small business, manufacturing Hollologs, or planters cut from logs. We cut a section of log from four to eleven inches long, then (leaving the bark intact) take out the core on a bandsaw. We nail the hollowed log back together, slice off a piece of the core for a bottom, treat it with preservative, and come up with a product somewhere between craft and manufacture—certainly far from art. Each pot is distinct and individual, and we especially enjoy making those which are somewhat crooked, knobby, slanted, or otherwise irregular: they are more of a challenge to make and each has a character and beauty of its own.

I do most of the bandsawing—on a huge old machine about eight feet high, its belt of blade spinning by at merciless speed. Imagine its power cutting longitudinally through eleven inches of solid, newly cut oak, or, even more dramatically, crosscutting the core to slice off a bottom. Sheer weight of the log section makes handling the large ones difficult, let alone much fine manipulation of the cut. My arms ache from the effort, and the muscles of my belly have tightened and flattened from the strain of twisting them round on the table. But I love the work so much I would do it even if we didn't make a living from it. After hours at the typewriter (I am currently writing a novel), I pick up and go happily to the saw. "Back to reality," I say.

Though this is, as I said, far from art, bandsawing helped me rediscover a principle of art the ancients had long proclaimed. As I gained skill at cutting pots I was more and more tempted to be fancy—e.g., to cut heart-shaped or other pretty forms. But they only detracted from the beauty of the pot, because they bore little relation to the shape of the log. It is better to follow the grain, but this is not always possible because, for instance, if the pot is at all slanted, the walls become too thin. Actually the shape of the bottom, which you cannot see when sawing, is much more critical than the shape of the top, which you can see—as the walls must be thin enough to get nails through and thick enough to make a strong pot. In general the pots should be as light as possible, consistent with strength, both for appearance and shipping weight. Nor can one take too long with a given pot, for increases in our costs increase doubly what the consumer pays, and there is a limit to how much any flowerpot is worth.

Suddenly it occurred to me that the better the bandsawyer I became, the more submissive I must be to the inalterable constraints in the process—the quality and shape of wood, the demands of time, the processes of nailing and finishing and shipping. Within each section of log stacked on the shelves is a perfect pot—but the perfection is not some abstract shape or design: it is a modulation of the demands of the wood and the equipment and the other workers and of unknown consumers who will use the pots for planting. As I set each one on the table of the saw I try to visualize that perfect pot—what will remain after the vertical blade has passed through it and removed all its internal excess. To make the pot I need skill and control, true enough, but skill in submission, control in restraint of whim or any impulse to "improve" upon the implicit design.

So *that's* what they are talking about, I said to myself, thinking of the claims of artists and poets in ages past, of what often seemed to me their mock humility in surrendering themselves to a mystic vision. Even in making so simple a product as these pots one needed to develop a computer-like capacity for calculation of dozens of variables, and to exercise it effortlessly, unconsciously, responsively, while turning heavy wood into the menacing whirr of the blade. I surged with joy at this discovery, singing now at my work, swinging up each new section, studying it briefly, marking it with chalk, ripping in and around, shaking out the core, chewing across the core to cut a bottom . . .

TWANG! With a bone-chilling rip the blade broke and chattered noisily in the heavy spinning wheels, sending me reeling (safe, though) back from the table, my heart pounding. It was as though a bolt from the gods had stricken my arrogance. You think you understand, now, do you Buster? the slowing wheels rasped at me. You have much to learn. Neither mind nor muscle will ever finally unravel my secrets. I cowered like Job rebuked.

My particular error that time was simple enough. I had not steadied the core sufficiently as I moved its round side into the biting blade for a crosscut, so that it spun the core round in my hands and whipped it like a twenty-pound marshmallow, snapping the blade. Hereafter I would hold it down with full weight—but the important lesson from the bandsaw was not that specific technique. It was to humble myself. It was never to think that I was fully in command. (If you want one or more of these pots, I'll be glad to fill an order—$5 for a middle-sized one, $12 for a huge one; other prices, including wholesale, on request. Write Downhill Farm, Hancock, MD 21750).

Another analogy for the submissive discipline of art is the chase of Moby Dick. Among all the other things the great white whale symbolizes, I wonder if one of them might be the book itself, a veritable white giant of a book, intact and breathing—and what a job, what a lifetime required, for Melville to have landed it. Even landed, printed, bound, it breathes terror, never mastered by the author himself or any reader or critic, an animate being not so much man-made as man-revealed. Like Melville, Ahab was an artist, cannily knowing that to capture his subject he must submit himself totally to it, reading its mind and darkest habits, but discovering only at the last that there is no mastery but being mastered by it, going down lashed to its dynamic plunging bulk.

I once mused on this theme, of the futility of trying to create great art while one remains on the bank safe, dry and rational:

WAITING AROUND FOR MOBY DICK

To me with my pole arched
above the brackish swill around the dock,
patient, patient as Indian wrestler sitting
all night with a forearm lock,
he will not come, nor nibble
my minnow bait. Should I then cast loose
over vacant, heaving seas and bore the mist
of the North, or the South's slow sun?
Should I run mad, as the mad have always run?
Ah, ease of the muscles, flexing of the fist!
Dreaming a wild war, I am trapped in truce,
   eroding in time's long dribble.

I read a book that promises defeat
even of Argosies supplied and skilled,
of subsequent misuse of golden fleece,
of Jasons, bluntly mortal, mocked and killed.
I read another saying that success
lay not in having done but in the doing,
that virtue made its way to heavenly banks
and lay secure, with interest accruing,

and now am tense (too dark to read)
with springs compressed and ready rod
waiting around in hope of going down
dead, silly, lashed to a sounding god.

There are two sides to the artistic mission: first the venturing forth, the willingness to risk, the honing of skills; second the submission, accepting the reward of the doing, surrendering all dominion over results and consequences, letting the art work finally speak for itself, committing oneself only to helping it say what it has to say.

The subject matter for a poem may be some innocent-appearing thing such as an incident of love or death or nature: the subjects are stacked like sections of log, waiting to be hewn. It takes a bit of pluck to take one up at all, and considerable skill to turn it. But these are incidental to the primary challenge—that of letting it happen to you. You think you are the one changing the raw topic into art, but in every poem well written it is finally the poet who is transformed.

LANGUAGE AND THE MEDIA

9

You work for an advertising agency that has just signed a contract with a new client. Their product is a small machine that sits in the middle of the floor and hums a single note very softly. It is in two parts, and the top part revolves slowly in one direction for five minutes, then reverses and revolves in the other direction for the same amount of time. *The machine has absolutely no use whatsoever.* Your job is to use the media to sell it, as follows:

a. Name the crazy thing.
b. Make up a magazine advertisement for it.
c. Write a 60-second radio commercial for it.
d. Write a 60-second TV commercial for it.

In their text, *The Mass Media Book*, Rod Holmgren and William Norton define the media as follows:

Media are communication channels that serve people. The mass media—newspapers, books, magazines, radio, television, and film—are channels which address their messages to anyone who chooses to read, listen or watch.

This is a narrow, but accurate, definition. There are many more media; for example, each of the following is a medium: circus, theater, rodeo, ballet, opera, mime. They are not mass media, however, because their "messages" are intended not for the general public but for specialized groups. Some of these non–mass media become the content of the mass ones on occasion, as when circus or ballet appear as the content of a television special, but the very fact that the term "special" is used to herald their TV appearances is an indication that they are not the everyday media and are somehow unusual.

The broadest current definition of media is that of Marshall McLuhan, who claims that media are extensions of our selves. As clothing is an extension of our skin, and the wheel is an extension of our legs and feet, so the communications media are extensions of our senses, of our nervous systems.

The telephone, according to McLuhan, is a medium that serves as an extension of our ears; the movies serve as an extension of our eyes. Television extends not only the eye and the ear but also the sense of touch as well; McLuhan tells us that the TV image is a "mosaic mesh of light and dark spots" and goes on to say that

> The TV image requires each instant that we "close" the spaces in the mesh by a convulsive sensuous participation that is profoundly kinetic and tactile.

The investigation of the proliferation of media, both mass and specialized, has led to a new academic discipline, the study of "popular culture." It has its own scholarly journal and all the rest of the academic paraphernalia that we are accustomed to associate with fields like physics and political science. Undoubtedly this new field is more *fun* than almost anything else around—where else could you study things like Mother Pillows and subway graffiti and Civil War corset covers and the music of the Beatles in a single course? (If this sort of thing interests you, you can find the *Journal of Popular Culture* in most college and university libraries.)

There can be no question about the importance of the role that mass media play in our lives. Take television, for one glaring example—

> Television is everywhere. There are, at present, roughly sixty million American homes with at least one TV set. That's nearly all the homes in the country. More families own televisions than bathtubs.

> And they use them more. The average TV is on for approximately six hours a day—42 hours a week, 2,200 hours a year. The average American spends three and a half hours a day sitting in front of a television screen. Some of that time he is doing other things as well —eating, reading, or talking. But he devotes 15 hours a week ex-

Drawing by Lee Lorenz. © *1971 The New Yorker Magazine, Inc.*

clusively to TV. That comes to 28 percent of his leisure time. It is more time than he spends at any other activity except sleeping and earning a living.—PETER M. SANDMAN

That means that if we were exposed to no other medium except television, we would be devoting more than *one-fourth* of our leisure time to the media. And it's a rare individual who isn't also spending plenty of his or her time with movies, radio, newspapers, magazines, and perhaps a favorite non–mass medium.

Now the question is obvious—what does this do to us? What happens to us as a result of spending more than a fourth of our leisure time in this way? What are the media up to? What effect do they have on society as a whole?

Many functions are commonly attributed to them. Just as we can make a long list of the functions of folklore—folklore having constituted the media for oral cultures—we can make a similar list for the media in our electronic society. They entertain, they teach, they inform, they persuade. It may well be that they corrupt.

McLuhan says that they are destroying Western society as we know it and replacing it with an entirely new society. In article after article we find the media, TV in particular, blamed for every evil of contemporary American life, from our penchant for violence to the disgusting way we overfeed and underexercise our bodies. It would take us a very long time to examine all these claims and the counterclaims that accompany them.

Cartoon courtesy *Better Homes and Gardens.* © *Meredith Corporation, 1972. All rights reserved.*

"I'll get on with the nonsense in a minute after this word about tired, aching muscles."

What we might do, however, is consider one factor that might be said to underlie all of the media effects, both bad and good. This single factor, the one thread that ties it all together, is the media's awesome power to create a world that does not really exist, and to create it so compellingly that people believe that it is real, or at least behave as if it were real.

If you read a book of fantasy, like Tolkien's *Lord of the Rings*, you suspend your knowledge that his creatures and places are make-believe for the duration of time you spend reading the book. This suspension of belief is part of your enjoyment of the book. But when you have closed the book and put it away you don't continue to behave as if the Tolkien world were real.

The media, on the other hand, have the power to change your behavior by causing you to behave in your everyday life as if the world they present were not make-believe at all. For example, every time a character on one of the daytime soap operas has a baby, the studios are flooded with gifts for that baby sent in by the American public. This happens despite the fact that the average American is surely aware that such a baby is a "television star" hired for the occasion and in no way related to its media mother.

We can see, then, that the media in this country constitute a kind of Magic Myth Machine. We will now take a long look at one of the principal myths it produces. The myth is on at least three levels. There is a surface-level myth that turns up overtly in commercials and other advertisements; there is a middle-level myth, somewhat more concealed but found everywhere, in drama as well as in advertising; and finally there is the deep-level myth, the one that is carefully hidden away. Here goes—

SURFACE-LEVEL MYTH

If you use Product X like the beautiful young woman in the picture, you can expect to appear equally young and beautiful.

MIDDLE-LEVEL MYTH

The word "beautiful" when applied to women is defined as follows: 5'2" to 5'9" tall, 100–120 pounds, skin that is unblemished and without a line or wrinkle, regular features, body hair visible on the head only, well-developed breasts set off by under-developed hips and thighs, and a good tan—in short, Miss Teenage America. In addition, this creature is not allowed to have any human odor of any kind.

DEEP-LEVEL MYTH

A woman is worthwhile as a person only to the extent that she can be described as beautiful.

It is interesting that this myth complex does not hold for men. While there is no real objection to a man's being young and conventionally handsome, it is not a requirement. Men are allowed by our culture to substitute any number of other characteristics in the place of beauty. If you're dubious about the truth of this, you might take a good look at Telly Savalas, star of the hit TV series, *Kojak.* Running down Mr. Savalas's physiology list, we get at least the following: bumpy bald head; pouches under eyes; big nose; features of a spectacular irregularity; jowls; wrinkles in all directions. (We can't say much about Kojak's body, since it is always covered by the most expensive and superbly tailored suits any policeman ever had the good fortune to wear, but there's no particular reason for us to assume that the body has weathered the ravages of time any better than the face.)

TEACHER.　Ferrabeau, what is an adjective?

FERRABEAU.　A thing that modifies a noun.

TEACHER.　For example?

FERRABEAU.　Well, say you have the noun *teacher*. If you put an *-s* on it and make it *teachers*, you've modified it."

With a description like this, nobody would hesitate to rate the man way down the Tony Curtis scale; nonetheless, we perceive him as a physically attractive man. The same can be said for Richard Boone, who—were the standards set for women applied to him—would be one of the ugliest males ever to cross a TV screen. Even if we get rid of the bald head in the list of Savalas characteristics, since women rarely go bald, can you imagine anyone in our culture considering a woman attractive if she has pouches under her eyes, an enormous bumpy nose, jowls, and a face full of wrinkles? Not likely.

Very well, then. We have this three-part myth which has been *created* for us and which is perpetuated daily by the media. No amount of ingenious argumentation will provide a logical reason for any part of it, while some parts are so blatantly illogical that close examination is embarrassing—for example, the demand that a woman have tanned skin. In a country where genetic possession of a dark skin has for approximately two hundred years entailed severe socio-economic penalties, how precisely do we bring ourselves to support —by our purchases—a demand that white-skinned women darken their flesh to increase their attractiveness?

The most terrifying thing about the way this job is accomplished by the media is that even when we know, with our minds, that we are being sold a bill of goods, we are unable to suppress our gut reactions. This culturally induced handicap is so severe that it constitutes the one reason why it might not be a good idea to have women running for president; that is, if one candidate met all the specifications for the Middle Myth, and the others were fat, or wrinkled, or otherwise non-spec, it might give the first candidate an advantage over all the others that no amount of intelligence and logic could overcome.

How is this done? How, precisely, can the media accomplish this miracle of imposed Mushythink? Let us count the ways:

1. In any TV drama, the heroine always meets the Miss Teen-age America (MTA) specifications. We sometimes see "beau-

Drawing by Robert Day. © *1970 The New Yorker Magazine, Inc.*

"Don't you understand? This is life, this is what is happening. We can't switch to another channel."

tiful" lady villains; there is in fact a traditional brunette cliche villainess. But never, never do we see an "ugly" heroine. It just doesn't happen. This is true also of the cartoons that constitute the major TV diet of our small children, at the age where their perceptions are most impressionable.

2. The only alternatives to MTA-standard heroines on our television are women who can safely be put into the Cozy Old American Grandmother category; such women are allowed to substitute their extreme *usefulness* for beauty. And even these second-stringers are never allowed to go to the kind of extremes we permit for Telly Savalas.

3. These characteristics hold for movies, comic books, and mass magazine fiction, as well as for TV. They are as rigidly held to in children's books as they are on the daytime soap operas.

And then there are the commercials that build upon the structure provided by the drama and the fiction and reinforce it. There was a time when the advertising industry made no attempt to be subtle about this myth, and when it was common to see ads that moaned about the fate of pathetic young girls left doomed to a life of single misery because they had failed to use Toothpaste X or Face Cream Y. In 1924, Listerine Mouthwash based an entire advertising campaign on just this premise. It would seem that this situa-should have changed drastically in fifty years, but has it?

1974 TV COMMERCIAL FOR CLOSEUP TOOTHPASTE
We see a beautiful young woman talking to a friend (an equally beautiful young woman). The first MTA is complaining that in spite of her expensive clothes the man she has in mind keeps ignoring her, and she ends her complaint by stating that she is going to go out and buy some even more expensive clothing to tempt him with. But her friend stops her cold, saying, "Put your money where your mouth is!" and presents her with a tube of Closeup toothpaste. The next cut shows us radiant First MTA telling her friends about her successful date with the reluctant male—all thanks to Closeup.

One of the oddest things about the flawless young skin sub-part of the MTA myth is that although you see many advertisements for products guaranteed to give you flawless young skin, not one suggests that you let that flawless young skin hang out. On the contrary, once you have achieved flawlessness, you are expected to purchase an extensive line of products to cover the flawless skin up, and to cover it in such a way that it looks as though you *hadn't* covered it at all. You wouldn't think anyone would fall for anything so illogical, but thousands do.

Recently we have seen a few advertising campaigns which try very hard to give the impression that they are actually working against the Middle Myth. In such advertisements we find fiendishly clever language telling us that getting older is not really bad, it's great, and that as a woman ages she improves like a fine wine. This looks on the surface like a step in the right direction on the part of the advertiser. But if you take a look at the illustrations that go along with the "matronly is beautiful" language, what do you see? Do you see a middle-aged woman manifestly contented with her aging face and body and glowing with her pleasure at being in the prime of life? Certainly not. There in the picture is your good friend and mine, Miss Teenage America. As usual.

As for the Surface-Level and Deep-Level myths, such ads are 100% behind them. Surface Level: Buy our product, and you, too—even if you're over 30—will look like the young girl in the picture. Deep Level: No woman is really worthwhile unless she's beautiful.

If you are wondering why the media don't devote themselves to promoting an image of "beautiful" defined by the characteristics of wisdom, compassion, and loving kindness, that's easy to explain. There are no *products* which can be trusted to impart these qualities, or even an appearance of these qualities. If tomorrow our scientists should discover chemicals which could do this, you'd see the most massive ad campaigns of all time. There'd be wrinkled women with gray hair (and jowls) looking pityingly at Miss Teenage America, all the while clutching their bottles of Little Wonder Wisdom Wafers, or their packages of Loving Kindness Loaf, Only 30¢ a Slice!

Every rhetorical device that we have seen in political language, every device that we have isolated in poetry, is used by the media in their advertising. The position of the poets and orators as top experts in the use of words has been taken over in American society by the group of men and women we often call "Madison Avenue," the advertising people. They use parallelism, rhyme, meter, antithesis, intricate patterns of sound and orthography, and every other technical device language offers.

Unlike the poets, the Madison Avenue people are extremely well paid. Without advertising, the mass media would disappear, since it is advertising that pays for their existence, and this lifeblood status is reflected in the advertising paycheck. Unlike the poets, the Madison Avenue people do not present their compositions in cheaply bound little books or read them aloud to half a dozen friends in a dimly lit coffeehouse. Their work is showcased by all the magnificent resources of our graphic artists, by color photography and printing that you literally cannot look away from. For example, take a look at the ad for Green Apple perfume. If there were a poem superimposed on that glorious apple, you'd read it.

Courtesy of Max Factor & Co.

You couldn't help yourself. The same thing goes for an advertising message.

The linguistic form of an ad will differ with the differing requirements and potentials of a given medium. For example, look at the following advertisement, a television commercial for Arrow shirts:

Arrow Shirts—60 Seconds

YOUNG AND RUBICAM, INC.

VIDEO	*AUDIO*
Open on chorus girls in dressing room.	ANNCR (VO): Some guys never know how good they have it. Well, that's show biz—maybe
Cut to Eddie the stage mgr entering.	Take Eddie.
Diss * to various backstage scenes: Eddie lighting cigarettes for girls, etc. He exits.	Day after day, a stranger in paradise. And nobody notices him. It's "Eddie hand me this." And "Eddie get me that." And nobody knows he's there.
Eddie re-enters via hallways, wearing new shirt.	Then one day, Eddie wears a new shirt. A blue and orange striped number—from Arrow.
He knocks, opens door and girls scream as they notice him. He exits hurriedly.	All of a sudden, *everybody* notices Eddie.
Eddie hesitates, walks over to locker, and looks at his old shirt. Scene diss to black, fades up on Eddie walking to door in old shirt. He enters.	Well, that's show biz—maybe Arrow shirts aren't for everybody after all. Especially if you have a job like Eddie's.
Cut back to new shirt hanging in locker.	But if you have a job like Eddie's . . . who needs Arrow?

---

* *Note:* diss means "dissolve;" vo means "voice over"—that is, voice superimposed over scene being shown.

All of the information that appears on the left side of the TV commercial is conveyed by the eye. The fact that Eddie is surrounded by girls, the fact that he's wearing a new Arrow shirt, the scene where Eddie changes back to his old shirt—all of these would have to be conveyed in words for a radio commercial. Someone would have to say, "Wow, Eddie, where'd you get the new Arrow shirt?" and "Look at Eddie, surrounded by beautiful girls, lighting their cigarettes for them!" Although the commercial lasts a full minute, it uses only 91 words. To convey the same amount of information that the TV commercial does on radio, we would unquestionably have to add another hundred words or so. And yet, although only half as much is being "said" by the TV commercial, this does not mean in sensory terms that there are empty spaces, "silences" in the sixty seconds. The time that we spend seeing the chorus girls, noticing Eddie's shirt, and watching the action of both Eddie and the girls fills up the available space with sensory input. You are not conscious, while watching such a commercial, of any delay between speeches. You don't sit and wait anxiously for the next vocal input to come along because the sight and sound are integrated into a unified whole.

If a radio commercial is to hold the listener's attention, it has to not only fill all the available sensory space, it must do so by exploiting the potentials of language to their fullest extent. If you think about radio commercials that you remember easily, you will notice that they use jokes, plays on words, comic dialects, strange sound effects, and many other attention-holding devices.

A television commercial, however, does not have to go to such lengths to hold its audience. Nothing that is said in the Arrow commercial is very clever. There's a mild joke at the beginning, relying on the "stranger in paradise" cliché, and a pallid kind of word play at the end with the following structure:

> Maybe Arrow shirts aren't for everybody after all. Especially *if you have a job like Eddie's*. But *if you have a job like Eddie's* . . . who needs Arrow?

This is possible for the TV commercial because the advertiser can count on the visual material holding the viewer's attention in spite of the downbeat dialogue. We see this pushed to its limit in commercials where the dialogue is confined entirely to a ditchwater-dull discussion of somebody's stomach acids, but the screen is covered with bursting bubbles and animated intestinal tracts and little colored arrows racing from organ to organ.

...like the baseless fabric of this vision,
the cloud-capp'd towers,
the gorgeous palaces,
the solemn temples,
the great globe itself, yea,
all which it inherit,
shall dissolve,
and leave not a rack behind.

Shakespeare said it, not us: Save the Earth.
WRNO-FM 99 NEW ORLEANS

Courtesy of WRNO

The magazine advertisement is relatively free from the constraints of language, and may use almost no words to convey its message. Look at the advertisement for Oneida sterling on page 175. This advertisement has only thirty-three words, and of those thirty-three it is probable that only the twelve in large type will be read. The picture does all the work. This does not mean, however, that language is not involved in any way. What the advertiser is counting on is that the person reading the magazine—say, Future Bride—will provide the language by going through a process something like the following in her head:

> Hmm . . . the sterling gets better with time, the way a bride's cooking does. Lord, I hope my cooking is going to be all right. Hey, look at that egg. Wow, is that a mess! And that toast . . . yecch, it's all burned. Nobody could possibly *eat* that stuff. But it might not be quite as repulsive if you had pretty spoons and things on the table with it. At least there'd be something else to look at until I learn how to make toast.

And so repulsively on and on. This is Future Bride thinking, but it would take little imagination to come up with the thoughts of Mother of the Bride, Nostalgic Father of the Bride, or even Chuckling Future Groom.

Ridiculous? Certainly. But it doesn't do a bit of good for us to talk about how silly it is that we can be manipulated in this way. Silly it may be, but as long as it can be done, it's dangerous. We should at least be aware of what's going on, or, as Marshall McLuhan has said, "Education is ideally civil defense against media fall-out."

Can you now redo your work on the Useless Machine described in the pre-problem for this unit? Can you improve the effectiveness and up the potential sales of the gadget by plugging it into the myth discussed in this unit, or one of the other common myths with which you are familiar? With your long years of training as one of the television generation, you should be able to make Useless Machine absolutely irresistible—even to the person who knows, logically, that he doesn't need it, can't use it, and will regret buying it. Consider yourself a Media Warden demonstrating what ought *not* to work, and produce the perfect advertising campaign for Useless Machine.

America's Number One Honeymoon Resort

Where It's Always a Young World . . .

It's true . . . Your first glimpse of Mount Airy Lodge by day or night will show you elegance in a dream-like seclusion. We've planned it that way. It's absolutely exciting. The most beautiful Bridal Suites you can imagine . . . feel the carpet beneath your feet . . . as luxurious

Like a bride's cooking,
Oneida's Heirloom Sterling gets even better with time.

◼ONEIDA

The silver cube. Our silversmiths' mark of excellence.   © 1973 Oneida Ltd.

as a wall-to-wall pillow. Control your contact with the outside world on a 21" Color TV with Stereo Sound . . . a bathroom so wondrous it deserves a description of its own. Our own Private Lake and white sand beaches . . . Our own ski slopes . . . ice skating, tobogganing and snowmobiling. We can please the most pleasure loving couple . . . at Mount Airy Lodge, the most complete year 'round honeymoon world you could wish for . . . in the Poconos, where sun, water and mountains create the perfect atmosphere for "just the two of you." Write for our FREE exciting 24 page color brochure and rate information.

EXERCISES

1. All of the following lines from recent ads involve the use of some technical device of language. Look them over and see if you can explain what makes them effective and memorable. (If you need to refresh your memory, refer to the poetry and political language units.)

BAYER ASPIRIN
We go to a lot of pains.

ROYAL DOULTON CHINA
Royal Doulton presents an English lesson in China.

OXFORD BONE CHINA
It wasn't designed with your grandmother in mind.

HOOVER VACUUMS
The vacuum, packed.

RATH HAMS
Where there's smoke, there's flavor.

PILLSBURY SPACE FOOD STICKS
Presenting the best thing that ever came between two meals.

SEARS (A LAMPSHADE AD)
Shades of the Tiffany look!

KRAFT FOODS
Seasonings Greetings. Ring in summer with free Barbecue Sauce from *Kraft*.

CARNATION HOT COCOA MIX
> Good old-fashioned
> cocoa without
> a good old-fashioned
> mess

PILLSBURY
> Add fruit and nuts to
> a Pillsbury Bread mix
> and next thing you know
> it's a holiday fruitcake.

BANKAMERICARD
> A dollars and sensible way to save.

LEEDS SHOES
> Your thong of thongs!
> Tuned up for high times.

2. Prepare a collection of ads like the one above, looking for as wide a variety of different technical devices as you can, and analyze them as you did in the first exercise.

3. In this unit we examined one of the standard Media Myths. There are lots more of them. Identify one and analyze it carefully. Does it have only one level or is it multi-level like the one described in this unit? Explain your answer briefly. Find examples of media ads that perpetuate your myth.

4. Remember the so-called rules of English grammar? The ones that can be suspended in poetry? Look at the following ad from *Ore-Ida* Potatoes:

> You'll find yourself eating these Tater Tots as hot nibblers any time of the day. Even serving them with dips. Easy to fix, too. In the oven. In your deep fry basket. In the skillet. They're good every-which way.

Find the grammar mistakes in this ad and rewrite the ad so that they are "corrected." Now compare the two versions. Which is more effective? Look at some more ads, listen to some commercials, and see if you can make a list of common deviations from the standard grammar of English.

5. Write a brief essay on the significance of the phrase "Only
_____ Dollars!"

6. Here is another quote from *Understanding Media:*

The young people who have experienced a decade of TV have
naturally imbibed an urge toward involvement in depth that makes
all the remote visualized goals of usual culture seem not only un-
real but irrelevant, and not only irrelevant but anemic. It is the
total involvement in all-inclusive NOWNESS that occurs in young
lives via TV's mosaic image. . . . The TV child expects involvement and doesn't want a specialist JOB in the future. He does want
a ROLE and a deep commitment to his society. It is, of course, our
job not only to understand this change but to exploit it for its
pedagogical richness.

"To exploit it for its pedagogical richness" means "to find a
way to make use of it in education." Using this paragraph as a base,
write a 1000-word paper on one of the following topics:

a. How Schools Should Be Changed for the TV Child
b. How English Classes Should Be Changed for the TV Child
c. Why McLuhan Is Wrong
d. Why the Teacher-Giving-a-Lecture Fails with the TV
Child

7. What are the three top status symbols in America today?
To support your choice give evidence from advertisements and commercials. The cost and style of the particular item is obviously going
to be different in a magazine intended for wealthy readers than in
one intended for blue-collar families, but does the choice of symbol
vary along socioeconomic lines?

8. Proctor & Gamble make Dash, Tide, Duz, Bold, Oxydol,
Cascade, Cheer, and Ivory Soap. What does this tell you about the
media claim that one soap product is different from another? Can
you find another example of this kind of production overlap? (Try
looking in the small print on boxes.)

9. Find the myths being presented in the ads on pages 179–
182. Are they single or multi-level?

10. There is an interesting question which has been posed by
William Blissett: If, as St. John Perse has said, a book is the death

of a tree, then "what is a TV program the death of?" Write an answer in about 500 words.

11.   Arthur Knight, talking of Western movies, says:

The Westerns devolved a formula that worked flawlessly for almost

When Cathy Cole and Peggy Burton saw Joan Emery's new floor, they couldn't believe their feet.

INTRODUCING G A F SOFSTEP VINYL FLOORS

Joan told her friends how much softer a GAF Sofstep™ Floor is than an ordinary vinyl floor. They felt the difference. With their own two feet. Sofstep is warm, quiet and comfortable. Thanks to deep foam cushioning, which makes it almost a quarter-inch thick.

And it never needs waxing. All it ever needs is an occasional light buffing to keep its natural shine and beauty. It makes sense to consider a GAF Sofstep Floor. But don't just use your head. Use your feet. For your nearest GAF dealer see the yellow pages. Or for further information, write GAF Floor Products Division, Dept. E113, Box 1121, Radio City Station, New York, N.Y. 10019.

Courtesy GAF Corporation

fifty years, with plots as predictable as a ballet and characters as precisely set as those of a fairy tale. No less rigid was their morality. The code of the West (or, at least, the code of the Western) demanded scrupulous honor for its heroes, an unsullied virtue for its heroines, and a nasty death for its villains.

Does this description still apply to movie Westerns? Does it apply

Courtesy J. P. Stevens

She covers the fastest men on wheels, tours the world throughout the year. She's not about to smoke a boring cigarette.

DAILY TRACK SUMMARY

Warning: The Surgeon General Has Determined That Cigarette Smoking Is Dangerous to Your Health.

Viceroy Longs has full-bodied flavor that doesn't flatten out. Always rich...always smooth...always exciting. Get a taste of Viceroy Longs. Get a taste of excitement.

Viceroy Longs.
Where excitement is now a taste.

VICEROY

17 mg. "tar," 1.2 mg. nicotine, av. per cigarette, FTC Report Mar. '74

© *Brown & Williamson Tobacco Corporation. Reprinted by permission.*

to TV Westerns? If not, what change has there been? Explain your position in a brief paper.

12. You have just heard that the government has appropriated two million dollars to support a National Opera Company. Write an angry letter of protest to your congressman on the grounds that opera is enjoyed by only a handful of people and the money should have gone for some more popular art form.

Courtesy Liggett & Myers Incorporated

13. Take the opposite position on the event described in exercise 12. Write an approving letter based on the fact that a medium enjoyed by only a handful of people is likely to die out altogether without federal support.

14. There's an organization called Videofreex which has a fleet of media buses, and which goes around communities making and showing video films. This sort of use of the media, for teaching

purposes and for community organizing of many kinds, is called "underground" media. Assume that you have the facilities of such an organization at your disposal for two hours in your community. What would you film? Write a brief description of the show or shows that you would prepare.

15. In *Psychology Today* for December 1973, Harvey Cox is described as claiming that the mass media are a kind of religion because they provide "images and icons" that "serve as contemporary myths of origin, identity and salvation." Do you agree? Write a 500-word defense of your answer.

© *The Hoover Company*

16. Draw a few sample "frames" and write a brief description for a Saturday morning television cartoon show for kids that might attempt to counteract one of the Media Myths.

17. Go back to unit 1 and look at our final definition of language. Now, arguing as logically and carefully as you can, write an essay explaining why the film medium (either cinema or television or both) is or is not a language. If you feel that a modification of the final definition would be appropriate, and if you can defend such a modification, that's fine.

18. Look at the Hoover magazine advertisement reproduced in this chapter. Would it work on radio? Would it work in television? Rewrite it as a 60-second commercial for either radio or television, being very sure you do not lose the information conveyed by the young man's facial expression.

Marvel Language: The Comic Book and Reality

ARTHUR BERGER

I would like to investigate some of the unique qualities of *The Fantastic Four* and the *Amazing Spider-Man* which we find in Marvel language. We are really looking at the work of Stan Lee, who plots and writes these stories. It is his innovations on the characterological aspects of the comic book—the flawed hero—and in the linguistic aspects—irony, self-parody, and hyperbole—that distinguishes these two comic books. Some of the other comic books of the Marvel Group, such as *Captain America,* do not have these elements and are as childish and uninteresting as most comic books.

The first thing we notice as we look at a Marvel comic (and I will use this term to mean either a *Fantastic Four* or a *Spider-Man* adventure) is the light tone, the frivolity, that we find on the opening page of each book, when the credits are given. A list of typical credits follow:

Extravagantly executed with ebullient erudition by Stan Lee and Jack Kirby. Inked by: Joe Sinnot. Lettered by: Sam Rosen. (61 April FF)

Contrived and crafted by the curiously creative, catastrophically compelling collaboration of Stan Lee and Jack Kirby. (62 May FF)

Let Marveldom Cheer! Let humanity shout! Stan (the man) Lee and Jack (king) Kirby have bestowed another masterpiece upon mankind. Exotically embellished by Joe Sinnot. Laconically lettered by Artie Simek. (73 April FF)

An awesome aggregation of airborne thrills by Smilin' Stan Lee and Johnny Romita, learnedly lettered by whammy Sammy Rosen. If you didn't read all about last ish, we're beginning to lose patience with you! . . . Stern Stan! (48 May SM)

These credits establish a certain levity right away, so that the stories themselves take on a status somewhat removed from what might be called "high seriousness." They say to the reader, more or less, "Yes, we do a lot of kidding around, and that's how you should take the stories, but let's see what we can do with our super-heroes anyhow. . . ." That is, the credits show that readers aren't to take the stuff *too* seriously.

There is another reason for this horsing around that has to do with the business of writing for comic books, an occupation that may have considerable rewards financially but that has little status in the literary world. By clowning around a bit Stan Lee also protects himself from criticism by "stating" to the world that he recognizes what's going on, and doesn't take himself seriously. The idea of a dedicated comicbook writer is somewhat hard to take; there are only two postures that (given contemporary American values) can "legitimate" writing comic books: money or satire. Thus by writing funny credits featuring remarkable displays of alliteration, he nods his head to society and convention and is then free to indulge himself in his science fantasies.

The use of alliteration is one of the outstanding qualities of Lee's writing. That in itself shows that he sees the comic book as having a particular quality or status, which he reinforces by recourse to a rather unnatural but remarkably intellectual use of language. Alliteration involves the use of words with the same letter or same sound, such as the famous "pick a peck of pickled peppers." Many of the characters have names that are alliterative such as Peter Parker, Betty Brant, Reed Richards, and Silver Surfer, and many of the titles use the same technique. Thus, we find such titles as *The Peerless Power of the Silver Surfer!* (55 Oct. FF), *The Tentacles and the Trap* (54 Nov. SM), *The Battle of the Baxter Building* (40 July FF), and *By Ben Betrayed* (69 Dec. FF). Alliteration when fused with the right rhythms tends to create slogan-like phrases that stick in our memories. It is a favorite technique of advertising and politics; "Beat Bensen with Burdick" was used to win a political campaign in North Dakota, and millions of Americans are implored to "Move Up to Mercury."

Alliteration is really a poetic device, and that is particularly important here, since there is no question in my mind but that the prose in Marvel comics is unusually poetic and at times quite lyrical.

The Silver Surfer is generally done in extremely poetical language, which is combined with overt moralizing about the deficiencies and

potentialities of man. Let's look at the way The Silver Surfer speaks to
see this. In the *Peerless Power* book the adventure featuring him is
called "When Strikes the Silver Surfer." The inversion of the language
in the title, together with the alliteration, is itself poetic; it has a much
more lyrical quality than the normal order of words: "When the Silver
Surfer Strikes." The Surfer describes himself in the following terms:

> I, who have crested the currents of space . . .
> who have dodged the meteor swarms, and
> out-distanced the fastest comets,
> I must resign myself to this PRISON which
> men call earth . . . Because I dared
> give up the freedom of the universe
> to aid the hapless humans!
> But I must have no regrets!
> Whatever destiny awaits me . . . I shall be true
> to my trust, though I am a stranger
> in a world I never made! (55 Oct. FF p. 3)

This description is really a prose poem involving a meditation upon
the human condition, the value of trust, and the mystery of destiny. It
is spoken on the top of an enormous mountain peak, surrounded by
other mountains and a vast landscape, as the Silver Surfer stands in an
heroic pose peering out over the terrain. The whole scene is romantic
and idyllic, as a nature-god (of sorts) ponders the future and what he
might do to aid humanity. The Silver Surfer is a Christ-like figure. He
gave up the freedom of the universe to come to the aid of mankind, and
yet, despite all his fantastic powers, he does not know how to get around
the greed and hatred that he sees in man. He is destined to eternal
solitude, to being a stranger, and like Twain's *Mysterious Stranger*, his
attempts to aid man, or force man to unite and realize his possibilities,
are characterized by violence and destruction.

There is also something lyrical about surfing, riding on the crests
of great waves, and the figure of a Silver Surfer, a creature from another
universe riding the air currents and glistening in the sun, is an emotionally
gripping one.

There is a vastness of scale here that is on the level of the epic,
and indeed a closer look at the comics leads me to believe that they
are modernized versions of the epic. In *A Glossary of Literary Terms*,
M. H. Abrams defines the epic as:

A long narrative poem on a serious subject, related in an elevated
style, and centered about an heroic figure on whose actions depends

to some degree the fate of a nation or a race. The "traditional" or "primary" epics were shaped from the legends that developed in an heroic age, when a nation was on the move and engaged in military conquest and expansion. In this group belong the *Iliad* and *Odyssey* of the Greek Homer, and the Anglo-Saxon *Beowulf*. The "literary" or "secondary" epics were written by sophisticated craftsmen in deliberate imitation of the earlier form. Of this kind is Virgil's Roman poem, the *Aeneid*, which in turn served as the chief model for Milton's literary epic, *Paradise Lost*. [p. 29]

Abrams says that the epic is an exceedingly difficult form which makes enormous demands on authors, and that consequently we have only a handful of unquestionably great epics. As he puts it, "It is certainly the most ambitious and most exacting of poetic types, making immense demands on a poet's knowledge, invention, and skill to sustain the scope, grandeur, and variety of a poem that tends to encompass the known world and a large portion of its learning [pp. 29, 30]." He lists certain characteristics of epics: a significant hero—of great importance; a world-wide (or even larger) scale; heroic actions and deeds in battle; the interest of the gods, who often take part in the action; and a ceremonial style, with a dignity proportionate to the subject. On the basis of this description of the epic I think we might claim that the comic book with its superheroes and supervillains and its scope is often close to the epic and might be considered a kind of modernized epic.

The adventures of the Fantastic Four who are "world-historical characters," whose actions are many times of importance to the whole world, often involve god-like individuals and are contemporary epics. We might call them "tertiary" epics, since they make use of other materials and are not "high literature" as we commonly know it. The interesting thing is that in a literary form that is generally seen as trash and seldom taken seriously we find poetic language, philosophical speculation, and the use of the epic form.

At the opposite extreme from lyrical and elevated language is the "language" used to create sound effects, an amazing collection of onomatopoetic creations. Onomatopoeia is a poetic device that uses words to simulate sounds, but the words in Marvel comics show a much greater range than in traditional poetic use. In addition the "words" used in comic strips can be given emphasis by being drawn in large letters, being brightly colored, or being given unusual shapes.

These sound effects play a rather dominant role in the panels that contain them. They spill over the boundaries of the panels, are as large as some of the figures, and are rather odd words. We find such creations as: "Krrash!," "Spkakk!," "Thoom!," and "Shoosh!," to name only a few.

These terms represent an attempt by comic strips to transcend the limitations of the medium, just as the individual terms violate the borders of the panels. They also form a sub-language of sorts, a language of sound-effects.

The accoustical terms give an indication of exactly what kind of destruction is taking place or what kind of blows are landing. They have a cacophony that mirrors the chaos that is creating them—and also, by their size and shape, tell us the degree of emotion (sound) we are to experience. They function like a playwright's notes on how his play is to be produced—telling what the characters are to look like, how they are to feel, and what they are to experience. All of the actions take place within a given sense of unreality and make-believe, which is carefully nurtured and which gives all the destruction and violence a particular status. This is the same kind of effect produced in a fairy tale by saying, "Once upon a time, long long ago, in a land very far away." This tells the listener how to feel about the story, regardless of what the story contains.

Perhaps the best way to see the comic book is in theatrical terms. Instead of thinking of the *Spider-Man* or *Fantastic Four* as comic books, think of them as illustrated plays. The dialogue is given in the balloons, the stage directions are given in the various inserts, and the thought (internal dialogue) of the characters are shown in balloons with fluffy edges. There are "conventions" to the comic book, and a reader has to learn them in order to understand what is going on.

Enticers, 1970; on TV, Who Do They Think You Are?

STEPHANIE HARRINGTON

Television commercials may be many things to many people, but two things are obvious—they're an index to our anxieties and a boon to anthropology. What better crash course in the values, mores, fantasies—and particularly the fears—of Americans?

How do Americans feel about sex? Consult your network television commercial. Consider the teaser about "Lovestick," a lipstick "men can look at but they can't taste." Are we overly concerned with surface appearances? Just try adding up the amount of television time spent on pushing make-up, hair spray, perfume, hair tonic, hair rinses, fashions, foundations, and the other products under which we seem determined to bury any part of us that's more than skin deep—not to mention the skin itself. Are we obsessed with cleanliness? If you have any doubts, they'll be quickly drowned in the flood of suds spilling out of the commercials for detergents, floor cleaners, soap flakes, shampoos, bath soaps, facial soaps, baby soaps, scented soaps, unscented soaps, hypoallergenic soaps, deodorant soaps.

What's the state of our collective nerves? Evidently, bad enough to support the headache remedies, tension relievers, and sleeping pills that are a staple of television advertising. In fact, we seem positively to enjoy our headaches. After all, two of the funniest commercials ever broadcast have been for Alka Seltzer and Excedrin.

On the other hand, the absence of commercials for certain items offers some indication of what does not particularly concern the mass of Americans. For instance, have you ever stopped to think why one of the few things not advertised on television is books?

But getting back to the question about sex. Just how do we see our attitude as it is bounced back to us through the television tube? Well, in addition to the look-but-don't touch message, there is the gamesmanship pitch: "A woman can taunt you, tease you . . . should you give her another tactic? Should you give her Ambush [perfume] by Dana?" And, of course, the big television tease of all time was the Noxzema Shave Cream commercial with a sultry blond Swede whispering over her bare shoulder, "Take it off, take it all off." It's all in the double entendre.

On the other hand, there's the sado-masochism of the misogynous message from Silva Thins (cigarettes) in which beautiful women get pushed out of cars or into descending elevators by a slick-looking stud in shades. And then there's the straightforward conquest by virile male of passive female implied in the Black Belt After Shave and Cologne [ad]. In that one, a fine figure of a karate expert brings his hand down on a pile of boards or bricks or something equally resistant and, as filmed in slow motion, gracefully, effortlessly—lovingly—slices right through it.

Sex, then, as projected by the American mind for the American mind (to persuade it to keep the American dollar in motion) is a game, a tease, a test of wiles versus brawn, of ego against ego. Or just plain conquest and submission.

If we can believe what our commercials tell us (and can all those psychologists, sociologists, market researchers, and pollsters be wrong?), the basic attraction that sets this *mano a mano* in motion is not the attraction of one human being for another, but of one product for another. It's really a case of Aqua Velva After Shave falling madly in love with Wind Song Perfume. "I can't seem to forget you," whispers the lithe, luscious man in the Wind Song (by Prince Matchabelli) commercial. "Your Wind Song stays on my mind." "There's something about an Aqua Velva man," croons the kittenish female in a pitch for "the after-shave girls can't forget." Love at first sniff. Indeed, Aqua Velva is presented not merely as the key ingredient of a man's surface charm, but as the definition of the man himself. Use it, advises the commercial, "to bring out the Aqua Velva man in you." Or, the essence is the essence. Essence of Aqua Velva, that is.

Of course, commercials indicate not only that there is a growing male market for cosmetics, but also that there is still considerable resistance among men to using sissy stuff like cologne and hair spray, for fear of calling their masculinity into question. The angst of this particular American dilemma is reflected in reassuring he-man commercials showing one rocky-looking male after another doing a real *man's* work—like running a pile driver or driving a truck—and telling you that he uses hair spray. And if hair spray is manly enough for a two-hundred-pound truck driver, it's manly enough, isn't it? This trans-sexual operation on the image of formerly women-only cosmetics involves christening the products with strong, virile names like Black Belt or Command. Command hair spray and Command Tahitian Lime anti-perspirant are "for men only," an aggressive male voice informs us, adding almost threateningly, "*And I mean for men only.*"

The American romance with superficiality as documented in our commercials does, however, have occasional moments of deeper meaning. As in the ad for Alton Ames men's clothes, in which another of those Swedish sex kittens practically blows in our ears on the subject of her man's (their relationship is naughtily but safely ambiguous) Alton Ames suits, fondling them as she purrs. It's clear that it's the suit she loves, not the man. Indeed, she would probably love any man who put it on (even you, Mr. Average Television Viewer). But at least in this case the relationship is not between two products but between a person and a product.

Flesh-and-blood people lead very precarious lives on television commercials. They are in constant danger of being rubbed, scrubbed, slimmed, trimmed, and deodorized out of existence, leaving no traces. There are certainly no clues remaining in our clothes, which can be purified with detergents like Dash, which not only gets out easily removable "outside dirt," but tough "ground-in body dirt" as well.

Body dirt! Under the influence of the staggering number of soap commercials on television, we were so busy using detergents, pre-soaks, bleaches, and enzyme-active stain removers to get out soil, grease, paint, blood, grass stains, food stains, and goodness knows what else, that we might have forgotten all about body dirt, if Dash hadn't come along with its anti–body dirt ingredient. (And if your husband cleans a lot of fish, you might like to know that, according to another commercial, a fisherman's wife washed his apron in Procter and Gamble's Gain and lo! the "set-in, dried-in blood stains were virtually gone, gone!" Which is the next best thing to bloodless fish.)

"To Keep Our Dark, Physical Secrets"

Of course, if we would only be provident enough to use a good anti-perspirant in the first place, we wouldn't have to worry so much about something like body dirt. There are certainly enough preventive products to choose from. Like Dial Soap "with AT7" (it always helps to throw in some scientific-sounding ingredient like AT7). Or "ice-blue Secret." The name itself promises to keep our dark, physical secrets.

The amount of television time taken up by commercials for products that clean, deodorize, disguise, and sometimes almost threaten to dissolve our bodies and whatever touches them seems to indicate that there is something about bodies that makes us nervous. True descendants of our Puritan forebears, we spend an impressive amount of time and energy—and pass a lot of money over the counter—trying to deny the animal in us. It scares us. And the American mind, both fashioner and product of the consumer society par excellence, has developed the notion that our fears and insecurities, like everything else, can be bought off. After all, as long as we have them, we might as well make a profit.

Scared of sex? Buy Ambush and turn it into a game. Do you worry about being drab, uninteresting? Afraid that beneath your surface there's just more surface? Terrified that your body odour will make you a wall-flower at the PTA or get you read out of the Rotary?

Afraid of being rejected by the opposite sex? Write to good ole Fran, paradigm of advice-to-the-wretched columnists. Sympathetic, motherly, solid. Fran knows best and Fran will tell you to buy Lavoris. Or, if you're a go-go type who hasn't the time to stop and gargle, chew Dentyne and, like the girl in the commercial, have "the freshest mouth in town." And, so the implication goes, like the girl in the commercial, look smashing in a bikini and get kissed by the dreamiest guy on the beach. So what if you have a mouth full of gum?

We seem to have convinced ourselves that there's no end to the relief that can be bought. Even political relief. When the kids complain about the System trying to co-opt the revolution, they know what they're talking about. When it became clear that youth was in revolt, that the black ghettos were organizing their own resistance, retaliation came with the Dodge Rebellion. If you can't lick 'em, join 'em. Join the Dodge Rebellion. Buy a Dodge. Feel like Che Guevara just driving to the country club.

Feel stranded on the far side of the generation gap? Relax. Buy a beer. A Ballantine. According to the commercial, the three-ring sign is "a happy sign" because "both the generations go for Ballantine." And to prove it, a neatly dressed young man, with hair just long enough to qualify as an under-thirty growth but not long enough to make anyone really nervous, is shown clinking glasses with someone definitely over thirty.

The ad men are even trying to buy off women's liberation by selling the resurgent female militants a cigarette: Virginia Slims. "You've come a long way, baby," says the commercial, as it traces the emancipation of the woman smoker who starts out sneaking a puff in the basement and ends up in a smashing sexy mod outfit, dangling a cigarette designed just for her.

The cigarette commercials in general have been rather subtle in their way. They seem to be selling fantasies. Smoke a Marlboro and be what you always wanted to be when you grew up—a cowboy. Or smoke a Salem and feel like you're in the country even when you're in the city. Smoke a Winston and find contentment by yourself in some secluded spot.

In Selling Fantasies, They, Too, are Buying Off a Fear

Fear of contaminated lungs. Of cancer. Of heart disease. For, you notice, almost all these fantasies take place in the great outdoors where the air is fresh and clean. Smoking, they seem to be saying—turning the threat into an asset—is good for you, as well as a way to find fun, romance, and *machismo*.

But two can play at the commercial game; and, ironically, some of the cleverest and most effective television advertisements now running are the anti-smoking commercials. And when it comes to working on a fear, they have the most obvious target. So until the cigarette commercials are finally off the air, the anti-commercials may provide a reasonably potent antidote.

There will always be other commercials to fill the breach. We start them young, after all. Probably the loudest, shrillest, densest concentration of commercials is to be found on children's programs, which hustle whole families of dolls and wardrobes of clothes to buy for them. There are miniature race tracks and garages and dozens of miniature cars to fill them with. There are miniature appliances, miniature pots, pans, dishes, plastic food to cook, dolls that crawl, walk, dance clap, drink, grow teeth. Anything to make a little girl feel that the doll she has is passé and simply has to be replaced.

But with all this emphasis on spending money to buy a sense of security one of the things we seem most insecure about is spending money. For one thing, we're afraid we'll be taken advantage of. Like the poor schnook in the Volvo commercial who can't even trade in his old car at the place where he bought it. After some quick calculations, the very salesman who sold him the car tells him its trade-in value is zero. Now he tells him. Taken again. (The point is, of course, that this doesn't happen with Volvos. They last.)

The fear of being conned, however, is secondary. The soothing commercials that comfort us with the assurance that we'll find a friend at Chase Manhattan or Irving at Irving Trust suggest that what we are really terrified about is that one day we may run out of money. And then how could we buy, buy, buy our anxieties away?

With worries like that, no wonder we get Excedrin headaches.

THE DIVERSITY OF LANGUAGE

10

This book began with the sentence: the subject of this book is human language. The first chapter defined human language, and we have gone on from that beginning to examine one such language —English—as it is used in a number of areas of daily life.

However, throughout the entire book we have behaved very much as if English were an undifferentiated monolithic *thing*. We can describe and measure and discuss the Golden Gate Bridge, or the sum of the numbers 3 and 6, or the distance from Albuquerque to Philadelphia; we have behaved as if the same processes could be applied, in the same way, to English.

This is a convenient method of going about things, and a practical one, and it is true that out of all the varied forms of English speech it is possible to extract a set of elements that most of us will agree somehow represent the "englishness" of English. The truth, though, is that there are many different kinds of English, that they are all constantly changing, and that no such thing as "standard" English really exists. In this last chapter we will try to set aside the convenient fiction that there is some one specific way of speaking that can be labelled once and for all, ENGLISH. We will try instead to examine the reality, something called ENGLISH-AS-SHE-IS-SPOKE.

We will begin with an example of your old friend and mine, The Multiple Choice Question. Mark your answer:

Do you speak a dialect?
a. Of course not. Only people from Brooklyn and New Orleans speak dialects. I speak English.

b. Sure. Doesn't everybody?

c. I used to, but in high school I finally learned how to talk right.

Answers *a* and *c* reflect two widespread misconceptions about what a dialect is. Answer *a* goes along with the idea that a dialect is a manner of speaking that is radically different from the way that you yourself speak, or from the way that television newscasters or college professors (or some such group) speak. Answer *c* reflects the idea that a dialect is just an incorrect way to talk.

Answer *b* is the right answer to this question. Strange as it may seem if the idea is new to you, every speaker of English (or any other language) has a dialect of his or her own, a particular way of speaking, that is unlike anyone else's way of speaking that language. For these individual dialects there is a special term—the *idiolect*. When a number of idiolects are similar enough that all their speakers feel that they are talking in much the same way, we can say that such a group of idiolects constitutes a dialect. Groups of dialects, in their turn, are recognized by speakers as sufficiently alike to be called a single language.

What does it mean, however, to say that people are speaking "in the same way"? The real meaning of the term *dialect* is to be found in the answer to this question. If we accept the idea that the shape of a language sequence—the sounds which it is composed of, and the order in which those sounds are arranged—is the result of the set of rules in the speaker's grammar, then we can say that to speak "in the same way" means to follow the same set of rules. By the same definition, if my dialect differs from yours it means that my grammar contains some rules that are lacking in yours, or that it lacks some rules that your grammar contains, or both. A dialect, then, is just a particular set of rules that determines the form of an individual's speech sequences.

Let's look at an example of a dialect difference that illustrates this definition.

1. **A.** You stole some artichokes from me, you know.

   B. I did not.

   A. Oh yes you did. You stole some artichokes from me and you're gonna pay for it!

   B. You're crazy. I didn't steal any artichokes from you, and if you keep saying I did, *you're* the one who's gonna do the paying.

2.   A.   You stole some artichokes from me, you know.

    B.   I did not.

    A.   Oh yes you did .You stole some artichokes from me and you're gonna pay for it!

    B.   You're crazy. I didn't steal some artichokes from you, and if you keep saying I did, *you're* the one who's gonna do the paying.

The B speakers in these examples have dialects that differ in at least one rule. In example 1, speaker B has in his dialect a rule called the *Some-Any Rule,* which says that "some" is changed to "any" in negative sentences, as in the following pair:

3.   A.   I ate some peas.

    B.   I didn't eat any peas.

Speaker B in example 2, however, does not have the Some-Any Rule in his dialect, and says instead

4.   A.   I ate some peas.

    B.   I didn't eat some peas.

The dialect split here is not just a two-way matter, either. There is a third possibility:

5.   A.   I ate some peas.

    B.   I didn't eat no peas.

All three speakers have the same structure in the affirmative sentence—"I ate some peas." And all share much the same structure in their negative sentences—"I didn't eat _____ peas." But their rules for the choice of the word to fill the empty slot in the negative sentence are different. One chooses "some," one chooses "any," and the other chooses "no." We say, therefore, that these speakers represent three different dialects.

Dialects differ from one another in two basic areas:

1.   The sounds of a particular language sequence

2.   The order in which the various elements of that sequence are arranged

Table 10-1 shows you a number of the ways in which the sound systems of two English dialects differ from the hypothetical standard.

Table 10-1

San Antonio, Texas *Anglo* Speakers	Northeastern Urban Areas *Black* Speakers
1. /r/ becomes a vowel like "a" in "sofa" at the ends of words	**1.** /r/ is deleted when it occurs before a consonant or at the end of a word
2. the vowel represented by "a" in "cat" is pronounced with a "y-like" offglide	**2.** /l/ is frequently deleted by the same rule as /r/
3. the sound /ay/, like "uy" in "buy," loses its offglide and becomes an /a/, like "a" in "father"	**3.** /t/ and /d/ are dropped at the end of the word when they follow another consonant
4. many unstressed syllables, like the second syllable of "Dallas," are pronounced with the sound of "i" in "bit"	**4.** when a word ends in a consonant followed by /s/ or /z/, either the /s/ or /z/ or that consonant is dropped
5. words like "tune" and "new" are pronounced "tyune" and "nyew"	**5.** at the end of a word there is no difference between /th/ and /f/
	6. for many speakers the two diphthongs /ay/ (as in "buy") and /aw/ (as in "house") are pronounced like "ah"

If your immediate reaction to lists like the two in Table 10-1 is "so what?" you need to stop and think about what a systematic set of sound differences like these might mean in terms of its effect. This is not the same kind of difference as that seen in speakers who say "vittles" for "food" or "taters" for "potatoes." Such one-word differences are easily changed, since a speaker has no difficulty learning to substitute one word for another. But *sound* differences affect every word in the language containing the particular sound.

Let's consider a daily language activity that is the common experience of every American child—learning to read. The idea behind learning to read, the idea that our teachers go to much expense of time and effort to get across to us, is that there is some connection between the sounds we make as speakers and the marks we see on the page as readers. Thus, we learn that when we see the letter "b" it represents the sound "b-" that we make in "boy" and "book."

Every English-speaking child dealing with this situation must struggle with the amazing lack of correspondence between sight and sound in long lists of words like the following:

enough
bough
through
one
know
sword
lamb
sign
pneumonia
debt

The child who speaks Black English has not only *this* difficulty but a similar one multiply extended. He or she must learn to recognize "that's" and "best" as their own "thass" and "bess," along with a host of similar examples. "Four" and "here" must be recognized as "foah" and "heah." In addition, the number of homonyms (words spelled differently but sounding alike) is greatly increased for the Black English speaker. For example, in this dialect all of the following sets are pronounced as homonyms:

Paris	pass	past	
mend	men	meant	
fine	find	found	fond
bind	bound	bond	
toll	toe		
hold	hole		
death	deaf		
Ruth	roof		

That this is anything *but* a "so-what" difference in the daily lives of children speaking Black English is tragically reflected in the failure of such children to learn to read in our schools, the high dropout rate resulting from that inability, and finally in the unemployment statistics.

Linguists tell us that all dialects are equally "good" and equally "right." That is manifestly true and has been demonstrated beyond quesion. The unfortunate thing is that this truth, like a lot of other truths, is not reality but an abstraction. Dr. Leonard Newmark, a language specialist at the University of California, has frequently illustrated this by saying that there is nothing "bad" or "wrong" about eating your soup with a fork—it just doesn't *work*. There is nothing either "bad" or "wrong" about speaking Black English, Chicano English, Appalachian English, Brooklyn English,

Charleston English, or any other nonstandard dialect. But when it comes to getting a good job, or being accepted by a good graduate school, these dialects are like the fork mentioned by Dr. Newmark—they don't work.

One of the major controversies in education today is whether or not speakers of these dialects should be taught to speak the hypothetical "standard" English, by which we mean Prestige English, middle-class White English from a limited urban area of this country, in the same way that they might be taught to speak French or Chinese; that is, should we concede the impossibility of changing the socioeconomic standards to fit the child and try to change the child to fit the standards?

Educators who advocate such change are also assuming that it is *possible* for teachers in an ordinary classroom to eradicate these differences in the sound systems used by their students, a hypothesis that has yet to be tested. Any teacher who has struggled year after year to force her or his students to make a sound distinction between "pen" and "pin" and seen them graduate from high-school still saying "pin" in both cases will look at this Double-speak hypothesis with some skepticism.

TEACHER. Ferrabeau, there are times when I wonder if you're putting me on.

FERRABEAU. . . . .

Early in this unit we discussed a difference not in the sound system but in the syntax. This difference, which in speakers of Black English results in sentences like "I didn't eat no peas," has the same kind of socioeconomic results as saying "thass" for "that's" and "bof" for "both." And this is by no means the only syntactic difference between the two dialects. Look at the following examples:

SE	BE
He is sick.	He sick.
She is gone.	She gone.
He is swimming.	He swimming.
She is singing.	She singing.
He speaks French.	He speak French.
She runs fast.	She run fast.

You can see from looking at this data that where Prestige English demands a form of the verb "to be" between the subject of the sentence and a predicate like "sick" or "gone" or a progressive form like "swimming," Black English has no such rule. You will notice that this does not interfere with comprehension in any way, since the information contained in the verb "to be" is totally redundant. Many of the world's languages show the same structural pattern as does Black English where this use of "to be" is concerned, and it is clear that the "be" form is only necessary in the sense that it is decreed to be so by the prestige grammar.

Similarly, Black English does not mark the third person singular form of the present tense verb with an "-s" as Prestige English does. And, as in the previous example, the information conveyed by the "-s" is redundant. Since no English third person singular verb can appear without a third person singular subject, it is not possible to be confused as to whether the verb itself is third person singular; that is, nobody is ever going to wonder whether "he walk" refers to one person or to more than one, because the presence of "he" is sufficient to make that clear.

Nonetheless, the English speaker who says "he sick" or "he walk fast" suffers socioeconomic consequences that have nothing whatever to do with logic.

THE FUNCTIONS OF DIALECT

For a dialect to be truly "bad" or "wrong," it would have to be like the nonexistent "primitive language" mentioned in the first unit. It would have to be inadequate for the purposes for which language is used by native speakers. There would have to be things that could be said or written in other dialects, but that could not be said or written in the "bad" dialect. Let's take a look at some examples of writing from a number of dialects of English, and see whether (1) they show that the dialect is inadequate for expressing the meaning of the selection and (2) the selection could be improved by being rewritten in the prestige dialect.

The first example is from Harper Lee's Pulitzer Prize novel, *To Kill A Mockingbird*. The black man speaking is on trial for assaulting a white woman.

> I was goin' home as usual that evenin', an' when I passed the Ewell place Miss Mayella were on the porch, like she said she were. It seemed real quiet like, an' I didn't quite know why. I was studyin' why, just passin' by, when she says for me to come there and help her a minute. Well, I went inside the fence an' looked around for

some kindlin' to work on, but I didn't see none, and she says, 'Naw, I got somethin' for you to do in the house. Th' old door's off its hinges an' fall's comin' on pretty fast.' I said you got a screwdriver, Miss Mayella? She said she sho' had. Well, I went up the steps an' she motioned me to come inside, and I went in the front room an' looked at the door. I said Miss Mayella, this door look all right. I pulled it back'n forth and those hinges was all right. Then she shet the door in my face. Mr. Finch, I was wonderin' why it was so quiet like, an' it come to me that there weren't a chile on the place, not a one of 'em, and I said Miss Mayella, where the chillun?

Would it have improved this speech if it had begun "I was going home as usual that evening and when I passed the Ewell home Miss Mayella was on the porch, as she has said that she was. It seemed very quiet, and I didn't quite know why. I was wondering about that, as I passed by, when she said that I should come and help her." Would the improvement in communication have been sufficient to keep this man from being hung for a crime he did not commit? Would the speech have been more powerful, more moving, more effective esthetically, if it had been in the prestige dialect?

How about the following example, from the recorded speech of Aunt Arie Carpenter in the *Foxfire Book.* Could you "improve" it by rewriting it in prestige-style English?

It's a whole lot easier today. I've hoed corn many a day fer a quarter. *Many a day.* An' we used t'pick huckleberries, me'n m'brother did, an' swap two gallons a'huckleberries fer one gallon a'syrup. Had t'do somethin' t'make a livin'. But we always had plenty t'eat. We always had plenty a'what we had. We didn't have no great stuff that cost a lot. We never did buy that. Well, we just didn't have nothin'tpay fer't, an' we always tried t'pay as we went. You know, if y'get goin' in debt, next thing y'know you can't pay it t'save yore life. I'm scared t'death a debts. I owe fer this road now, an' it worries me t'death. Used t'be I didn't have enough money t'mail a letter with. An' you know how much candy I bought in my life 'fore I's married? I bought one nickel's worth a'candy in my life. I just didn't have nothin' t'buy *with.* Poppy hired a girl t'stay with Mommy 'til I got big enough t'do th'work, an' y'know how much he'd have t'pay? Seventy-five cents a week. They'd work all week fer seventy-five cents.

Do you think that Mark Twain's book, *Tom Sawyer,* would have been improved if the English in it had been "cleaned up and corrected"?

This is the sort of point that need not be belabored, surely. The nonstandard dialects of English, whether they be black, white, red, yellow, or green, have a quality of vivid *life* that makes them powerful and beautiful, and to "eradicate" them from our culture would be to impoverish our language, not to purify it.

ACADEMIC ENGLISH

We will end this chapter by taking a look at a kind of English that *might* profitably be eliminated, just to see what the possibilities for killing all the good things in a language are. The next example is not from a dialect, but rather a specific *style* of English. When a style of speaking becomes associated with a specific role of the speaker—for example, when a child learns to say "He is good" at school but continues to say "He good" at home—we call that style a *register*. The following selection represents a particular register.

> A significant number of the relevant factors which must be taken into consideration in order to achieve those behavioral objectives selected for optimum maximization in the subject areas (see above) exhibit tendencies whose primary pragmatic effect is an inverse function of the economic stability of the target population. Isolation of such factors tends to proliferate in those sectors where the profitability of conformity has been demonstrated through the application of known laws of demographic confluence and their accepted correlates, the enumeration of which can safely be glossed over in view of their familiarity to the scholar and the sociologist.

This particular selection is not a quote; it is an example constructed by this writer, who is able to go on like that for pages and pages and pages. If the selection has any meaning at all, it is an accident. This is the *academic* register, and is all too often used primarily for one of the following reasons:

1. Anything written by a scholar in clear and comprehensible English would be looked upon by other scholars as trivial.

2. The writer has very little to say and has learned from experience that a very little goes a long way when written in this register.

3. The writer really has nothing to say, but feels obliged to publish something anyway.

This should not be taken to mean that there are not good and sufficient reasons for using polysyllabic words and a learned vocabulary. There are times when the word "pragmatic" is the precise and only word to use. It would be a great step forward, however, if the scholar would wait for those times to come along.

As things stand today, it is very difficult to write a scholarly article or a textbook in anything *but* the academic register, because of the pressure of the academician's peers. That is, just as the street child will suffer peer pressure if he insists on saying "I beg your pardon, are you ready to leave?" instead of "Hey, man, you ready to split?", so will the scholar suffer such pressure if he tries valiantly to say "we know" instead of "a consensus of scholarly opinion would seem to indicate a significant probability that . . ."

This is particularly unfortunate because most of the language a student has to deal with in school is written in this academic register and it often sets up an almost impenetrable communications barrier. The student who wades through five paragraphs of sentences bristling with long and unusual words, intricate clauses, extra material in parentheses and footnotes, sections in foreign languages, and with every other sentence written as a passive rather than an active, has good reason to be outraged when he finds out that the same thing could have been said in half a dozen straightforward words. The appropriate reaction is—and should be—*Why on earth didn't he say just* that *instead of all this gobbledygook?"*

We might just look at one of the standard language phenomena of academic language to see what lies behind it and whether there is really a reason for it. Let's take one of the characteristics mentioned above—the passive—and see why it is so overpoweringly common in the academic register.

An ordinary English active sentence has the order Subject-Verb-Object, as in the following sentence:

1. Phyllis ate the pickle.

A passive sentence, on the other hand, alters this order to Object-Verb-Subject, resulting in

2. The pickle was eaten by Phyllis.

The ordinary reason for doing this sort of thing lies in the fact that the subject position in an English sentence is assumed by native speakers to contain the part of the sentence you really want to emphasize. Given no other information (such as a heavy stress on some other word, for example) an English speaker who hears "Phyllis ate the pickle" assumes that the speaker is primarily interested in talking about Phyllis. If the speaker really wants to talk about the pickle instead, the second sentence is one of the common and appropriate ways to convey this information. But what about a sentence like the following:

3. Particle X has been proposed as the most likely reason for the strange behavior of the chemical.

It may be that the speaker wishes to emphasize Particle X over the chemical in question. But it is even more likely that this

---

Q. Last night a flaming red sky in the north could be seen from every part of the United States. Also last night, millions of Americans saw on all three networks the mile-high figure of an angel with a sword in his right hand. Do you feel that the term "alleged apparition" is still the proper language for this?

A. I'm not authorized to change the language of the announcement.

Q. Is the White House aware of the possibility that the apparition may spell the end of the world?

A. It seems to me that the use of alarmist language is counterproductive in this situation.

PETER BERGER
from "The Briefing"

---

is an example of the academic passive. The problem here is that scholars, who often know a remarkable lot, are supposed to *pretend* that they know very little. This is a kind of academic good manners, like pretending not to notice when someone belches at the table. It makes no difference that the scholar who wrote sentence 3 is the world's foremost authority on the behavior of the mentioned chemical and particle; it makes no difference that every individual in his field recognizes him as such an authority and knows that if anyone's knowledge about these items is reliable, his is. Nonetheless, he *may not say* the following sentence instead of sentence 3:

4. Particle X is the most likely reason for the strange behavior of the chemical.

Worse yet would be:

5. One thing I know for sure is that Particle X is the reason for the strange behavior of the chemical.

Once in a great while this can be done, but if it happens very often the writer is—in the academic sense—belching again and again and again, and pressure will be exerted to remove him from the academic table.

Does this seem odd to you? It may seem more familiar if we take it out of the academic context for just a moment. Look at the following sentence:

6. Laundry is placed in the hampers at the end of the hall.

This is the "military" or "summer-camp" passive. It has the same purpose as the academic passive; it is there to allow the speaker to disclaim all responsibility for what he or she is saying. It is a way of saying "Look, *I'm* not the one giving you guys this order, it just came from somewhere and I'm stuck with passing it along." It is a way of saying "after all, we all know you people are adults, and of *course* no one is going to try to order you around." A quick switch to the passive follows.

7. These suggestions are made for your own safety.

The same sort of problem of manners lies behind the use of such stuff as "this writer believes" for "I believe." In the same way that it is unmannerly to announce your own discoveries, it is unmannerly, in a sequence of academic writing, to say "I."

Is there anything that you, as a student, can do about all this? Probably not. So long as your texts are chosen for you, and so long as academic fashions remain unchanged, you will have little chance of changing textbook language into everyday English. What you can do, however, is become skilled at quickly translating the stuff into everyday English form as you read it. You can learn not to be impressed by it, just because long words and ponderous grammar *look* as if they signalled something of major importance. When you find a paragraph in a text that turns out, after translation, to be nonsense, you can write to the author of that text in care of his or her publisher and complain as loudly and as lengthily as you feel inclined. The knowledge that students are actually bothering to interpret the scholarly paragraph with a view not to pleasing the instructor but to determine whether the paragraph itself is worth reading might come as a real shock to some of the perpetrators of academese. It might even give the poor writer some kind of backing when he or she tries for the umpteenth time to drop the academic register and aim for clarity rather than mystification.

EXERCISES

1. One of the activities of the American Dialect Society has been the preparation of dialect maps like those in the following extract, which show the geographical distribution of particular words —for example, the use of "movies" versus "picture show." Nowadays such maps are not as useful as they once were, because of the extreme mobility of Americans and their wide exposure to the language of the mass media. The days when a man might spend his whole life within a geographical radius of three or four hundred miles, and never hear any dialect other than his own, are over. However, there are still many words which are characteristic of particular areas, even though they may no longer be the only word a speaker uses to convey a given meaning.

Do you think that dialect differences of this kind—differences in particular lexical items—are as significant as the differences in sound and syntax? Would they be easier to eradicate than the differences in sound and syntax? Write a brief paper explaining your position on this matter.

2. Look at the first list of words on page 198. For most of these words (all but the word "sign") the difference between their sound and their written shape has a historical explanation. Choose three of these words and find out what this historical explanation is.

3. You may feel that almost everyone in your class speaks the same dialect of English. To check your judgment, ask everyone in the class the following questions, and then tabulate the answers:

    a. Do the following pairs of words rhyme?
      star/war
      Mary/berry
      hoarse/coarse
      leg/plague
      barn/corn
      often/soften
    b. Do the following pairs sound the same or different?

knotty/naughty
sot/sought
cot/caught
tot/taught

    c. Are the following sentences grammatical?
       (1) John was shot by himself.
       (2) Mary told Bill that shaving himself would be difficult.
       (3) Tabs were kept on the students by the FBI.
       (4) Which hat did you believe the rumour that Tricky Tom wore?

    d. What does the following sentence mean?
    Not all of the rabbits were brown.

    4. How do you feel about the idea that all American children should be taught to speak Prestige English, even if it is only a second dialect for them? (That is, even if they use it only as a register.) This is a difficult question; try to think of at least three valid reasons for your position on the matter instead of writing five paragraphs of vague emotional wanderings. Look up the word *polemic* and be sure you don't write one of those.

    5. Can you isolate the various registers in which you normally speak or write? Describe each one in terms of (1) when or where you switch to it; (2) how it differs from your other registers in sound, syntax, and/or lexical items; and (3) where you think you acquired it—at home, school, or somewhere else.

    6. In some societies it is possible to speak of "men's language" and "women's language," either because the two are very different or because a particular area of the language is obligatorily restricted to one sex or the other. Many American Indian languages have systematic language differences based on sex; for example, in Lakota Sioux the word that ends an interrogative sentence is different for men and for women. Do you think that American English has any separation of language into such sexual areas? Is it possible to determine someone's sex just by reading a transcription of his or her speech? Write a brief essay either (a) describing a phenomenon that seems to you to be sexually determined language or (b) explaining why you feel that no such phenomenon exists for American English.

    7. Look at the following quotation from Douglas Bush's article "Polluting Our Language":

We know that language is always changing and growing (and

also, in a much smaller degree, shrinking), but acceptance of the perpetual process does not or should not mean blind surrender to the momentum or inertia of slovenly and tasteless ignorance and insensitivity. Ideally, changes should be inaugurated from above, by the masters of language (as they often have been), not from below.

There is of course an undefined-terms problem here, since "above" and "below" are given without any kind of explanation other than that among those who are above are the "masters of language"—presumably educated scholars and writers. However, you can probably do a good job of determining what is meant by these terms from the vocabulary and tone of the paragraph. How do you feel about the views expressed by Mr. Bush? Write a paper of about 600 words either supporting or arguing against his position.

8. In order to achieve the goal expressed by Mr. Bush in the preceding exercise, France has a formal organization called a language *academy,* whose official function is to authorize change in the French language, hold back unauthorized change, rule on the suitability of new words, and so on. Assume that the U.S. Congress has created an American English Academy to do these same things in this country. You, as a taxpayer, consider such an academy a grotesque waste of your money. Write a letter to your congressman explaining your objection and demanding that the AEA be dissolved at once, if not sooner.

9. You will remember that in an earlier unit we talked about "body language" and various systems of gestures. Do you think that body language also has dialects? For example, are the gestures and body movements of a surfer different from those of a bank executive, or does it depend on the individual? Do body language dialects exist for various age groups or ethnic groups? If you think they do, try to isolate and describe one such dialect.

10. It has frequently been proposed that an individual's effectiveness in communication depends as much upon his or her body language as upon the actual words used. It seems logical that if this is true it would matter greatly for the effectiveness of teachers. Observe at least three of your instructors' body language carefully for a week and take detailed notes. Do they seem to exhibit a "teaching dialect" of body language? Or perhaps a "teaching register?" (That is, do they use a system of body language in the classroom that they do not seem to use in other social settings?) Do you see any particular kind of body language as characteristic of a "bad" . teacher or a "good" teacher? Explain your answer carefully.

11. In *You and Your Language,* Charlton Laird talks about a dialect phenomenon as follows:

> Consider the word *bull.* It designates a common farm animal, but perhaps for reasons of modesty many other words have often been used to designate the creature.

He then goes on to list a number of these words—*top cow, top ox, top steer, critter, male cow, beast, male beast, stock beast, brute, male brute, stock brute, male cow, ox steer,* and *masculine* pronounced to rhyme with *mine.* Given the fact that when a speaker from Vermont or New Hampshire says *top ox* he, as well as everyone listening to him, knows perfectly well that *top ox* is equivalent to *bull,* what do you think is the function of such a substitution? Write a brief statement explaining your position.

Rules from *The Grammar of Jargon*

ROBERT WADDELL

Nouns

1. Never use a concrete noun in its original concrete sense.

2. Use one of the Ten Basic Nouns of Jargon in every sentence, if possible. The Ten Basic Nouns are: *aspect, case, character, condition, factor, feature, instance, nature, phase, situation.*

Verbs

3. Avoid verbs wherever possible: for example use *prior to the Vanderpool committee investigation* rather than *before the Vanderpool committee investigated.*

4. In the main sentence, where a verb is unavoidable, use the most colorless verbal construction. Use *to be* as much as possible. Never say, for example, *believe* or *emphasize;* use *have the belief* or *put the emphasis on.*

5. Use all transitive verbs in the passive voice. Avoid mentioning the agent who performs the action, that is, the subject of the active voice.

6. Always use vaporized common verbs in a vague abstract sense, never in the original concrete sense. For example: this situation *arises* . . . ; religion *was begun* by man as a solution for . . . ; devaluation *will bring* or *make for* better trade relations . . . ; the field *embraces* both electronics and chemistry . . . ; factors *provide* or *give rise to* a new outlook . . . ; radar *falls under* the heading of electronics; *speed* moral reorientation; *build* confidence.

7. Where verbs are unavoidable, use dignified latinate terms; avoid vulgar informality. Use *state* for *say*, *imbibe* for *drink*, *ensue* for *follow*, and so on.

8. Avoid using simple adjectives in the vulgar manner. Whenever possible use nouns instead of prepositional phrases. For example, *psychological research* is flat and tasteless; prefer *psychology research* or *research of a psychological character*.

9. Avoid placing adjectives before the nouns they modify; put them after the nouns in prepositional phrases: e.g., *of a detrimental nature*. Avoid simple adjectives as complements: turn them into prepositional phrases. (The quarrel was *of a feudal rather than a religious nature*), or turn them into noun objects of colorless verbs (e.g., the presentation *has compactness*; not *is compact*).

10. Always insert the category of modification to which a simple adjective complement belongs: e.g., rectangular *in shape*; efficient *in operation*; steel blue *in color*; gigantic *in size*. Otherwise, the reader has to pause to figure this out.

11. Avoid using nouns in old-fashioned prepositional phrases to modify other nouns. Place them directly before the other nouns like old-style adjectives: *economy purposes*; *control method*; *competition sphere*; *transportation facilities*; *personality traits*; *population increase*; *situation significance*; *group situation*; *air worthiness requirements*.

Connectives

12. Avoid old-fashioned simple connectives like *because, before, of,* or *as.* Always prefer *due to the fact that, prior to, in connection with, in a manner similar to,* and similar forms.

About the language outlined in this grammar of jargon, there are three or four things we may observe. The first is the heavy preponderance of nouns (the list of nouns in jargon could be extended almost indefinitely beyond the vocabulary given above; the list of verbs and adjectives could not). Many of the verbs and adjectives are only the same nouns in

different grammatical functions. And all abstract! Jargon does not dramatize or describe anything concretely. It is concerned only to name and
label things and then to indicate, very foggily, certain kinds of relations
between them.

These relations constitute the second point worth noticing—the
pseudoscientific air of jargon. Most of the vocabulary is concerned with
four apparently technical but really very simple, even basic, ideas or
ways of thinking.

1. Many of the words indicate little more than mere occurrence
or nonoccurrence: *absence, presence, appearance, condition, data,
element, fact, item, lack, phenomenon, situation, state; is, exist,
enter in, lie in, occur, eliminate; apparent, essential, positive.*

2. Another group is devoted to classification: *category, class, area,
field, line, character, nature, orientation, phase, role; classify, com-
prise, include, embrace, typify, fall under.*

3. A large group is used for measurement of one sort or another:
*addition, decrease, increase, extent, level, majority, maximum, rate;
add, approximate, balance, culminate, precede, outweigh; broad,
great, initial, moderate, outstanding, partial, predominant, primary,
superior, ultimate.*

4. A fourth group is devoted to what we shall here call abstract
lubrication: Do the factors in a case slither together in a comfort-
ing way? Then use words like *adjustment, aid, function, influence,
medium, motivation, solution, trend, assist, effectuate, facilitate,
expedite, ensure, maintain, make for, result, utilize; adequate,
available, efficient, favorable, feasible, satisfactory.* But if things
are not so satisfactory, tack *dis-, in-, mal-, non-,* or *un-* onto the
same words. The only sign of life in jargon is this unctuous, flabby,
mush-mouthed eagerness that everything shall be, in a broad general way, smooth and well greased. Nobody has to work for anything; things simply *tend, function, combine,* and *result in.* Everything must turn out to be *easy, available,* and *expedient*—or at very
least *favorable* or *adequate.*

These four ways of thinking—take them honestly—are important
and even essential to any kind of thought whatever, especially to scientific thought, which specializes in them. But in jargon none of them are
actually performed in a precise or illuminating manner. They are only
blurrily suggested; jargon goes vaguely through the motions. It all sounds
very technical, and there is much clatter and hum from what we are
meant to believe is scientific machinery. But the scientific results are very

meagre. And so are any other results. Jargon is quite without means of suggesting much about color, tone, or visible motion. It cannot deal vividly with feeling, temper, opinion, or personality. It cannot indicate relations in simple, exact, or familiar terms, and it is helpless to cope with precise details. The universe of jargon is a dusty, gray, general fog, in which various factors may be said to exist. Jargon is concerned only to assert this existence and to classify it (more or less), and check the oil.

A third characteristic of jargon is its verbal inefficiency. It never uses one word where three or four will do. It never says *if*, it says *in the event that*; it never says *because*, it says *due to the fact that*; it does not say *in, by, of, for,* or *about*, it says *in connection with* and *with respect to*. These phrases are not only several times longer than the English equivalents but also much less precise. Jargon seldom commits itself to any single meaning in particular; instead it evasively alludes to any meaning that is vaguely relevant or possible in the context. The heavily worked phrases *for the most part* and *in many cases* (or *instances*) are examples of this inclusive ambiguity:

> *For the most part* college students have little trouble in getting rides. [Does this mean *most students* have little trouble? Or that *students usually* have little trouble? It means neither—not exactly. The writer couldn't make up his mind. It means both—more or less.]
>
> Engineers in the past have failed *in many instances* in designing the highway for speed and safety. [*Many engineers? Engineers have often?*]
>
> Experimenters in the past, in treating heat transfer from vapor to cooling water, have devoted their efforts to steam and water, *with the exception of a very few cases*. [Cases of what? experimenters? efforts? steam and water? And what would any of these mean anyway?]

The single verbal economy that jargon can boast of is the plentiful use of nouns as adjectives, which cuts down on prepositions. But the saving in words is lost many times over through clumsiness and obscurity. The use of noun-adjectives is common in English (*stone* wall, *morning* paper, *business* letter, etc.), but it is usually confined to relatively short nouns, and the relation between noun-adjective and noun modified is usually clear and simple (time, place, purpose, composition, etc.). But in jargon, the longer the noun-adjective the better; and its relation to the noun modified can be anything—or, better yet, everything. Consider the sociologist's phrase *happiness adjustment*. Does this mean adjustment *to* happiness? *in* happiness? *for* happiness? or what? It means none of these, and all of them. It means, with beautifully sweeping vagueness, *adjustment in connection with happiness*.

A fourth, and pitiful, characteristic of jargon is its shuffling pace and arhythmic gait. Since a sentence in jargon is almost nothing but nouns, noun-adjectives, and other noun constructions strung together with relatively meaningless connectives (and somewhere or other at least an *is* among them to make things grammatically legal), there is little reason for it to stop anywhere in particular; it can pad itself out rearward with *in relation to*'s, and other prepositional phrases until it runs out of breath. Since such a sentence is never trying to dramatize anything and since almost everything in it is as emphatic as everything else, there is no need for it to have a special shape, length, or pattern. Its parts are not very clearly distinguishable. Its subordinate clauses, for example, rarely begin with simple subordinate conjunctions like *since* or *before*, but rather with long prepositional phrases like *in view of the fact that* which looks simply like more nouns and prepositions among the many nouns and prepositions already in the sentence. Or the clause becomes a noun construction—*prior to the committee's investigation of the charge* instead of *before the committee investigated the charge*. Its precious noun-adjective is its only change of pace. It sometimes likes to pile up three or four of them, as we might in a parody of the sociologist's phrase mentioned above: *pre-high school age group happiness adjustment factors*. Slap something like this into the middle of the ordinary sentence in jargon and the sentence is galvanized into a series of spastic mechanical jerks, very welcome after the somnolent slow plodding of the paragraphs or pages preceding. . . .

Language like this, besides being feeble and obscure, is morally reprehensible because it is irresponsible. For jargon, which lacks all sharpness, clarity, and force, is beautifully designed, as George Orwell points out, "to make lies sound truthful and murder respectable, and to give an appearance of solidity to pure wind." * The apprentice writer who imitates it through laziness, incompetence, or gullibility, has of course no thought of murder or of any deception, but in using it he casts his vote for deceptive vagueness, abstract inhumanity, graceless bad manners, and confusion of thought. He becomes in effect a support and a willing listener to those who use this sort of language to bulldoze

* "Politics and the English Language," *New Republic*, June 17, 1946. Orwell illustrates the respectability of murder as follows: "Consider for instance some comfortable English professor defending Russian totalitarianism. He cannot say outright, 'I believe in killing off your opponents when you can get good results by doing so.' Probably, therefore, he will say something like this: 'While freely conceding that the Soviet regime exhibits certain features which the humanitarian may be inclined to deplore, we must, I think, agree that a certain curtailment of the right to political opposition is an unavoidable concomitant of transitional periods, and that the rigors which the Russian people have been called upon to undergo have been amply justified in the sphere of concrete achievement.'"

and deceive; through him the muddy vagueness spreads. For as Orwell continues, "an effect can become a cause, reinforcing the original cause and producing the same effect in intensified form, and so on indefinitely. A man may take to drink because he feels himself to be a failure, and then fail all the more completely because he drinks. It is rather the same thing that is happening to the English language. It becomes ugly and inaccurate because our thoughts are foolish, but the slovenliness of our language makes it easier for us to have foolish thoughts. The point is that the process is reversible. Modern English, especially written English, is full of bad habits which spread by imitation and which can be avoided if one is willing to take the necessary trouble. If one gets rid of these habits one can think more clearly, and to think more clearly is a necessary first step towards political regeneration; so that the fight against bad English is not frivolous and is not the exclusive concern of professional writers."

The writer who writes well writes like himself. For the apprentice writer this means first of all sorting himself out from the anonymous public background, examining the scene about him and his own manifold relations to it, judging his own and others' values, accepting, rejecting, changing his mind, but always trying to see the object as it really is to him—which may or may not have anything to do with what it is generally said to be.

His first writing about these preliminary efforts may be plain, bald, and inadequate, but if it is honest it will display individuality and perhaps even a blunt charm. With practice this individuality becomes clearer and more assured. This is not to say that the writer need be concerned at all with "expressing himself" all over the page; the writer entirely preoccupied with himself is more often than not a bore; there are other subjects. It is in attempting to report accurately his own observations and convictions and in honestly trying to make others see and agree that the writer's personality most naturally and pleasingly exhibits itself —quite by the way—as a kind of unearned increment to the rewards of writing honestly—as style, in a word, or the beginnings of style.

The man who can write a decent informal style can with a little patience develop a responsible formal style, and his example may encourage others—to the vast improvement of our intellectual, moral, and political thinking. Oceans of bilge by and for the intellectually limited and the irresponsible will continue to surround us. Which provides all the more reason for the honest and intelligent to cultivate accuracy in observation, lucidity and force in statement, and good manners in persuasion.

American Dialects Today

Finding the Dialect Areas of American English

Dialectologists record on maps the pronunciations, words, and grammatical forms which they find in an area. These items are represented by various symbols. Map 1, a map of several Eastern states, illustrates this procedure. The circles indicate the communities investi-

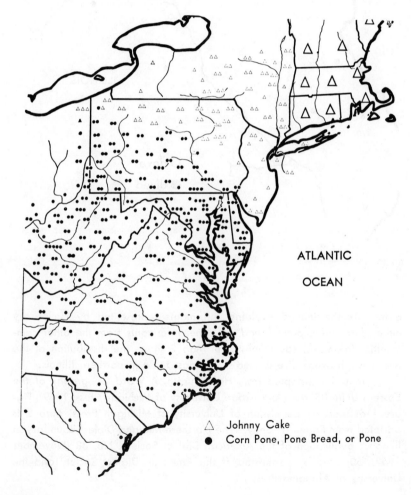

△ Johnny Cake
● Corn Pone, Pone Bread, or Pone

ATLANTIC

OCEAN

Map 1

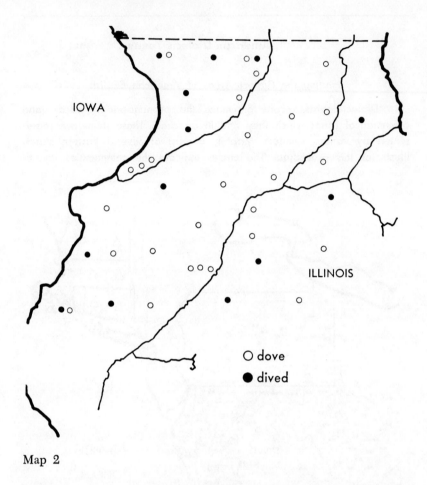

Map 2

gated. As the legend explains, informants represented by circles say either *corn pone, pone bread,* or *pone.* Informants from the other communities (triangles) say *johnnycake.* Map 2 shows the distribution of the two ways the verb *dive* is used in the past tense in northern Illinois.

[Map 1 is adapted from Hans Kurath, *A Word Geography of the Eastern United States* (Ann Arbor: University of Michigan Press, 1949), Figure 116; used by permission of University of Michigan Press. Map 2 is adapted from Roger W. Shuy, "The Northern-Midland Dialect Boundary in Illinois," publication of the American Dialect Society, No. 38 (November 1962), 50; used by permission of the American Dialect Society and the University of Alabama Press.]

The Validity of Black English and What to Do about It

J. L. DILLARD

Significant research on Black English in the United States is almost entirely a product of the 1960s. In this decade a group of linguists, freed of preconceptions about the geographic provenience of American dialects, has shown that Negro Nonstandard English is different in grammar (in syntax) from the Standard American English of the mainstream white culture. They maintain that there are sources for varieties of English elsewhere than in the British regional dialects. Like the West Indian varieties, American Black English can be traced to a creolized version of English based upon a pidgin spoken by slaves; it probably came from the West Coast of Africa.

The grammar of Black English is so similar to that of certain other Afro-American varieties of English that the temptation to look for historical connections has been irresistible to the small band of linguists who have interested themselves in the problem. But the most immediate solution that suggests itself—direct influence from the African languages spoken by the slaves—proves to be too simple and is made to seem unlikely by the language-mixing practices of the slave dealers.

For the mixing of African language groups, we have the evidence of statements like that of slave ship Captain William Smith in 1744:

As for the languages of *Gambia,* they are so many and so different, that the Natives, on either Side the River, cannot understand each other: which, if rightly considered, is no small Happiness to the *Europeans* who go thither to trade for slaves . . . I have known some melancholy Instances of whole Ship Crews being surpriz'd, and cut off by them. But the safest Way is to trade with the different Nations, on either Side the River, and having some of every Sort on board, there will be no more Likelihood of their succeeding in a Plot, than of finishing the Tower of Babel.

(A New Voyage to Guinea)

Thus, language mixing developed after some of the crews learned the hard way that the Africans did not welcome being enslaved. It therefore seems entirely probable that some of the earliest slave ships contained relatively homogeneous linguistic groups. In some cases the circumstances of slave trading brought further mixing after the arrival of the slaves in the New World. In other cases slave buyers came to prefer

Africans from specific tribes and areas, and the language mixing practiced on the slave ships was counteracted in the markets of the Americas.
Consequently, African languages survived in the New World for a time.

Although many of the slaves may not have had to relinquish their
African languages immediately, they all found themselves in a situation
in which they had to learn an auxiliary language in a hurry in order
to establish communication in the heterogeneous groups into which they
were thrown. This mixing of speakers of a large number of languages,
with no one language predominant, is the perfect condition for the
spread of a pidgin language, which is in a sense the ultimate in auxiliary
languages.

It is often maintained that a pidgin is a simple language, and this
may be accurate in a way that is all to the credit of the pidgin. It is
designed to be used by diverse linguistic groups. It tends to "lose" or
"rid itself of" (whichever expression you prefer, since both are meta-
phorical) the more finicky, trivial features of language. Pidgin French
doesn't have all those troublesome masculine and feminine forms for
adjectives, and Pidgin English doesn't have all those irksome irregular
verbs. In more important language features—like the formation of questions, commands, subordinated sentence patterns and even in the potential for sentence complexity—a pidgin is very like any other language. It
may come to be used primarily for trade, since it is used entirely with
outsiders. And nobody gets sentimental or emotional about a pidgin or
rebukes you for misusing his language. Since children do not grow up
using it, it is a language primarily for adults.

When the African slaves produced children, there was no one
African language that those children could use with their peer group.
Even though the mothers (or fathers) spoke African languages and may
in some cases have taught them to their offspring, the children would have
found little use for those languages. With their playmates they would
have used the common language—in some cases Pidgin English, which
is classified as a creole as soon as it has such native speakers. (Gullah,
or "Geechee," of the South Carolina—Georgia Sea Islands, survives in
the creole stage today.) English Creole now acquires developmental forms,
since there are young children who are learning to speak it. People can
now become sentimental or emotional about it, since it is "their" language.
It fills all the purposes of the normal speech community, including different styles and different modes associated with greater or lesser prestige.
Vocabulary needs ("deficiencies") will be made up by borrowing from
other languages, from Standard English or from the African languages
of the adults, just as it's done with all other languages. The creole is
now a full-fledged language like any other. It just happens to have a
pidgin in its ancestry.

Since statements like the above are not usually made except by specialists in pidgin and creole languages, we do not expect to find a document saying "West African Pidgin English completed the creolization process in Blacksburg, Virginia, on April 2, 1698" or anything to that effect. Drawing historical conclusions requires a certain amount of ingenuity on the part of the language historian, including, one hopes, an ability to interpret the statements of nonprofessionals. Perhaps the very first such statement helpful to the historian of Black English is the reference to the use of English on the West Coast of Africa in a Portuguese text of 1594. In view of the general conditions of the West African slave trade, it seems reasonable to believe that Pidgin English was in use in the slave trade by the beginning of the seventeenth century, if not slightly earlier. Its chief competitor was Pidgin Portuguese, which almost certainly antedated it by at least a few years and which had an amazing worldwide spread during the sixteenth, seventeenth and eighteenth centuries. The English-based pidgins have a certain amount of vocabulary (*pickaninny*, for example) from the Portuguese Trade Pidgin, and those forms of Afro-American English that have undergone least decreolization (Saramaccan, in Surinam) have the greatest amount of Portuguese vocabulary.

Slaves coming to the New World by 1620 must have had some means of communicating with their masters and among themselves. A little reflection will show that the latter is probably the more important consideration. Spokesmen could be appointed who would convey the orders of the master to the great masses of slaves, and the spokesmen may have been more or less fluent in the language of the masters. But the masses of slaves still had to communicate among themselves and with the spokesmen, and a lingua franca or the European language of the masters constituted almost the only alternatives. Since there is an abundance of documentary evidence that they did not use the latter, it follows that they must have had some language of wider communication—the job for which a pidgin is eminently qualified. The surviving texts of the speech of slaves corroborate the hypothesis that Pidgin English was the language of the masses of slaves in what is now the continental United States. The early evidence suggests that it was as widespread in the northern states as in the South.

These were the beginnings. Today the best evidence we have—and it is admittedly incomplete—indicates that approximately 80 percent of the black population of the United States speaks Black English. (*Black population*, in this case, would mean all those who consider themselves to be members of the "black" or "Negro" community.) There are others who speak the same dialect; for example, many members of the Puerto Rican community in New York City have learned Black English in addition to Puerto Rican Spanish. In the past, there were many white speakers of the black variety of English, especially among the southern plantation-owning class. At an earlier period, the pidgin stage of Black English spread to the Seminoles and to other Indian tribes. But, in the twentieth century, this particular dialect came to be identified almost exclusively with the black community.

APPENDIX:
SOURCE PARAGRAPHS

The following source paragraphs should be used as material for writing papers of any length or type that you choose. They are from many different publications and on numerous topics.

1. It should now be a truism that everyone uses language, in some shape or form. What might be less obviously a truism is that quite a large proportion of the time dedicated to language-using could have been spent a lot more satisfactorily.

DAVID CRYSTAL

Linguistics, Language and Religion
Hawthorn Books, N.Y., 1965. p. 116.

2. Seventy feet under the surface of suburban Rochester, N.Y.—unknown to most of the residents living above—a massive mole is eating its way through the earth. It's been down there since spring of last year, and right now should be under Thomas' Creek. It's chewing its way through 5½ miles of hard siltstone and shale, leaving an 18-foot sewage tunnel in its wake. . . . It can chew its way through up to 100 feet of hard rock a day, and through more than twice as much softer rock (the record is 403 feet). You can tunnel without surface-blast vibration or fumes. It's safer, too, and it gives a nice smooth hole as well.

ROBERT GANNON

"Deep in the Earth with the Monster Moles"
Popular Science, 8/73. p. 84

3. Perversely, men have always valued their poor—valued them enough to insure that they will be numerous. And men have always punished their prophets. This is because the poor and the prophet force others to look at themselves in different mirrors, the former showing men as they are, the latter as they can be. Since both reflections are painful, both are hated, along with those who show them. When men no longer use their poor to exalt their own egos, when they no longer destroy their prophets, then justice will have come to the poor, and prophecy will be as treasured as power is now. Having banished the ancient call to strife and blood, man can begin to compete in love and service. Then we will begin to live.

PHILIP BERRIGAN
Prison Journals of a Priest Revolutionary
Ballantine Books, N.Y., 1970. p. 103.

4. A biological community is the collection of organisms that live in a given area. An ecosystem is a community taken together with the physical surroundings with which it exchanges nutrients and energy. People familiar with an Eastern deciduous forest, Western chaparral, or tropical rain forest know that these collections of different kinds of plants, animals, and microorganisms will persist for long periods of time if not destroyed by fire, bulldozing, or some other form of catastrophe. The stability of these biological communities is in sharp contrast to the instability of those in man-made agricultural ecosystems. As farmers and gardeners are only too aware, stands of a single crop require constant attention if they are to survive. It is accepted among ecologists that, in general, complexity leads to stability in ecological systems and simplicity produces instability.

PAUL R. EHRLICH AND JOHN P. HOLDREN
"The Negative Animal"
Saturday Review, 6/5/71. p. 58.

5. There are many stories to be told about the way black newspapers get started, from the most famous of them, how John H. Johnson started *Negro Digest* by mortgaging his mother's furniture to raise five hundred dollars for an advertising campaign, to the story of James H. Anderson's starting the *Amsterdam News* with, according to newspaper historian James Booker, "a dream in mind, $10 in his pocket, six sheets of paper and two pencils." All of these stories, however, document the fact that it takes money to start a

newspaper or to buy a radio or TV station, and that money, for the most part, is precisely what black people haven't got.

RICHARD G. HATCHER
"Mass Media and the Black Community"
Black Scholar, 5/1. pp. 2–10.

6. Here's how don Juan explained it to me. In the rearrangement of the world, nothing as it stands is 'real.' You see, what I'm perceiving right now is really a recollection of what you were a fraction of a second ago.

CARLOS CASTANEDA, TO GWYNETH CRAVENS
"Talking to Power and Spinning With the Ally"
Harper's, 2/73. pp. 91–94.

7. Q: This unending work to be done—does it flow from the need to communicate, into an indeterminate end product? Or do you start each project with a specific idea and then try to translate it?

Angelou: It starts with a definite subject, but it might end with something entirely different. When I start any project, the first thing I do is write down, in longhand, everything I know about the subject, every thought I've ever had on the subject. This may be 12 or 14 pages. Then I read it back through, for quite a few days, and find—given that subject—what its rhythm is. 'Cause everything in the universe has a rhythm. So if it's free form, it still has a rhythm. And once I hear the rhythm of the piece, then I try to find out what are the salient points that I must make in the piece. And then it begins to take shape.

MAYA ANGELOU
in an interview by Sheila Weller, "Work in Progress"
Intellectual Digest, 6/73. p. 11.

8. What does it mean to say that a scientific discovery is 'ahead of its time'? Molecular geneticist Gunther S. Stent, writing in *Scientific American*, December 1972, gives some classic examples: Gregor Mendel's discovery of the gene in 1865, unacknowledged for 35 years; Michael Polanyi's adsorption theory in physics, ignored from 1914 until its rediscovery in the 1950's; Oswals Avery's identification of DNA as the basic hereditary substance years before James Watson and Francis Crick discovered the double helix. These were all valid scientific discoveries: Why did they fail to have an immediate impact? Stent suggests that "a discovery is premature if its

implications cannot be connected by a series of simple logical steps to canonical . . . knowledge"—that is, the already existing body of accepted knowledge—about the subject.

(STAFF COLUMNIST)
"Newsletter/Science"
Intellectual Digest.

9. I've often said school for most children is like playing bingo with no prizes. You're asked to do a routine task with small reward, and nobody in his right mind plays eagerly unless he believes he has a chance for a prize. . . . Now if I'm playing real bingo with 50 people, I know that every time I play the game I have as good a chance to win as everyone else. But in the school bingo game, most of the cards have a little green dot at the bottom. The kids play for a while without winning and finally say, "Why is there a green dot on my card?" And the teacher will say, "Oh, I forgot to tell you. If you've got a card with a green dot, you'll never win." And they don't—and they resent it but they can't leave the game.

WILLIAM GLASSER, TO LOUIS DOLINAR
"A Talk with William Glasser"
Learning, 12/72. p. 58.

10. In a recent study of the odds on hitchhiking, psychologist Margaret M. Clifford of the University of Iowa and Paul Cleary of the University of Wisconsin found that hitchhikers who wear neat sports clothes are much more likely to get rides than those who wear grubby jeans and T-shirts. . . . At one point, a male experimenter turned down seven rides in 30 minutes while a nearby genuine hitchhiker with beard, long hair, dirty jacket and backpack had no luck at all. Obviously perplexed by the odd behavior of the bogus hitchhiker, Clifford and Cleary report, the real one walked over and asked disgustedly: "Hey man, what's your problem? You waiting for a ride to your goddamn livingroom?"

KENNETH GOODALL
"tie line"
Psychology Today, 10/71. p. 32.

11. Among the various experiences of our senses, tone is the only one that belongs exclusively to life. Light and color, sound, odor, and taste, solidity, fluidity, and gaseousness, rough and smooth, hot and cold—all these are also to be found in nonliving nature. Only life can produce tones. Living beings, out of themselves, add tone

to the physical world that confronts them; it is the gift of life to nonliving nature. A scientist, the first man to tread another planet, not knowing if he would find organic life there or not, would only need to hear a tone and his question would be answered.

VICTOR ZUCKERKANDL
Sound and Symbol
Princeton University Press, 1956. p. 1.

12. Even today when broad-band community cable could put fifty or sixty channels into every home, could end the constricting limitations of the VHF quasi-monopoly, could change television as much as television changed radio, we are bogged down in jurisdictional controversies between cities and states, between the states and the FCC, between the FCC and the White House. Cable television, the wired city, could virtually eliminate limited access and the other problems that now make it difficult to apply all of the principles of the First Amendment to broadcasting.

FRED W. FRIENDLY
"Television and the First Amendment"
Saturday Review, 1/8/72. p. 47.

13. The word which has been erroneously translated as non-violence is *satyagraha*, the word which Gandhi himself used. And when translated accurately it means something totally different from 'non-violence.' *Satyagraha*—with the force of ones' soul. This is more than not being violent. It is an act of creative love. With the force of my soul, I will change yours.

JULIUS LESTER
"Aquarian Notebook"
Liberation, 4/70. p. 38.

14. Every project for self-transformation is a vicious circle. Dogen, a Zen master of the thirteenth century, said that spring does not become summer and, in the same way, firewood does not become ashes: there is spring, and then there is summer; there is firewood, and then there are ashes. By the same argument, a living being does not become a corpse, and an unenlightened person does not become a Buddha. Monday does not become Tuesday; one o'clock does not become four o'clock. Thus to try to become a Buddha, to attain enlightenment or liberation or supreme unselfishness, is like trying to wash off blood with blood, or polishing a brick to make

a mirror. As Chuang-tzu said, "You see your egg and expect it to crow."

ALAN WATTS
"Planting Seeds and Gathering Fruit"
In *Does It Matter?*
Vintage Books, N.Y., 1968. p. 108.

15. The poet often knows that some part of his history is contributing to the poem he is writing. He may, for example, reject a phrase because he sees that he has borrowed it from something he has read. But it is quite impossible for him to be aware of all his history, and it is in this sense that he does not know where his behavior comes from. Having a poem, like having a baby, is in large part a matter of exploration and discovery, and both poet and mother are often surprised by what they produce. And because the poet is not aware of the origins of his behavior, he is likely to attribute it to a creative mind, an "unconscious" mind, perhaps, or a mind belonging to someone else—to a muse, for example, whom he has invoked to come and write his poem for him.

B. F. SKINNER
"On 'Having' A Poem"
Saturday Review, 7/15/72. p. 35.

16. The women's-lib theologians are overly optimistic, really, simplistic, in hoping that "feminizing" God will do away with the repression of women in the church and in Western society. . . . Notwithstanding Samuel Johnson's opinion that while all wise men have the same opinion of women they do not divulge it, most wise men—not excepting Dr. Johnson—have derogated woman-in-the-flesh while spinning "feminine" imageries. The Greek and Roman pantheons were about equally apportioned to goddesses, but the worship of the female deities did not sway the males who knelt before them to identify the women of Olympus with their earthly counterparts. I don't think one is overly pessimistic in prognosticating that referring to God as "She" and substituting "Eve" for "Adam" in the creation story will not *really* liberate women.

TRUDE WEISS-ROSMARIN
"Is God 'She'? And So What?"
Commonweal, 7/23/71. p. 374.

17. The Zodiac which is used in our astrology has very little, if anything at all, to do with distant stars as entities in themselves. It is

an ancient record of the cyclic series of transformations actually experienced by man throughout the year; a record written in symbolic language using the stars as a merely convenient, graphic way of building up symbolic images appealing to the imagination of a humanity child-like enough to be more impressed by pictures than by abstract and generalized processes of thought. The essential thing about the Zodiac is not the hieroglyphs drawn upon celestial maps; it is not the symbolic stories built up around Greek mythological themes—significant as these may be. It is the human experience of change. And for a humanity which once lived very close to the earth, the series of nature's "moods" throughout the year was the strongest representation of change; for the inner emotional and biological changes of man's nature did correspond very closely indeed to the outer change in vegetation.

DANE RUDHYAR
"The Zodiac as a Dynamic Process"
In *The Pulse of Life*
Shambala Publications, Berkeley, 1970.

18. When a person who is used to being healthy gets sick, he thinks, This won't last; I'll soon be up and about. A person who is used to being ill, exhausted, and in pain, if he does have a spell of feeling well, thinks, This can't last.

    This is in part why children who are used to failing are so little cheered up when now and then they succeed.

JOHN HOLT
What Do I Do Monday?
Dell Publishing Co., N.Y., 1970. p. 33.

19. I believe none of us dreamers realized in the beginning what difficulties would arise. For instance, we hadn't foreseen the problem of uniting Jews coming from such different countries who had lost contact with one another for centuries. Jews from all over the world have answered our call, just as we wanted: true. But each group had its own language, its own culture, and integration proved much more laborious than foreseen in theory. It isn't easy to form a homogeneous nation with such different people . . . there was bound to be a crash. It sorrowed and disappointed me. Moreover —you'll think me silly, naive—I thought that a Jewish state would be free of the evils afflicting other societies: theft, murder, prostitution. I was encouraged to believe it because we had started so well. Fifteen years ago in Israel there were hardly any thefts, and

there were no murders and no prostitution. But now we have them all. And that's a thing that cuts to the heart: it hurts one even more than the discovery that one has not yet succeeded in creating a society with more justice and more equality.

GOLDA MEIR
in an interview for Ms. Magazine,
4/73. p. 75.

20. Most people understand the language of tones without further ado; they are capable of hearing successions of tones as melodies, of distinguishing between sense and nonsense in tones. The lack of this ability, so-called tune deafness, is a very rare anomaly. . . . When a tune-deaf person listens to a melody, he hears tones succeeding one another; he does not hear melody. He hears music as we hear a lecture in a language we do not understand. The tones themselves, the sound, he perceives exactly as the normal person does; he lacks the organ for the *meaning* in the tones. To him our Beethoven melody is a succession of tones, what the cat produces on the keyboard is another succession of tones; the distinction between sense and nonsense, between music and nonmusic, escapes him completely. Were we in a position to demonstrate exactly what it is that a normal person hears in a melody and the tune-deaf person does not hear, we should presumably have isolated the factor that makes tones meaningful and makes music out of successions of tones.

VICTOR ZUCKERKANDL
Sound and Symbol,
Princeton University Press, 1956. pp. 16–17.

21. The mathematician or the physicist looks for principles which are persistently operative in nature, which will hold true in every special case. If you can find principles that hold true in every case then you have discovered what the scientist calls a *generalized principle*. The conscious detection of generalized principles which hold true under all conditions, and their abstraction from any and all special-case experiences of the principles, is probably unique to humans.

BUCKMINSTER FULLER
"How Little I Know"
Saturday Review, 11/12/66. p. 30.

22. The fearful person, on the other hand, does not care whether his model [of the world] is accurate. What he wants is to feel safe.

He wants a model that is reassuring, simple, unchanging. Many people spend their lives building such a model, rejecting all experiences, ideas, and information that do not fit. . . . Such people, and they are everywhere, of all ages and in all walks of life, fall back in many ways on the protective strategy of deliberate failure. How can failure be protective? On the principle that you can't fall out of bed if you're sleeping on the floor. . . . If you can think of yourself as a complete and incurable failure, you won't even be tempted to try. If you can feel that fate, or bad luck, or other people made you a failure, then you won't feel so badly about being one. If you can think that the people who are trying to wean you from failure are only trying to use you, you can resist them with a clear conscience.

JOHN HOLT
What Do I Do Monday?
Dell Publishing Co., N.Y., 1970. p. 35.

23. Men triumph by being courageous, inventive, enterprising, intelligent; women, before the twentieth century, have triumphed most often by being 'good.'

PATRICIA MEYER SPACKS
"Reflecting Women"
The Yale Review, Autumn 1973. p. 27.

24. Unconvinced by theology of any sort, which along with theory of all sorts is dismissed as a 'head trip,' the young especially are looking for experience: direct, unmediated God-awareness through altered states of consciousness. They want the end without the means, kernel without husk, soul without body, spirit without letter.

HUSTON SMITH
"The Relation Between Religions"
Main Currents, 11/12/73. p. 56.

25. It is easy to believe that religions which concern themselves with inward rather than outward solutions to suffering encourage callousness toward hunger, injustice, and disease. It is easy to say that they are aristocrats' methods of exploiting the poor. But it is, perhaps, not so easy to see that the poor are also being exploited when they are persuaded to desire more and more possessions, and led to confuse happiness with progressive acquisition.

ALAN WATTS
Nature, Man and Woman
Pantheon Books, N.Y., 1958. p. 51.

LIST OF SOURCES

page *

xiii   Lee Loevinger, "The Ambiguous Mirror: The Reflective-Projective Theory of Broadcasting and Mass Communications," *Journal of Broadcasting,* (Spring 1968).

xiii   Alan Toffler, *Future Shock* (New York: Random House, 1970).

xiv   George Gerbner, "Communication and Social Environment," *Scientific American* (September 1972), pp. 153–60.

10   Mary Breasted, review of *SDS* by Alan Adelson, *Saturday Review* (12 February 1972), p. 75.

11   Paul Ehrlich and John P. Holdren, "The Energy Crisis," *Saturday Review* (7 August 1971), p. 50.

15   Timothy Leary, "Languages: Energy Systems Sent and Received," *ETC.* (September 1965), p. 437.

29   James E. Churchill, "Food Without Farming," *Mother Earth News* 18, pp. 87–90.

29   John M. Murray and Annemarie Weber, "The Cooperative Action of Muscle Proteins," *Scientific American* (February 1974), pp. 60–61.

32   Michael J. Arlen, "Notes on the New Journalism," *The Atlantic Monthly* (May 1972), pp. 43–47.

32   Edmund Carpenter and Marshall McLuhan, "The New Languages," *Explorations in Communication* (Boston: Beacon Press, 1960).

32   Terry Southern, "The Rolling Stones' U.S. Tour," *Saturday Review* (12 August 1972), pp. 25–30.

35   Jerry Friedberg, "Convert Your Car to Propane," *Mother Earth News* (May 1972), pp. 78–82.

* Selections mentioned in the Acknowledgments section beginning on the copyright page are omitted from this list.

38 Denis Hayes, "Can We Bust the Highway Trust?" *Saturday Review* (5 June 1971), pp. 48–53.

39 Torsten Husén, "Does More Time in School Make a Difference?" *Saturday Review* (29 April 1972), p. 32.

45 Lloyd Linford, review of *The Underground Guide to the College of Your Choice* by Susan Berman, *Earth* (July 1971), p. 24.

52 Archer Taylor, "Folklore and the Student of Literature," quoted in Dundes, *The Study of Folklore* (Englewood Cliffs, N.J.: 1965), pp. 34–42.

54 William R. Bascom, "Folklore and Anthropology," quoted in Dundes, *The Study of Folklore,* pp. 25–33.

55 Paul D. McGlynn, "Graffiti and Slogans: Flushing the Id," *Journal of Popular Culture* (6:2), pp. 351–56.

61 Ernest Baughman, *Type and Motif Index of the Folktales of England and North America* (New York: Humanities Press, 1966), pp. 17, 64.

66 Son House, "I Can Make My Own Songs," *Sing Out!* (July 1965), pp. 38–45.

85 Robin Scott Wilson, ed., *Those Who Can: A Science Fiction Reader* (New York: New American Library, 1973), p. 177.

87 Norman Martien, "Getting Out of Schools," *New American Review* (New York: Simon & Schuster, 1971), pp. 96–116.

88 *Writer's Yearbook 70,* p. 146.

88 Loretta McCabe, interview with Kurt Vonnegut, *Writer's Yearbook 70,* p. 103.

88 J. Robert Moskin, "The Commune Way: Israeli Version," *Intellectual Digest* (February 1973), p. 20. (Interview with Yehiel Shemi)

89 Suzette Haden Elgin, "Final Exam."

94 Wayland M. Parrish and Marie Hochmuth, eds., *American Speeches* (Westport, Conn.: Greenwood Press, 1954), p. 3.

106 Burnham Carter, Jr., "President Kennedy's Inaugural Speech," *Contemporary Essays on Style,* Glen A. Love and Michael Payne, eds. (Glenview, Ill.: Scott, Foresman, 1969), p. 246.

112 Virginia Armstrong, *I Have Spoken* (Chicago: Swallow Press, 1971), p. 79.

120 Martin Luther King, "I Have a Dream," *The Crisis* (August/September 1973), p. 239.

129 George B. Leonard, *Intellectual Digest* (September 1972), p. 27.

131 Robert Nisbet, interview in *Psychology Today* (December 1973), pp. 50–64.

132 Rita Guibert, interview with Octavio Paz, *Intellectual Digest* (December 1972), p. 69.

132 Herman Kahn, interview in *Intellectual Digest* (September 1972), pp. 16–19.

132 Carl Gorman, "Navajo Vision of Earth and Man," *The Indian Historian* (Winter 1973), pp. 19–22.

133 Bruce A. Rosenberg, "The Formulaic Quality of Spontaneous Sermons," *Journal of American Folklore* (January/March 1970), pp. 3–20.

137 Suzette Haden Elgin, "Cluster Code."

151 Suzanne Massie, "The City of Six Thousand Poets," *Saturday Review* (12 August 1972), pp. 42–45.

151 William Heyen, a review of *Straw for the Fire* by David Wagoner in *Saturday Review* (11 March 1972).

160 Rod Holmgren and William Norton, eds., *The Mass Media Book* (Englewood Cliffs, N.J.: Prentice-Hall, 1972), p. 1.

161 Marshall McLuhan, *Understanding Media* (New York: New American Library, 1968), p. 273.

161 Peter M. Sandman et al., eds., *Media: An Introductory Analysis of American Mass Communications* (Englewood Cliffs, N.J.: Prentice-Hall, 1972), p. 269.

179 Arthur Knight, "The Way of the Western: More Mire than Myth," *Saturday Review* (March 1973), p. 38.

197 Janet B. Sawyer, "Social Aspects of Bilingualism in San Antonio, Texas," *Publications of the American Dialect Society* 41 (1964), pp. 7–15.

204 Peter Berger, "The Briefing," *Worldview* (March 1973) [also in *Intellectual Digest,* July 1973].

207 Douglas Bush, "Polluting Our Language, *The American Scholar* (Spring 1972), pp. 238–47.

215 Roger W. Shuy, *Discovering American Dialects,* National Council of Teachers of English, 1967, pp. 43, 44.